38·00

Developing
Successful
New Products

A Guide to Product Planning

DAVID ALLEN

FINANCIAL TIMES

PITMAN PUBLISHING

Pitman Publishing
128 Long Acre, London WC2E 9AN

A Division of Longman Group UK Limited

First published in 1993

A CIP catalogue record for this book can be obtained from
the British Library.

ISBN 0 273 60150 4

Typeset by Pantek Arts, Maidstone, Kent
Printed and bound in Great Britain by
Biddles Ltd, Guildford and King's Lynn

*This book is dedicated to
product planners everywhere, in all kinds of
industry. Your fine work has been sometimes
unappreciated and, until now, unheralded.*

CONTENTS

11 PRODUCT PLANNING AND ITS CROSS-FUNCTIONAL RELATIONSHIPS   269

PREFACE

My introduction to product planning came in 1966 when I was working for the Rootes Group, later to become Chrysler United Kingdom. My experience of the quite new product planning function was extremely positive and has been a definite influence on my working life ever since. It was then a leading edge technique for planning profitable products. It remains so today.

I started in automotive sales and marketing with Rootes in 1960 and later was invited to join the new product planning function to bring in some sales and customer experience. I remained for six years in product planning, starting as a product manager on the car side. Eventually I became director of car and truck product planning in 1969. During this period we were intensively involved in trying to build the best possible product planning organisation to plan, create and introduce new and profitable car and truck programmes for Chrysler UK. This was necessary to strengthen the business position of Chrysler UK, but we were also pushing the boundaries of managing new programmes in new ways, to introduce new models in a quality-, cost- and time-effective manner. Product planning in the UK was a relatively new management discipline and we were keen to develop it and see it produce results for the company.

During this period we launched five new car model ranges and several model improvements, and on the truck side we created the product strategy and plans that produced the Dodge 100 Series and 50 Series ranges.

Many of the ideas and techniques we tried and adopted during that period are even now hailed as the way forward in improving new product development processes for European industry. Both during and after my time with Chrysler I have felt sure that this product planning experience and the principles of product planning in general were worth spreading to a wider business audience.

Since then I have twice headed up business and product planning functions with major European automotive firms, once with Perkins Engines in the 1970s and once with Volvo Holland from 1988 to 1992. I have also had spells in sales and marketing, distribution and general management at OEM companies and major suppliers to the automotive industry. I have seen from many sides the effectiveness of product planning and the contribution it can make to the overall new product development process. My belief in product planning as a key driver for the eventual manufacturing of successful products has been much reinforced.

Product planning departments have not always been seen as effective contributors to a company's success. This can be due to inter-departmental rivalry: a new department may not be fully accepted by the entrenched line functions. The cross-functional style of working, so essential to effective product planning, has caused many relationship problems when departments still see themselves as individual islands of excellence. Lack of success has also been due to bad product planning; this ranged from the use of subjective judgements instead of analysed opinions of market needs to continuous changes of mind about what a new product needs. Everyone is an "expert" on what a new product should be: in many companies the subjective product planning opinion was demonstrated to be no better than anyone else's. To avoid this, product planning must be a professional discipline where the work and requirements of product planners deserve the same consideration as the inputs of the more established functions.

I am sure of one thing: properly staffed and performing product planning can be a major asset in a high technology, fast-changing, competitive world where creativity, excellence of planning, good decision making and execution are the essential ingredients of success.

This book is a complete appraisal of the product planning process and function, based on my experience, but I have also tried to extend its scope to show how good product planning principles and practices can be applied to a variety of situations in various industries. I also point out the pitfalls through examples of ineffective product planning because I believe that successful examples are not the only way to learn good new ideas. Analysis of problems or even failures can also teach many lessons.

Product planning can mean both an *organisational* entity or the *process* of planning the product which can involve many more departments in a company. It will be necessary to cover both aspects because product planning is a truly cross-functional activity and there are many actions that contribute to the product plan or to a new product programme that are not necessarily performed by someone who calls himself a product planner.

Many companies have product planning departments. Some companies have departments with other titles, such as project planning or product management, that perform what I consider to be product planning tasks. At the same time, the front end of the product creation or product development process is often called the product planning phase. Involvement in this is not limited to one functional department but should, in a well-run company, be a combined effort of all the necessary functions. I believe, however, that in some types of industry, product planning should exist as a separate department in the organisation in order to gain advantage from its cross-functional operating style and because of the need to focus on the professional techniques of planning new products effectively.

Quite apart from my belief in the value of product planning as a primary business process, another reason for writing a book on product planning stems from an absence of descriptive literature, whether academic or practical, that deals directly and specifically with the product planning purpose, process and function. Checking through the reference sections of well-respected books such as *The Machine that Changed the World* by Womack, Jones and Roos[1], *Product Development Performance* by Clark and Fujimoto[2] or Philip Kotler's *Marketing Management: Analysis, Planning and Control*[3], reveals mainly passing references to product planning as a concept or as part of the product marketing process. Only Clark and Fujimoto effectively describe the product planning process at the start of a new programme. But even there, the role of a product planning function as such is not emphasised. In fact, in many of the books that describe world class product development processes, the indication of who, apart from top management, should be driving the process is not always clear.

The emphasis in the first two books rests more on the complete product development process and, in particular, on simultaneous or concurrent engineering, which covers part – but not all – of the necessary scope of successful new product development. In Kotler and other major marketing textbooks, product management is described as a part of marketing. A separate product planning activity is not clearly defined.

I believe, however, that product planning deserves separate treatment. I have attempted to set down the origins of product planning as a specific discipline, with all of its benefits, scope, organisation and development. This can provide a frame of reference from which useful conclusions can be drawn by companies looking to improve their industrial performance. It may also suggest further avenues of research in the academic field. If product planning is an important industrial discipline then it should be taught both as a strategic subject and in terms of its individual tools and techniques. Product planning could be included in MBA courses, in engineering degree courses and technical training of all kinds. Most product planners have a technical background. Engineering is the department with which product planners do much of their work. Therefore, a sound knowledge of product planning should be part of an engineer's armoury.

Today there is much discussion of what can be learnt from the best practice in Japanese and western automotive firms in world class or "lean" product development. There are important lessons to be drawn from studying successful Japanese companies both in Japan and in the way their transplants are operating in Europe and North America. However, it has also been my experience that there are few really new techniques that can improve the industrial process.

The current focus on improving the product development process in engineering-based industries has fostered a whole host of apparently new management ideas such as programme management, parallel and cross-functional working, improved timing and time to market and better up-front planning. In my experience, however, these are not completely new ideas or business practices. In 1968 I was a programme manager in product planning with the responsibility for getting a new product programme in on time against all its programme objectives. In the mid 1970s, I participated in a study group at Perkins Engines which came to the conclusion that a matrix, product-based organisation, instead of a purely functional one, would provide a better market and profit focus for each group of products. Perkins later went further and divided itself into profit centre management entities based around different product ranges.

Programme timing expertise, and the compression of development programmes by overlapping activities to reduce time to market was a constant concern through the 1970s. I have found that timing functions and the development of timing expertise has been necessary for improved programme implementation efficiency. Often this has been done in the face of considerable opposition from people who regarded timing as an unnecessary overhead or thought it should be part of a central engineering function. I say much more about the importance of timing later.

Parallel working between different departments as a means of achieving better quality, up-front planning of programmes was certainly used successfully on projects with which I was involved as early as 1968. The parallel process itself was not formally the focus of attention but our ideas were based on a common sense approach of always trying to get maximum input and commitment from colleagues at each decision stage of a new programme.

All of these techniques and practices are now gathered under the general umbrella of improving the product creation process, but each technique, on its own, is not new. What is new perhaps, is the realisation that no single magic technique or buzz word will bring about guaranteed success. Everything must be done well and with an intelligent approach at the time and, each time the process is repeated, it must be done better. Continuous improvement must be the aim. This is the single most important message we can extract from Japanese industrial performance in Japan, the US and UK. It is as if we have been looking at the Japanese companies' success for years and focusing on the wrong things.

As indicated above, the idea of efficient product development and good up-front planning was in existence in the late 1960s. We were, however, only at the beginning of the continuous improvement learning curve. The difference between Japanese and western companies in the intervening period has been efficiency and speed in making best use of, and improving, available ideas and techniques rather than creating anything really new.

I shall return to these issues in later chapters, but it is interesting to note here that the Hillman Avenger, launched by Chrysler United Kingdom at the beginning of 1970, was an all-new car (new engine, body structure, transmission and axle) produced in a new manufacturing facility. It took four and a half years from programme start to launch and met its original timing, product development, product performance and piece-cost targets. Despite its newness, the Hillman Avenger was a reliable vehicle, accepted by large vehicle fleet users in an era when new models were regarded with suspicion because of past experience of unreliability. Effective programme timing performance and cost control still form the holy grail sought in Western engineering industry. These factors are recognised as two of the main determinants of profit performance during a product's life cycle. The Avenger project was very successful in both these aspects.

It achieved this successful launch thanks to an effective product planning organisation and a management team (product planning, styling, engineering, manufacturing, marketing, purchasing) which believed in, and actually achieved, working together and recognised the overriding importance of the programme, the company's needs and the requirements of individuals or functional specialist departments. This theme of company versus functional priorities is also one that I return to later.

The techniques of product development improvement are widely known in Europe and North America but their effective use or combination is not sufficiently developed. Some companies have already started down this road and are achieving success but for the rest the time is now... or never. If the study and adoption of an effective product planning process, in its broadest sense, can help bring about necessary improvements, the objective of this book will have been realised. The end result of any new product development process is a product. If that product does not successfully meet or exceed the customer's needs and expectations, no amount of non-product frills will produce adequate results.

Most of the material in this book comes from my own automotive OEM and supplier industrial experiences. I am indebted for many of my views on product planning to all those colleagues with whom I have worked, arguing and deciding about how best to perform the product planning task. It has been a constant challenge for all of us to refine our approaches and techniques in striving for ever better products within a dynamic, multi-functional environment. However, to include a view of the current status of product planning in other companies, and industries, I have also used material from several other sources including the product development organisations of non-automotive companies. I am grateful to these sources, each of which is acknowledged separately in the book.

I do owe a specific debt of gratitude to certain people who have helped by discussing the book's contents and in challenging me on style, presentation and content. I would particularly like to mention Professor Jean Phillipe Deschamps of Arthur D.Little (Brussels) who encouraged me initially to write the book; Dave Schoch, Manager of Business and Strategic Planning at Ford of Europe, for clarifying the development of the Ford product, business planning and programme management organisation; Professor John Chelsom of City University for his all-round helpful comments and critique; Alan Martin, Director of Business Strategy, Rover Group, for sharing with me many aspects of his own wide experience of product planning techniques and principles. Finally, I would like to thank Sir Terence Beckett, who was one of the originators of product planning in Ford of Britain in the 1950s, and who has made available to me material and views that I have used in the book. In particular, he has encouraged me with his own enthusiasm for product planning as a modern business management technique that deserves a wider audience at all levels in industry.

Notes

1. Jones, Womack and Roos, *The Machine that Changed the World*, Macmillan Publishing Company, 1989.
2. Clark and Fujimoto, *Product Development Performance*, Harvard Business School Press, 1991.
3. Philip Kotler, *Marketing Management: Analysis, Planning and Control*, Prentice Hall 1984.

1 THE INDUSTRIAL ENVIRONMENT FOR PRODUCT PLANNING

The present industrial environment in Europe and the US encourages strong concentration on product development. Each company needs to be more effective at producing customer-oriented products because consumers are becoming more varied and more demanding. The pressure of competition from domestic and foreign competitors makes this need all the more urgent. Nowhere is the pressure stronger than in the automotive industry.

Product planning is widely used in the automotive industry and is gaining increasing acceptance in other industries. Japanese companies, which are in the forefront of the competitive battle with ever more, better and technically advanced products, use product planning extensively in almost all industries, especially those with a strong customer focus.

Product planning is placed in its industrial context and is presented as a top management concern and, ultimately, responsibility. The key features described can be a major factor in helping top management achieve the necessary improvements in a company's new product development performance.

CHALLENGES FOR INDUSTRY

The business atmosphere for manufacturing companies in Europe and North America presents two major challenges: first, for companies to become more capable of handling the international or global nature of their markets; second, to meet ever-increasing competition from all sides.

Neither of these conditions is new. Both have existed throughout the 1980s but as the world economic situation becomes more difficult in the 1990s, the companies which successfully deal with both challenges will have the chance to succeed in the long term.

Company strategies must be based on what is happening in both domestic and global markets. Economies of operation, research or production scale, as well as the need to be financially strong, force companies to consider a broadening of the markets in which they attempt to be successful. Competition comes from established players in developed countries who seek ways of strengthening their positions and from new firms in developing countries that have started with domestic production as part of a drive for self-sufficiency and have followed up with aggressive exporting campaigns to the markets of the developed countries.

This pressure to develop strategically comes at a time when there is overcapacity in many industries, severe economic and political instability in many markets and strong pressure from the financial community for companies to improve short term financial results.

THE PRIORITIES OF INDUSTRY FOR THE 1990s

It is not surprising that the response of industry and those involved in helping industry has covered a wide range of business activity. In the 1970s and 1980s the emphasis was on improving logistics through material requirement planning (MRP), reducing inventories through just-in-time deliveries (JIT), increased use of big information technology (IT) systems for basic company operations and the improvement of manufacturing efficiency itself through automation technology and the use of robots.

These actions were followed by attention to personnel resourcing, quality circles, a general search for excellence, total quality, cell manufacturing and the flattening of organisations by cutting out levels of management. In the UK particularly during this period, productivity in manufacturing industry rose strongly – sometimes through genuine efficiency improvements and sometimes by cutting out all but essential core activities. This involved direct and indirect labour, as evidenced by the UK's historically high levels of unemployment in the 1980s.

In the Nineties, almost for the first time, we are seeing a greater concentration on product development as one of the key areas of company operations where improvements can show results. Developing new products in a different way became necessary after successive attempts to reduce costs by cutting overheads or by improved manufacturing efficiency for existing products were found to have limited potential. This realisation began to grow at the end of the 1980s and was reinforced by studies that showed the gulf in total manufactured cost that still existed between the average Western company and the majority of its Japanese counterparts. Studies pointed out that it was not just labour efficiency, harder work, smooth-running logistic systems or lower design cost products that gave Japan the edge, but rather, their whole way of conceiving, designing and producing. Fully competitive products from Japan were covering the bottom and top of every sector. These were competitive in price but also capable of competing with the most technically advanced products of the West.

The automotive industry of Europe and North America has been in the front line of this competitive struggle. The rate of development of customer-oriented, profitable new products is a major weapon. In the past, the automotive industry has been the source of ideas, technologies, processes and management techniques that have given an inspirational lead to other industries. Hence the experience of automotive companies in Europe and North America with new techniques of efficient product development, under the influence of severe competition, can be useful in a wider industrial arena.

In addition to product development, another four priority areas identified for corporate improvement in the 1990s seem to be: integrated logistics, continued work on manufacturing efficiency involving process, technology and people, organisation structure development and integrated information technology.

These five fields of improvement are cross-functional. It is now realised that the single function improvement programmes used in the past have not produced the desired long term results. There is now a strong realisation that improvement must be implemented across a complete company system or process to achieve real progress. This is one of the major aspects of the new product development process regarded as critical for future success. Cross-functional working has been found to be one of the keys to improving product development in the automotive industry, although it was not always accorded the right priority in the past.

FOCUS ON NEW PRODUCT DEVELOPMENT

New product development is a complete system involving most departments in a company. At the same time, the characteristics of a new product influence the operations of the rest of the company once the product is in production. The benefits of getting it right are company wide.

- If a new product meets the expectations of the customer it will be easier and more profitable to sell.
- Research and development efforts can be focused on the requirements for future product ranges and not just on challenging new technologies.

- Tools and techniques for improving the internal and external engineeering processes involved in designing, testing and manufacturing new products must be acquired.
- A product designed for ease of manufacture will be easier to deliver profitably to customers and will make the overall task of running a manufacturing operation easier both technically and from a personnel viewpoint.
- The regular launching of products planned to position a company effectively against its competitors in international markets will ensure the success of that company.
- The components of a product, created with the help of suppliers, will be cheaper to buy and to procure in volume with quality and reliability of supply.

That the new product development process as a whole is at last receiving the attention it needs is evidenced by the large number of academic and business books describing good practices found in the most successful companies, both Japanese and Western. Many companies in the West are able to demonstrate their experiences of achieving measurable improvements by changing their old product development practices. In the UK particularly, the DTI Enterprise Initiative is focusing on improving the new product process as one of its key promotional programmes for 1992 and 1993. Business schools, universities and consultants are adding new product development techniques such as simultaneous engineering to their teaching and consultancy portfolios.

Among all this activity, the product and its planning need to be given prominence if only because an efficient development process working on a wrongly or inadequately positioned product will not give the desired results. Within the product and its characteristics reside all the cross-company benefits described above.

PLANNING THE PRODUCT FOR MARKET AND CUSTOMER

Product planning is the necessary starting point for any successful new product development. Products must be planned to meet the needs of a wide variety of customers in different markets. Despite the concept of the global product, it is still necessary to match local needs, preferences and legislation in each market sector. This means product proliferation rather than standardisation and the creation of many variations and options within a product family.

This is particularly true in industries such as the motor vehicle industry where, despite many attempts at producing a "world car", most major regions of the world market require unique product solutions in size, style, quality or price levels. Even Japanese car manufacturers are finding that they need quite different versions of the same basic model to compete in, for example, Japan and Europe. Consumer durables such as cameras, video and audio products can have a more global character because their usage patterns are more international. But even here, variations between markets and nationalities must be recognised.

To meet the needs of these varying international markets, product planning should be a significant company response to the challenge of global operations and increasing competition.

I plan to show that product planning work is an essential preliminary and part of successful product development and that it should therefore be considered as a discipline equal in importance to other participating functions such as engineering, purchasing, manufacturing and marketing.

PARALLEL AND SEQUENTIAL WORKING

Figures 1.1 and 1.2 show the involvement of all functional areas in a new product programme. Involvement can be sequential with each department handing over or releasing its work to the next downstream department in relay style as shown in Figure 1.1. This is referred to, not without good

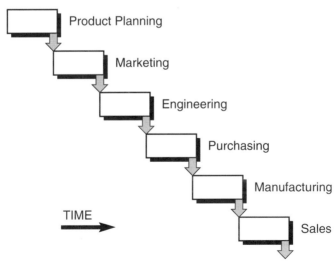

Figure 1.1 Sequential or 'Over the Wall' Programme Execution.

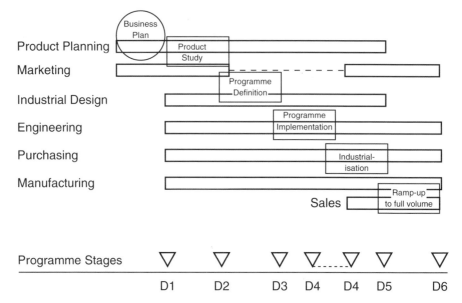

Figure 1.2 Simultaneous Programme Execution.

reason, as "over the wall" or "ivory tower" product development, in which each participating department tries to finish its work before handing it over to the next in line. Usually, the work has been carried out with minimal reference to other departments' needs. Successful programmes carried out in this manner require much longer to implement. They also absorb more resources because of the constant need to back-track in downstream phases to correct mistakes made earlier due to lack of cross-functional consultation. In general, such programmes are unsuccessful because there is never enough time or resources to get everything right.

The modern approach requires that all departments work simultaneously, in an integrated manner, to achieve a successful programme, as shown in Figure 1.2. Product planning is one of the truly cross-functional departments that can facilitate an integrated, simultaneous product development approach, starting at the beginning of the process and staying involved right to the end. Almost all successful product programmes today use some form of this parallel approach.

The whole process of creating new products is often referred to as simultaneous or concurrent engineering. While I have nothing against engineering processes or the engineering profession, I find that this title is somewhat misleading. Although engineering and technical disciplines lie at the heart of effective product development, the process embraces much more than just engineering.

Project teams are one of the most widely recommended recipes for success in simultaneous engineering. They put design and process engineers together to ensure that the two aspects of technical input are blended. Some companies see the formation of these engineering-led project teams as the way to perform simultaneous engineering. The results can be disappointing. Trying to implement product development programmes in teams that do not include representation from non-engineering departments has been one of the reasons. Successful simultaneous engineering is a discipline that must involve marketing, purchasing, product and business planning as well as engineering. For this reason, a more appropriate title for simultaneous engineering could be *integrated product development.*

Another title used to cover activities connected to product planning and the implementation of product programmes is programme management. This organisational concept for managing new product programmes has a very strong link to, and sometimes an overlap with, product planning. Where teams are formed, the programme manager heads up the team. The job of the programme manager is broader in scope than that of a product manager in product planning. The programme manager has hands-on responsibility for the programme right through its life. In some organisations he also has line authority over those working on a new programme that overrides the authority of functional area heads.

In many companies that have moved from a functional structure to a matrix or programme and project structure, product planning activities form an essential part of the dedicated programme management team. The "product" focus is all-important in successful programme implementation. This is the main reason for the overlap of responsibilities. A good product planner must be experienced in cross-functional working – one of the key skills required to manage programmes. The relationship between these two disciplines is so important that I devote the whole of Chapter Seven to a description of programme management and the key aspects of its relationship with product planning.

The difference between a conventional, function-based organisation and one that has adopted programme management in its fullest sense is shown in Figures 1.3 and 1.4. Instead of having the responsibility for implementing the new programmes spread between the different functional heads, the programme manager is responsible for the implementation and the functional heads provide the resources and the input of functional expertise, as seen in Figure 1.4.

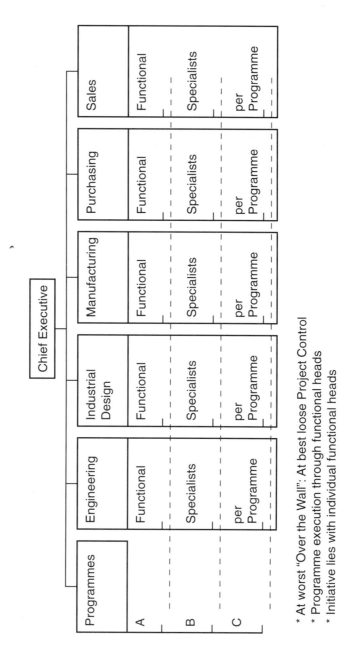

Figure 1.3 Conventional Product Development Organisation.

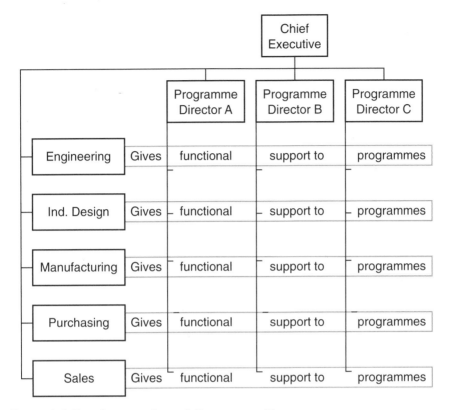

Figure 1.4 Development through Programme Management.

THE MAIN PRODUCT PLANNING PRINCIPLES

The following points encapsulate the aims of an efficient product planning process. At this point, it doesn't matter whether these principles are embodied in a large or small product planning department or simply in a process to which a company works. Without them, however, the starting point for new product development activities will not be well established:

1. Product planning should be seen as acting on behalf of the board as a secretariat of the new product creation process. This is, in a way, taking over the product creation role of the old-style entrepreneurs because businesses have become far too complex for the board to get involved in the details of new products without some help.

2. Product planning is always trying to strike a balance between the conflicting requirements of the old style line functions of a company such as engi-

neering (design), manufacturing, finance, sales and marketing. The following quotation comes from a discussion with a journalist in which I tried to describe concisely the new function of product planning.

> 'Product planning acts for the company in reconciling the conflicting needs of the different departments of the company with regard to the introduction of new products. To exaggerate a little, engineering departments want to design products as perfect as a Swiss watch; manufacturing departments want them to be made of no more than three component parts; sales departments want them to be full of fine technical product features at a low price. The finance department only wants them to be profitable. Product planning is needed as an honest broker to manage the trade-offs and to recommend to management what should be decided.'

3. Product planning has the role of product requirement definition, stating what new products the company should make and what changes should be made to existing ones. This leads naturally to the creation and control of the company's long term product plan together with all the associated actions and decisions needed to implement the various parts of the plan.

4. As a result, product planning usually runs the product planning committee (PPC) which, in many companies, is the central management organ and the means by which it determines a large part of its future not just on products but on product-related matters such as market and technology diversification, joint ventures and capacity expansions. A PPC is normally composed of the board or executive committee members plus co-opted specialists.

5. From being initiators and definers of new product creation, it is only a short step to becoming monitors and even controllers of the implementation process. In 1967, Chrysler UK changed titles in product planning from product line managers to programme managers with the idea of stepping up to this more difficult – but equally important – role of managing trade-offs during the implementation process. In this area, the product planning role overlaps with the management of programmes.

A programme manager should have an innovative concern for customer requirements and should strive to preserve the tone, quality and content of the programme throughout its life. Hence success and profit result from cannily getting into production or into a finished state as near as possible what was imagined, planned, calculated and even hoped when the programme was committed.

Thus there are two factors important to the product planner:

- The planning of the product and the commitment of the whole company to that product programme decision has to be of a high quality.
- The execution has to be excellent.

These concerns are illustrated in Figure 1.5, which is often used to illustrate a key aspect of improved product creation and which is said to represent something we can learn from Japanese companies. The chart illustrates that the difficulty of making good decisions is highest at the beginning of the programme. This emphasises the need for high quality up-front planning. On the other hand, the cost of correcting bad decisions rises as the programme progresses. So it is worth spending more resources at the front end to avoid costly second and third development loops in the downstream phases to correct mistakes or take account of late changes.

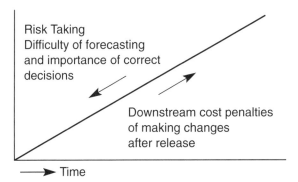

Figure 1.5 Early Planning in New Product Programmes: Cost of Changes versus risk.

Certainly this is the way that successful Japanese, European and American companies work. For me, however, this represents an old product planning principle that has perhaps been forgotten or overtaken by other issues. I return to this point in Chapter Five when discussing product planning's role in the new product development process.

The budgetary effects of this concept are shown in Figure 1.6. Line A is a typical product development spend curve, starting slowly and continuing after production start due to late product corrections or changes of mind. Line B follows the prescription for more efficient product development; more early work and completion of the job prior to production. More cost is incurred up front but the direct development costs later in the programme can be lower and the indirect costs to the rest of the company from a bad product launch will be much lower. This is "lean-clean product development".

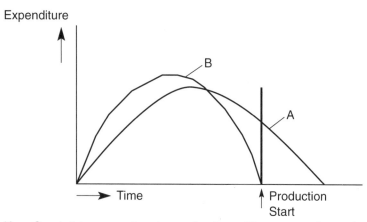

Key: Graph A is conventional spend pattern. Changes continue after
production start
Graph B is "Lean-clean" spend pattern. Development task complete
by production start

Figure 1.6 Conventional vs. "Lean-Clean" Development Expenditure.

Short term budgetary management will certainly work against any move
to apply more resources early in product development programmes without
a corresponding and guaranteed return. Often there has to be, initially at any
rate, an act of faith. However, many companies who have tried to implement
lean-clean product development know that the savings are there to be won in
terms of lower total programme cost, faster time to market and the freeing of
resources earlier to start on the next new programme.

Figure 1.5 is also an argument for recruiting only the highest calibre
people into the front ranks of product planning – and rewarding them appro-
priately. The most difficult and serious decisions are those taken a long time
before their implementation point: here, the cost of correcting wrong decisions is very high. Hence the product planning responsibility is correspondingly large. The quality of the professional product planners' input to new
programmes is something I return to in Chapter Three.

These points encapsulate the product planning task that we were trying to
implement in the late 1960s, 1970s and early 1980s. Only now is this being
recognised as the driver of successful new product development. If product
planning has not managed on its own to transform the product performance
of European industry during this period, it is not because the approach is
wrong but more because of the way a "new" cross-functional working
process has been viewed by many companies.

PRODUCT PLANNING PITFALLS

The five main elements outlined above contain the main themes which have developed during the last twenty years leading to the different examples found in several industries today of the product planning function and process.

It is necessary to see both sides of the coin, to understand why wider recognition of something which seemed clear and obvious to some of us has taken twenty years. There are some pitfalls in the development of product planning which were not always easy to avoid.

1. Reporting Levels

For product planning to operate effectively as an extra arm of the board, it needs to report to the board full-time. Most product planning departments of the time reported to the head of product development or the vice-president, engineering. Some were more like departments that only did product requirement planning, a simple statement of what the product should be or should contain, and reported in to the head of sales and marketing. The less effective departments lacked strength outside their own division. They tended to do the bidding of their functional boss when the chips were down rather than serving the needs of the company as a whole. The departments that succeeded did so because of their own strength or because of a particularly favourable working atmosphere in their companies. The reporting level of product planning is a key issue and I shall return to it in Chapter Six when dealing with organisation.

2. Defining the Product

Product planning departments nominally had the role of defining the product. This led to a risk that their views would become overly influenced by the subjective and not based sufficiently on real customer requirements. In many companies, subjective and emotional opinions on possible new products still hold sway, especially where the product has a strong consumer or fashion element. These opinions can assume a life of their own and become more important than finding out what the customer really thinks and wants.

Product research techniques were available from the consumer goods industry but were not widely accepted until the 1980s in technically-based industries such as durable consumer goods. Here the subjective views of senior members of management, engineering, marketing and the views, both professional and subjective, of product planners all played a role in arriving at the decided product. Clinics were used to research the acceptability of new product concepts, especially in styling model form, but clinic results were often mistrusted or simply double-guessed. Product planning's role actually became discredited in some companies: planners became too subjective and not sufficiently analytical or professional in determining the nature of the new product. The rest of management thought they could double-guess anything the product planners came up with. In this way, in a lot of companies, the influence of product planning in this phase of a programme diminished.

A second problem area was that defining the product was often seen as the territory of marketing departments. Product planning either became a part of marketing or disappeared altogether, leaving marketing far too focused on the future product, instead of selling the current product.

3. Managing Programmes

The concept of managing as well as planning the product programme was a good and logical one. In the early stages it cut across much hallowed turf and many cherished views of functional responsibility in other larger departments such as engineering, manufacturing and purchasing. The concept was prevented from working in some companies; even now, many firms need to go through a major upheaval in organisational responsibilities and work processes in order to reap the benefits of cross-functional working. Thus even the embryonic attempts of product planning to act in a programme co-ordination role, especially in the downstream parts of a programme after the final decision to implement, met with resistance from the strong functional departments. Later attempts at a solution in some companies merged product planning functions into a programme management organisation (see Chapter Seven). However, getting people to work cross-functionally without totally separating them into programme or project teams is still a problem.

4. Product and Business Planning

A little learning can be a dangerous thing. Creating and publishing the long term product plan was not enough. A product plan that did not recognise its full implications throughout the company would soon lose credibility. For example, one requiring resources that the company simply did not have. Thus product planning could suffer from the same ivory tower problem as many early attempts at corporate planning. This was unfortunate, because an effective product planning function should be firmly rooted in the real operating life of the company. Its activities should form a bridge between medium- and long-term planning and programme implementation action. It should also be a department that constantly works hard at being accepted as a working partner by all other functional areas of the company.

Only later did companies discover business planning as an adjunct to, or a separate part of, the product planning process. In business planning the full impact, company-wide, of a given product plan or strategy had to be planned and evaluated including resource, financial, manufacturing, purchasing and other company feasibility issues.

Business planning, as a strongly related part of the product planning process and therefore overlapping with product planning's own task, is covered in Chapter Eight.

5. Cross-Functional Working

In theory, the perfect company should not need a cross-functional co-ordinating and planning activity. However, more and more of a company's main streams of activity are cross-functional in nature. Generally, it is also impossible to implement a complex project through the successful interaction of strong, competent and independent operating divisions or departments without strong management or co-ordinatory intervention. This is not a task that the board or a co-ordinating committee can easily achieve as part of its normal management function. Therefore, some organisation structure has to be put in alongside the divisional barons. Thus we have seen, in successful product companies, the rise of various forms of matrix and the increasing importance of people who oversee the total programme – not just as administrative co-ordinators but as programme directors, decision makers and entrepreneurs who take over project responsibility from the specialist departments. In Japan this programme supremo is called a *shusa*. Japanese companies have been among the first to get the full potential out of the organisational concept.

LESSONS FROM JAPAN

Japanese companies are regarded as setting the standards for the most effective ways of developing new products. Many expeditions have been made to Japan by Western companies. Many reports have been written about Japanese conditions, techniques and working practices. The well-publicised Ford programme *After Japan* is one such example. Ford realised the need to organise its development and manufacturing more efficiently to remain competitive after studying the performance of its Japanese competitors. Many incredible things about Japanese performance have been uncovered through joint ventures with Japanese partners. Yet Western-based parent companies have not always been able or willing to implement the lessons at home.

Much of these deliberations focuses on techniques such as *kanban*, quality circles, *taguchi*, QFD, and even programme management itself without getting to the heart of the Japanese experience. The real Japanese skill is in constantly trying to find ways to do things better – whether or not the technique or idea was originally home-grown or acquired from a Western source. Some Japanese quality techniques in fact originated in North America. Programme Management itself was not originally invented by the Japanese. It is the working approach to industrial efficiency, almost the industrial philosophy, of the Japanese that we should learn from rather than just trying to apply those techniques that appear to be the basis of their success.

In studying these various ways to improve, we are also beginning to learn that it will take a lot of effort to change prejudices, ingrained habits and defensive working attitudes before the full effect and benefits of these improved product development techniques can be realised. What is needed – in addition to the continuous improvement idea – is the removal of a whole host of other obstacles that prevent some Western companies from behaving in an optimum way. These obstacles include concentrating mainly on short term financial results, distrust of bright "staff" departments and attachment to divisional parochialities rather than to the interests of the company as a whole or the requirements of a new product programme.

With their constant seeking after improvement, the Japanese have gained maximum benefit from these ideas. They have woven them together with ideas of their own to produce the highly competitive ranges of products with which they are challenging Western companies in all markets.

Akio Morita, chief executive of Sony, noted in *Made in Japan*[1] that there are three key forms of creativity in any successful company.

- Technology creativity.
- Product planning creativity.
- Marketing creativity.

By technological creativity Morita means the development or acquisition of technology appropriate to the businesses and markets that the company is in, or wants to be in. This will provide the opportunity for the company to produce products with characteristics that attract customers and beat the competition. This approach implies focusing R&D efforts away from blue sky research and towards market opportunities and product needs – a feature of the latest thinking on how to manage research and development programmes for profit.

The second form of creativity, and the most important in the context of this book, resides in product planning. Here Morita is referring to the complete product development process that builds a bridge between the availability of necessary technology and the conversion – through a mixture of creative, engineering and management processes – into a saleable and competitive product. It is not clear whether he sees product planning as a process or as a specific organisation but its importance to Sony is clear. Elsewhere in the same volume he shows how some of Sony's successful products had their origins in a product planning technology committee. It is this bridge between the developing of technology and the creation of a profitable and marketable product that is often said to be lacking in Western and, particularly, British companies. This problem is not confined to large companies but can be seen and heard in all sectors of industry. More focus on all aspects of product planning would pay dividends.

Marketing creativity is only in small part the concern of this book. Understanding the market and customers is a prime requirement for the product planner but I think that Morita is talking more about creative ways of organising the marketing chain to maximise the customer's wish to buy and to make it easy for him to do so. It is possible to market a bad product superbly, but a good product can be irretrievably harmed by inept marketing. Necessarily, creative marketing is a last link in the chain.

I find that Morita's definition of the three creativities fits well with my own experience of product planning. In the chapters that follow I show more fully how effective product planners can contribute to the first two of these creativities.

It is appropriate that Morita shows his understanding of the product planning process in this way – not least because I believe that product planning in its nature and origins should be the concern of the chief executive. I shall keep coming back to this point. Nowhere else are there so many aspects of a company's operations, organisation and future prosperity bound up so closely together.

PRODUCT PLANNING AS THE DRIVER OF THE NEW PRODUCT PROCESS

There are four areas where product planning should be seen as the initiative taker and not just another co-ordinating, staff department. It is these features that drive the new product development process.

Voice of the Customer. A company must listen for the voice of the customer before all other things. It should not impose its own internal vision or its management's subjective view of the product. It has to understand where its products should be positioned in the market in order to attract the numbers of customers needed. It must aim to produce a product that both looks and behaves in line with customers' wants and needs.

Managing Technology. To satisfy the customer at the lowest cost a company must have proven technologies on the shelf to fit into new product programmes at the appropriate point, thus saving time, development duplication and ensuring quality of execution. A company must also strive to make maximum use of its own or others' proven technology so as not to have to reinvent the wheel, which unnecessarily absorbs precious resources and time.

Creating a Product Strategy and Plan. It is no good starting a new product programme with a poorly thought out plan. The best, most successful products are those where the producer gives as much emphasis to planning as to implementation. The results are a more economical product programme, faster time to market, fewer running changes and less disruption after production start.

Managing Progress and Decisions. One of the most important profit drivers is to ensure that what was decided at the beginning of a new product programme gets into production while meeting the original targets. This can only be achieved with a logical, well thought out process in which all company functions work smoothly together. The objective should be always to start and finish on time – and, preferably, to finish before your competitors.

Of all the many strategic management initiatives over the past twenty years – optimised manufacturing, quality circles, total quality, strategic planning, cost reduction, just-in-time, employee empowerment – none offers the same end-to-end improvement potential as product planning and an efficient total product development process. It is possible to manufacture a mediocre product superbly, or severely to cost reduce it after it has started in production. How much better then to get it right first time and to optimise customer requirements, costs and manufacturing design as part of the original new product programme. Total quality can only be meaningful if it comes down to the level of doing something with every aspect of the business and, therefore, paying attention to the new product development process. Quality circles and empowerment programmes are a good and necessary way of harnessing the talents of employees but such programmes don't in themselves create anything except a co-operative work environment and the ability to optimise products and processes that already exist. Strategic planning is useful only if linked through a hands-on project planning and project implementation process to the daily operating life of a company. This is exactly what a good product planning process must do.

THE LAYOUT OF THE BOOK

The approach I have used takes various slices through the new product development process, to provide, in each chapter, a different cross-section that allows me to illustrate different aspects of product planning.

This chapter makes clear why product planning should be more widely understood. It is also a first look at some strategic aspects and factors for success. Chapter Two says something about the history of product planning, its origins and development. This chapter gives some clues about the relations between product planning and chief executives. It also demonstrates that the original reasons for product planning are just as valid today.

Chapter Three is the first cross-section through the process. It describes the building blocks that make up the product planning function and responsibilities. All major parts of the total process are covered. Various forms and degrees of product planning are shown made up of different combinations of the building blocks.

In Chapter Four, I show what kinds of other industries, besides automotive, are ripe for product planning strategies and techniques. I try to draw out the industrial factors or characteristics that could lead a company to consider adopting a formal product planning organisation. Although much of my own experience is drawn from the automotive industry, I reach the conclusion that product planning techniques are appropriate to a wide variety of industries.

Chapter Five describes the new product development process itself – a fundamental part of a company's operations that determines its product-related profitability. I try to give only a high-level view, defining that part of the process relevant to the product planner in order to show how the product planning actions are involved in the process and how they both guide and support it. At this level emphasis is placed on the decision-making aspects of the process – a major product planning concern – and the essence of managing the stage-by-stage decision-making. I also touch on risk management and quality aspects of the whole process.

Chapter Six provides an organisational cross section, taking some examples of product planning organisations in automotive and other industries and commenting on their particular features, working methods and likely advantages and disadvantages. There is no fixed blueprint for a product planning organisation structure: it must develop over time to address ever-changing operational needs or to meet competitive threats. There are, however, many similarities between product planning and product management organisations in different industries.

Chapter Seven contains an overview of programme management as an organisational entity in its own right – a relatively new and important development. It has its origins in the product planning process and relates strongly to the cross-functional workings of product planning. Programme management is used by Japanese companies such as Toyota and Honda and more advanced European and North American firms such as Ford, Rover, Xerox, John Deere and Hewlett Packard.

Chapter Eight describes the key aspects of business planning, which has strong affinities with product planning. This is a very significant part of the overall company planning process and provides the front end of the new product development process. The creation of a business plan defines the conditions under which an individual new product programme may be successfully started. Often the two departments go hand-in-hand.

In Chapter Nine, I say something about the approach of a product planner to his work and take a critical look at some of the tools and techniques of the trade.

I have tried to include a range of case studies from as wide a cross-section of industries as possible. These illustrate good and bad points of the product planner's art. Inevitably some of them are from the automotive industry since that is where the product planning function is most often found, but I have included studies from other industries, from Europe and one from Japan, where product planning as a function is used more widely. These case studies make up Chapter Ten.

Chapter Eleven is another cross-section describing the relations and main functional interfaces between product planning and other line functions working together on product programmes. This is important to clarify, since product planning is a truly cross-functional departmental form that owes its success to effective interfacing with most other departments, whether staff or line. This chapter also contains my concluding comments about the overall value of product planning. In each chapter, however, I try to draw out relevant conclusions so that the content of that chapter speaks for itself.

Notes

1. Akio Morita, *Made in Japan*, William Collins, 1987.

2 THE ORIGINS OF PRODUCT PLANNING

Where did the need for product planning first arise? Product planning belongs to a creative form of entrepreneurial activity and can
be found in its earliest forms in the US and UK. The basic working
of product planning and its main principles can be seen in these
early examples, confirming the thesis that product planning is an
activity carried out on behalf of a company's chief executive.

Why has product planning not been more widely adopted in
Europe and US compared to Japan? What lessons can be learnt
from the Japanese approach to planning new products and the total
product development function?

EARLY PRODUCT PLANNERS

The first product planners were those early entrepreneurs – William Lyons,
Walter Bentley, Henry Ford, Henry Morgan and many others – who founded
the great product-based companies. Since the 1950s, significant Japanese
product-based companies have also been established by figures such as Akio
Morita and Sochiro Honda. Most of these entrepreneurs were also engineers
who were revered for the engineering excellence of their products. Yet this
did not make these early pioneers product planners in our sense of the word.
For, as already noted, product planning in the fullest sense is more than pure
engineering excellence. It is the ability to build the necessary bridges between
engineering excellence, customer need and a profitable market opportunity.

In the days of Bentley and Morgan, creating a business was relatively
simple: these were the days before mass production, dedicated product
tooling and facilities, complex product legislation specific to each country
and the internationalisation of both production and markets. It was possible
to define the vision and concept for a new product quite simply and quickly.
Execution could follow through the technical and manufacturing staffs of
the organisation. Certainly the planning and control process was simple
enough not to need a separate department. The competitive excellence
needed to succeed was more based on the creative flair of the original

product concept than on attention to fine detail and optimisation during planning and implementation.

Neverthless all the basic ingredients of the product planning mix can be seen in the work of these entrepreneurs of the pre- and immediate post-war period – even if the concept of a product planning function as such was still not needed or recognised. Later, due to the growing complexity of companies and markets and the need for company heads to devote time to more international or operational issues, the initial entrepreneurial task itself became more complex and the planning of new products came to require a more formalised approach.

PRODUCT PLANNING MGs IN 1953

As an illustration, look at these extracts[1] from internal memos by John Thornley, then general manager of the MG Car Company, written in 1953 to his board. Thornley was trying to create understanding of, or obtain approval for, his product ideas. These memos were written when the MG sports car was widely revered throughout the world and especially in North America. The then currently popular product was the MG TD, a successor to the TA/TB/TC models which spanned both the pre- and post-war period. The product design configuration and technology were also very much derived from the pre-war standards. In the marketplace, however, things were changing[1].

'SOME THOUGHTS ON THE FUTURE OF THE MG 2-SEATER
To say that the USA is our most important market is, of course, a platitude, but it seems improbable that, if the American market were lost, the whole of the rest of the world would be able to absorb much more than half our present output. In thinking in terms of future design and development, therefore, we must base our thoughts entirely on the USA.

It must not be forgotten that when the TD was introduced into the USA its performance was such relative to the average American car that it could beat them from the traffic lights and on the open road. It is probable that this feature alone did more to popularise the model and bring it to the attention of the American public than any other single factor. During the last three years, however, there has been a revolution in American power unit design and the TD, having remained unchanged, is now at a disadvantage.

It is probable that the American market can be held with the existing TD through the summer of 1953 but unless there is some change of model it is doubtful whether the present rate of sale can be maintained through the succeeding winter.

On the basis of the TC and TD MG, the marque has an extraordinarily high reputation in the USA for reliability and for withstanding punishment and its continued success is largely attributable to this fact. Whatever mistakes we make with regard to the American market we must not submit to them anything which is untried or in which there is the slightest possibility of epidemic defect.

The first point which arises from the foregoing is that we must be careful about the introduction of the BMC B series engine. If there is any doubt about it by the due date of its introduction, i.e. September 1953, then it would be preferable to consider the continuance of the XPAG engine for a few months (if this is possible from a production point of view) or even to provide the increased engine power by means of an over-bored version of the XPAG engine (samples of which are on test at this present moment) and despite the objections to siamesed bores.

In order to derive maximum advantage from the increased power of the larger engine an attempt has been made to improve the shape of the TD without destroying its essentially characteristic appearance and the blue car which is to be submitted for scrutiny by the joint boards on 8th January is a sample.

It is believed that this model will not only meet the immediate requirements of the USA, as expressed by the distributors there, but, by representing a change from the TD, will fill a ready market consisting of most of those who at present own TDs (and there are over 10,000 of them) who will wish to change for change's sake.

A new series of small MGs has been designed by Mr Palmer. From the fact that these are, at the present moment, not beyond the drawing board and rough mock-up stage, one would be entitled to draw the conclusion that these could not be in production before September 1954. A statement has been made, however, that they could be ready by March 1954.

Undoubtedly these motor cars or something like them, provide a very suitable long-term development from the TD, but bearing in mind what was said above about the need for sending to the USA only well-tried designs, we must be careful not to place ourselves in the position where we are utterly dependent for a continuance of the market upon the premature introduction of an untried motor-car.

If credence is given to the suggestion that this car could be ready in March 1954, it might well be decided that the existing TD, or the existing TD with the 1.5 litre engine in it, could run on until that date. If then the new model proved to need more extended development, we should be forced into a position either where we were sending an unsatisfactory vehicle for sale in the USA, or where we were leaving a big gap in the continuity of our supplies to that market, either of which would be disastrous.

The sensible answer to these potential problems would appear to be to introduce the re-designed TD (the blue MG which has been tentatively called the TF) in September 1954, or even earlier, if possible, and allow it to run on for at least a twelve-month or perhaps even 18 months, during which time Mr Palmer's new motor cars can be fully developed and tried and "all the bugs taken out of them".'

This all new model eventually became the MG A and was not introduced until 1956. The modified TD – the TF model – came in towards the end of 1953 and, together with a 1.5 litre version of its engine, lasted until 1955.

John Thornley continues:

'No review of this kind would be complete without some reference to a "buzz-box" by which term is meant a small, light, inexpensive vehicle of the nature of the original MG Midget of the 1930s.

It must be said at the outset, however, that such a model has little future in America where long distances and high cruising speeds call for larger engines. For this reason the cars mentioned above must take pride of place.

For Britain and for the rest of the world there is undoubtedly a big market for the "buzz-box", and we would do well to think about it now.

The basic minimum requirements of such a car are: 70 mph with commensurate acceleration; 2 seats with luggage space; basis price £350-£375 at current levels.'

This line of thought probably resulted in the Austin Healey Sprite, which was developed by another arm of The British Motor Corporation with help from Donald Healey. This was not an MG until the MG Midget version was introduced some years later.

There are several internal memos written by John Thornley in the same period in which the same creative product planning principles shine through clearly. These can be summarised as follows and cover many of the points with which a product planner should concern himself in evaluating potential new product programmes or product improvements.

CONSIDERATIONS FOR THE PRODUCT PLANNER

- What is the customer reaction to our present products in our most important markets?
- What alternatives do we have to improve that situation with new product action?
- What are the chances of getting the various new product projects approved by our management?
- What are our competitors doing?
- Should we go for a re-vamp of our existing product, so saving time and money, as well as getting a product improvement into the market quickly? Or should we introduce that all new and much more advanced product that the advanced engineering specialists have been working on?
- If we go for the large-step improvement with an all new product, what is the risk of damaging our reputation in key markets? We certainly should not be hurried into launching an undeveloped and unreliable product. Perhaps we should carry on with small-step improvements until the all new product is thoroughly tried out.
- There are other market opportunities that we should address to broaden our market coverage. The board should consider the implications of these.

Clearly, one of the important tasks of the MG general manager was to do the product planning and to present the results to the BMC board for approval.

PRODUCT PLANNING THE LANCIA LAMBDA

Some quite different considerations are highlighted in this *Autocar*[2] article about Vincenzo Lancia and the creation of his revolutionary Lancia Lambda in 1922. Lancia's product decision issues were bolder and more risky than those of MG but the same combination of technical understanding and creative product flair was required for success[2].

'Imagine the effect if today, right in the middle of a recession, Aston Martin was to introduce a Sierra-sized family car with a carbon-fibre composite body shell, active suspension and an ultra-compact, two-litre, six valve per cylinder engine that immediately made all cars in its class obsolete. That, essentially, was what happened in 1922 when Lancia launched the Lambda.

To understand the Lambda, you have to know what came before. Until then, the Italian manufacturer had, on the whole, been making straight forward, up-market machines. This meant ladder-type chassis with strengthening cross members, relatively big, lazy, side-valve engines, solid beam axles fore and aft, brakes on the rear only, and any body you liked as long as someone else built it. The difference was that Lancias were beautifully made and had a fine reputation worldwide, notably in the US and England.

The Lambda, on the other hand, was as radical as you could get. It had a unitary body/chassis, an extremely advanced and compact overhead cam V4 engine, independent front suspension and four wheel brakes. Quite why or how the concept of the Lambda arose is unclear. It is said that a boat hull gave Vincenzo Lancia the idea for the body, and with his background, he was fully familiar with technical developments throughout the world. Individually there was little in the Lambda that hadn't been seen before – it was the combination of its features that set it apart.

The Lambda, though, is famous not just for its technical breakthroughs, but for the fact that it worked. It was truly a major technical milestone in the history of the motor-car.'

In a profile of Vincenzo Lancia himself the article continues:

'He was a good example of the Edwardian, self-taught, intuitive engineer in the mould of Ettore Bugatti or W.O. Bentley, but if he is to be compared to anyone it would have to be Colin Chapman, since he had the same technical flair. On top of all that, in his younger days he was a world-class racing driver.

He was not a hands-on engineer or draughtsman, but he put his ideas across in broad brush strokes, to which others applied the details. Thus the Lambda chassis, after Lancia's brief, was actually concocted by Battista Falchetto. Nor was he (Lancia) a one-car man, for the Lambda was followed by the even more advanced Aprilia, this time with true monocoque construction, all independent suspension and streamlined body work.'

Here again we can see some of the basic approaches of the best product planners.

- Combining known technology in a creative way to produce a unique product to beat the competition. Creativity is a very important part of a product planner's approach and often this factor, more than technical or product excellence, provides the competitive edge.

- Describing the new product vision in overall terms and principles but handing it over to the engineers to implement in detail.
- Having a love for and experience of the product – Lancia was formerly a tester with Fiat and a racing driver – as well as an understanding of the engineering principles involved without necessarily being qualified as a design engineer but having good engineering colleagues to whom the implementation could be entrusted.

PRODUCT PLANNING: A TOP MANAGEMENT CONCERN

It is clear from just the two examples above that the first product planners must have been top managers: almost all the early entrepreneurs and founders of successful product companies based their success on products they themselves conceived. Judging by some of the products which have seen the light of day, not all of these entrepreneur product planning efforts were successful. Often, where one founder of a successful company was the product ideas man, another partner could be the salesman or financial brain. This provided a business balance. Business balance is also a required characteristic of a product planner.

I have no doubt, however, that the original responsibility for product planning must have lain with the head of the company. It also follows on from this that even today the initial product planning conceptual work and the decision making surrounding it should be seen as company-wide activity. This means it should be carried out on behalf of top management or the board, not performed separately from the main line, strategic thrust of a company.

Perhaps it is a lack of understanding of this key principle that has led to the fall of many product planning dynasties in British, American and some European companies. This would explain why, although the value of basic product planning principles has been known for a long time, there has been a failure to implement them effectively and consistently in a broad spectrum of industries. Had this not been so, product planning should have become widely established as a major part of company management. Often a product planning department has reported too low down the organisation so that it has been seen as the tool of a functional department such as product development or marketing rather than as a company-wide activity. I give some further analysis of this in Chapter Three; the role definition of product planning and programme management and their reporting levels in any organisation are of crucial importance.

EARLY PRODUCT PLANNING DEPARTMENTS IN EUROPE

A very early version of a product planning department can be found in the Ford Motor Company in the UK in the mid-1950s. Product planning was one of the management techniques used during development of the first Ford Cortina model, which was launched in 1960. It was said to have played a major role in the Cortina's success.

Sir Terence Beckett, a former chairman of Ford of Britain and subsequently the director general of the Confederation of British Industry, is credited with being responsible for product planning the Cortina. His comments on the origins and basic principles of Ford's product planning organisation, given to me in a series of discussions, are of some interest.

'Product Planning started at Ford UK in the mid 1950s at the instigation of the then managing director, Sir Patrick Hennessy. From experience of working with his US Ford colleagues, who had a product planning committee, and from his own Ford UK operational needs, he perceived the need for a full-time group of managers who would first define, and then monitor, the success of all new product programmes. Accordingly he set up a division called Product Planning Staff.

I was head of product planning from 1955 to 1963 and at that time it consisted of about sixty multi-disciplinary specialists: engineers, finance and marketing analysts, buyers and so on. These were divided into several product teams and were responsible for product definition, cost control, timing control, competitive analysis and for co-ordinating the important views of all divisions working on new products as an input to the programmes.

Sir Patrick Hennesy recognised that he needed such a staff reporting to him for three reasons. First, they could receive guidance from him on the strategic outline of the next new product and turn that into a detailed product programme brief for engineering, manufacturing and marketing to implement. Second, they could provide the Product Planning Committee (in fact the board with their product hats on) with the tools and information to control the implementation of product programmes and to eliminate or at least control product drift, that tendency for new models to vary widely from their initial objectives during the development phase. Third, and of increasing importance, the product planning group took on the task of actually proposing to the PPC what the forward product plan should be, based on a study of the market, the competition and what Ford could or should do according to its internal needs. Product planning acted as the secretariat of the PPC and, in this last proactive role, actually performed tasks that had previously been the preserve of the board itself, or certainly of the chief executive; the proposals for new products.

Initially, the product planning group was inexperienced and the first two projects did not go as well as we wanted. However, the Cortina programme was the first one where we had really developed our product planning techniques to the required level, especially in terms of product definition, cost and time control. The story of the Cortina programme is well documented in Graham Turner's book, '*Industry, People and Cars*' but it is worth mentioning here some of the important principles that I learnt as part of that early product planning experience regarding the importance of product planning to the whole industrial process.

1. It is essential that the chief executive of a company believes in the importance of, and gives support to, the product planning function. This is vital because of the fundamental importance of new products to a company's future. Only the chief executive can ensure that all other functional areas play their part properly in the new product creation process.

2. Product planning is an essential discipline in industries characterised by long lead times for new products, high investments, high volume complex products, and a long time between the taking and the implementing of a decision. This latter point emphasises the high quality of the decision making that is needed because of the high cost of later changing wrong decisions.

3. The recognition of product planning as a separate discipline within a company which co-ordinates all the relevant activities to develop competitive and profitable new products is vital to a company's future prosperity.

I still hold these views strongly on the importance of product planning for British industry.'

PRODUCT PLANNING IN THE UNITED STATES

As Sir Terence Beckett notes, product planning already existed in the US automotive industry and at Ford UK in the 1950s. I was aware of it at Chrysler in the 1960s. However, from my recollections, the US style of product planning only contained some of the characteristics of full product planning as Sir Terence defined it and as I am trying to describe it in this book.

The US car market in the 1960s had already settled down to relatively well-defined product segments with each of the major OEMs competing directly against its competitors on a model for model basis. This was certainly not yet the case in Europe, where each auto company was still trying to find the right market positioning for each of its models. European auto manufacturers were still trying to develop a full model range to cover the market. Annual product changes in the US market were based on cosmetic facelifts and feature changes, perhaps with the introduction of new options, but with very little fundamental reappraisal of a product's cost, design, configuration or market positioning. There were very few all new products breaking new ground. Product planning changes, therefore, were in the main incremental to a known base product that was assumed as proven. They were not subject to the same comprehensive planning and targetting activities as were applied to the Cortina.

These product planning departments were much more concerned with product requirement planning, with product release authorisation to cover the annual new model upgrades, with the introduction of American-designed vehicles into overseas CKD (completely knocked down or disassembled) territories and with planning minor current model facelifts that normally had a heavy visual content. They were seldom the departments responsible for creating wholly new products to satisfy new customer needs in line with real market trends. They were also much less concerned with programme timing, cost targetting and the structuring and management of product programmes for optimal total results. Although there were exceptions, such activities tended to be left to engineering groups or were not done at all in a co-ordinated way. There were, however, some all new product concepts introduced such as the Ford Mustang programme, where some more fundamental product planning principles could be seen at work.

The Creation of the Ford Mustang

A study of Robert Lacey's *Ford*[3] and of Lee Iacocca's *Iacocca*[4] gives some fascinating insights into the Ford Mustang's creation. This was a new model, in a new market segment, developed with a typical product planning multi-disciplinary team approach. It was undeniably successful. The Mustang was based on an existing platform, the Ford Falcon, for time and investment economy reasons: therefore, it relied on a lot of carry-over engineering. As a pure product idea, it was directly stimulated by a General Motors' product styling exercise, the Corvair Monza, which was exhibited at the Chicago

Motor Show in 1960, and which captured the attention of the public and of the design and product planners at Ford.

As Robert Lacey notes, the main product planning ingredients were all there.

> 'The Ford product planners went into action to see how they might match the Monza and the Ford design studio was already thinking along the same lines. Gene Bordinat, just taking over Ford's design vice-presidency from George Walker, had been discussing the sporty-type Corvair with Don DeLaRossa, his chief of advanced design, and the two men decided to try to put Ford's 289 cubic inch V8 engine of the day into the light and resilient platform of the Falcon. They then devised a totally new body shell to give this car a power-packed appearance in the traditional way – "lotsa hood" – and they rounded the two-seater off with a squared roof and low flat rear deck.'

The styling proposal was presented to Lee Iacocca, then vice president of the Ford Division, in autumn 1961. The next months were spent in a scramble of product planning and engineering activity to turn this attractive concept into a viable programme. A political campaign was launched to persuade Ford's top board to provide the funds and approve the programme: no small task in view of the relatively recent Edsel fiasco. In fact, Henry Ford II at first rejected the whole idea when it was presented to him.

Iacocca himself acted as "product champion" or what would today be called the programme director. His situation offers a good illustration of the kind of reporting levels and strength needed by a programme manager to get what he wants, especially when trying to drive through a really creative new product idea against strong opposition from more traditional factions in a company. Not every programme needs an Iacocca; but many programmes fail today because their backers fail to recognise the need for high level attention and support.

After a full review of the programme and the proposed styling model, including one or two top management-inspired design changes, the go ahead was given and the vehicle was launched at the New York World's Fair in the spring of 1964. It cost only $2,368 but looked much more expensive and handled more like a sports-car. In 1965 and 1966 the Mustang sold over 500,000 units; a market penetration of 6.1 per cent.

Iacocca's memoirs give much more information about the nuts and bolts of the product planning process that went to make up the success of the Mustang programme; the demographic research that revealed the growing and more affluent demands of the post-war generation; the problems of squeezing two more inches into the rear legroom to meet Henry Ford's demands; the brand new idea to offer a wide range of options and packages that would allow different customers to tailor the car to suit their pockets and lifestyle; the struggles to plan more capacity as the car's full volume potentials were realised; the constant vigilance to hold the cost and weight and price targets, and above all the motivation of a team of people fired by a common vision of their new product creation.

Iacocca captures the urgency of the situation in the aftermath of the Mustang's launch.

> 'After only a few weeks it became clear to me that we had to open a second plant. The initial assumption had been that the Mustang would sell 75,000 units during the first year. But the projections kept growing, and before the car was introduced we were planning on sales of 200,000. To build that many cars we had to convince top management to convert a second plant, in San Jose, California, into producing more Mustangs.
>
> Our annual capacity was now 360,000 cars and soon we were converting a third plant, in Metuchen, New Jersey.'

Illustrating that one product planning swallow does not make a summer, Iaccoca reports that from 1968 the Mustang's success was waning and the latest versions were being criticised by customers. Driven by successive product efforts to upgrade the car, by 1971 the Mustang was far distant from the original concept. Iacocca describes it as being eight inches longer, six inches wider, almost six hundred pounds heavier and carrying a much more powerful engine than the original 1965 model.

> 'It was no longer the same car, and our declining sales figures were making the point very clearly. In 1966 we sold 550,000 Mustangs. By 1970, sales had plummeted to 150,000 – a disastrous decline.'

There is clearly good product planning and not so good product planning. I shall attempt to point out the route to consistent, effective product planning in the rest of this book.

DEVELOPING PRODUCT PLANNING SKILLS

Considering the breadth of functions needed to cover the whole product creation process, it is perhaps surprising that no comprehensive body of teaching literature exists on product planning and the process of product development, as it does on engineering, finance or marketing. Perhaps with the emergence of the matrix organisation in more companies, with the product and programme axes being given at least equal, if not greater, weight than the old functional specialisations, we shall see the emergence of these product disciplines taught in business schools and universities. The need for better product planning is very current. With the emphasis on competition through new product development, most companies need a thorough overhaul of the complete product planning process. Many companies need to establish some of the key building blocks that lie at the heart of world class product planning.

As the last of my remarks on product planning's history, the experience of Japanese automotive companies reinforces the view that there is little in the way of new techniques but much to be gained in the way of more effective technique utilisation. During my period with Volvo Holland, I was involved in negotiations between Mitsubishi and Volvo up to September 1991. Ultimately, these talks led to Volvo Car BV being renamed NedCar after Mitsubishi acquired a one third share in the company.

During the many product discussions, I learnt that Mitsubishi use a product structure and specification system – the UPG (Universal Parts Grouping) system – that is very similar to a system developed by Chrysler in the early 1970s and also used within Chrysler UK. Chrysler took a 15 per cent share holding in Mitsubishi Motors in 1971 and helped with product planning by stationing one of their senior product planners in Japan, where Mitsubishi already had a formal product planning department. In working together with Chrysler, Mitsubishi must have become familiar with many of Chrysler's product planning practices and techniques. The fact that Mitsubishi still uses these same techniques, no doubt in a significantly developed form, is a tribute both to the quality of the original concepts and to Japanese competence in adapting and improving what they learn from other people. Western companies have had these techniques for a long time, but have not always created such a succesful platform for their use.

Japanese companies have also developed the possibilities of product planning, cost targetting and programme co-ordination activities into the successful *shusa* programme management concept. *Shusa* is specifically identified with Toyota and is believed by many to be the cornerstone of Toyota's world-wide success. Honda call it the Large Programme Manager but the operation is the same. Programme management is also used very widely in non-automotive Japanese companies that make technical products such as consumer electronics. To an increasing degree, it is also used in leading

European companies, although implementation is not without its difficulties in Western management climates.

If there is nothing new in the techniques and ideas, and if some of them have been in partial use in various European automotive companies since the 1960s, why, in Europe, has no industry-wide improvement in product planning and product development efficiency matched that achieved by most Japanese companies? I can suggest some pointers from my own experience, especially as regards the effective development of a product planning mentality and approach in European companies.

REASONS FOR INSUFFICIENT USE OF PRODUCT PLANNING

In some Western companies, the development of product planning, with all its separate product definition, project planning and control ideas, created an adverse reaction in the large well-established organisational units such as engineering or marketing. In the past, these units had seen themselves as the true line functions responsible for the "doing". Advice, input and control were only very reluctantly accepted from what was seen as a small staff department. A line role or a combined line/staff role for product planning was not clearly understood. Certainly the cross-functional role of an effective product planning activity was not clearly understood or accepted. Instead of strengthening its position, the fact that product planning usually had a direct line to the board through the product planning committee only made the resistance to change stronger. Better planning, more parallel working and a more efficient process fell by the wayside. Inter-divisional wars and power plays between "the product planners" and "the engineers" or "sales and marketing" became the norm.

In some companies, hands-on chief executives found delegation of the "simple" task of directing product plans to another "staff" department an expensive luxury. The chief executive would keep the job for himself or for the board in committee. That approach works where a company can live off the fat of previous effective product planning and product development. However, the time usually comes when subjective, unresearched, off-the-cuff decisions are insufficient or when the next major new product development is due and the required knowledge of the processes and techniques has been allowed to fade away. The slimming down of many British companies in the past ten years has cleared out many such resources seen as not directly productive or contributing to this year's bottom line.

I say this not to take sides with product planners versus "the rest", but to show what often happened in a variety of automotive and other engineering product companies. However, I would also like to emphasise that the time for this kind of corporate behaviour is past. High quality planning and preparation, parallel co-operative working and the sharing of responsibility between people and departments must become the order of the day if European companies are to meet and counter the threat from the highly efficient and competitive Japanese and other Far Eastern companies.

Product planning must establish itself as a professional discipline alongside engineering or marketing so as to get away from subjectivism in product decision-making: the situation where everyone is a product "expert".

The artificial division between staff and line functions should also be swept away. If a job needs to be done, someone should have the responsibility for doing it properly. There should be no stigma attached to it being done outside the traditional large "line" functions. If the job doesn't need to be done there is no issue. There is no longer any doubt as to the kinds of things which need to be done to improve new product development processes. The key question is how to make them happen. Perhaps more difficult, we must make them stick so that a company is consistently able to generate customer-oriented and profitable new products. The building blocks of product planning, which form a major part of these drivers of successful new product creation, are described in the next chapter.

Notes

1. John Thornley has kindly agreed to my use of these extracts which were first published in the MG Car Club magazine, Safety Fast, in March 1991.

2. These extracts are reproduced with the permission of Autocar and Motor, from an article in the September 1991 edition about Lancia and the Lancia Lambda.

3. Robert Lacey, *Ford*, William Heinemann Ltd, 1986.

4. Lee Iacocca, *Iacocca*, Bantam Books, 1986.

3 THE BUILDING BLOCKS OF PRODUCT PLANNING

> The many different aspects of a product planning process may be organised in a single department or shared by different departments. The various functional tasks and responsibilities – the building blocks – of the product planning mix are critically examined and described. Six distinct groupings of product planning activity are suggested as representing the different organisational forms in which product planning can be found. These range from the simplest product requirement planning to an all-embracing product and programme management organisation.

THE DIFFERENT FORMS OF PRODUCT PLANNING

In the Introduction and in Chapter One, I talked about aspects of the role and purpose of product planning. Here, I would like to summarise all the different elements so that a complete picture may be gained of the scope and activities of planning the product. This section covers the potential of product planning to help a company develop the competent and effective processes that ensure the creation of profitable products that customers will want to buy again and again.

Potentially, there are almost as many forms of product planning organisation as there are individual companies. Chapter Six describes the approaches that several different companies, in several different industries, have taken to arrive at an appropriate product planning organisation. No two organisations are the same. Each company must find its own way. However, to give some structure to this review of the total scope of product planning, I have distinguished between six types or grades of product planning, most of which can be found in European companies.

1. Product Requirement Planning.
2. Product Management.
3. "Normal" Product Planning.
4. Extended Product Planning or Programme Planning.
5. Product and Programme Planning and Programme Implementation.
6. Product Planning and Product Cycle Planning.

1. *Product Requirement Planning* is a relatively simple form that concentrates on what the consumer, the industrial customer or the user wants from a proposed new product. Sometimes this function is the only part of a company with a specific "product" responsibility and may operate as part of a marketing department rather than being closely tied to a product development organisation. The evaluation of the impact of the product requirements on the rest of the company's operations is left to other people, often engineering or finance personnel. For some reason, this form of product planning is often found in the truck industry, perhaps because the product requirements can be precisely defined by a legislative framework combined with a quantifiable view of needed characteristics such as payload, dimensions, productivity factors and driver features. Subjective or mass consumer considerations are less prominent.

2. *Product Management* can be a stand-alone function with responsibility for the product or product family throughout its life as well as during its creation or development phase. This function is widely found in consumer goods companies where the marketing, selling and advertising emphasis is much stronger than the technological or product development aspects of company activities. Product managers exist also in engineering companies, but often as part of a larger product planning, marketing or product development organisation rather than standing on their own.

3. *"Normal" Product Planning* is the lowest level at which one can speak of a product planning department in its own right rather than as planning activities that belong to another department. This should also include advanced product planning; longer term research into suitable products and product characteristics. The advanced function can be a separate department or carried out by the product management department itself.

The key characteristic of a product planning department deserving the title is the capability and the responsibility to act as if representing the board (regardless of whether it reports at that level) in studying and recommending product action and taking into account the implications of that action for the rest of the company. This is more a creative and business task than a problem of pure financial evaluation, although financial evaluation and justification retain an important role. But the most important aspect of it is managing the trade-offs between the conflicting demands of other departments. The distinguishing feature of what I call "normal" product planning is this multi- or cross-functional role. This causes confusion in companies and organisations used to the comfortable and clear divisions of line departmental responsibilities. A staff function, which product planning is often incorrectly seen as, defines its requirements as a form of advice to the rest of the company: the responsible implementing departments are left to get on with the job. In such cases, the concept of shared or company responsibility for an activity has not been accepted. More of this later.

4. *Extended Product Planning or Programme Planning.* Product planning responsibilities can be extended to include planning the details of the product programme such as the programme timing plan, the resource plan and the decisions and main actions necessary to bring the new product on stream. Programme timing may be a separate department attached to product planning.

In planning the product and evaluating the possible effects of having that new product idea turned into a product programme, it is impossible for an effective product planner not to concern himself with all the aspects of the plan to introduce the product, regardless of which department is responsible for covering that aspect. How else can he be sure that what he is asking for is feasible? How else can he stand up in front of the product planning committee or board and present a new product programme and not be shot down for failing to consider all key cross-company implications? In particular, the timing framework for a new programme is vital, in that it allows management to see how the programme fits together, how it links to other activities, what the levels of risk are, when costs will be incurred, resources used and profitability realised.

Having worked in a product planning department that included an effective timing function, I firmly believe that up-front programme timing responsibility must lie in product planning, especially in terms of setting objectives for the programme. Timing is a skill not sufficiently understood across all departments in industry. Therefore it needs a separate focal point at the centre of the programme.

This idea of having certain types of expertise in a product team does not necessarily have to be extended any further. A product planning department does not necessarily need to include marketing, manufacturing planning or purchasing people to ensure that detailed programme planning in those areas is properly done. These are tasks to be performed by the functional areas themselves. However, product planning must include people with a broad understanding of all company operations. This enables an effective cross-functional dialogue in the programme planning task and ensures that all the company-wide implications are taken into account. I have seen two organisations where product planning additionally took on the roles of long-term market planning and initial manufacturing planning. These two extra responsibilities added a dimension of quality to the up-front planning that product planning as a whole was able to deliver. These are evaluated in Chapter Six.

I consider this form of product planning to be the ideal basis for effective planning. In turn, it provides the foundation for speedy and profitable programme implementation.

5. *Product and Programme Planning and Programme Implementation.* If the planning task has been done well and all the participating departments have committed to the programme in its approval stage, management must then maintain continuity so that what was agreed is implemented. If product planning has been responsible for negotiating and co-ordinating the content of the programme at the front end, it can be sensible, in the interests of continuity, to keep the implementing responsibility with product planning. The planners have the most detailed knowledge of the discussions, commitments and decisions that make up the programme. In this scenario, the product planning department has been extended to cover what are often described as separate programme management functions. Under certain circumstances, placing responsibility for implementation alongside planning can work well. But this is not the only solution, and I discuss the question further in Chapter Seven.

6. *Product Planning and Product Cycle Planning.* This comprises normal or extended product planning with the additional responsibilities of product cycle planning. Product cycle planning involves defining future product changes and renewals for all products in a company's range over a defined planning period. This task also includes the evaluation and definition of the implications of the product plan for the whole company in resource, feasibility and financial terms. In some companies this function is also called business planning; it may or may not include the additional responsibilities outlined in sections four and five above. However, it should not be confused with corporate planning or with forms of business planning concerned with just the financial expression of a company's plan without responsibility for the hard assumptions behind the figures. Since this is a crucial subject in its own right, I describe the full extent of business planning and its relation to product planning in Chapter Eight. In fact, product cycle planning is one of the most important activities at the creative end of the product planner's task. But, for some reason, in some companies it is performed separately. In showing it as a possible form of product planning, especially when combined with the evaluation and creation of the product-based business plan, my preference for its position in the organisation is clear. Product cycle planning as a technique is dealt with more fully in Chapter Nine.

THE BUILDING BLOCKS OF PRODUCT PLANNING ACTIVITY

The above six forms or groupings of activity give an overview of the main forms in which product planning is found. Within each main group different activities go to make up the whole. They are functions that should occur in all successful product-based companies, whether or not they are grouped together in a single product planning department. I call these activities the building blocks of product planning.

There are specialist business books that deal in detail with several of these, especially where they are a recognised business technique – such as business planning in its widest sense or product management, which is a common organisational feature of fast-moving consumer goods companies. It is not the intention to give a full description here but rather to show enough about the importance of the activity to the overall product planning process to provide a complete picture of that process. Activities that tend to be more specific to product planning are covered in more detail with examples.

Figure 3.1 identifies the main building blocks which are described below. This can also serve as a high level overview of the product planning process from the first concept work through to a successful product programme implementation.

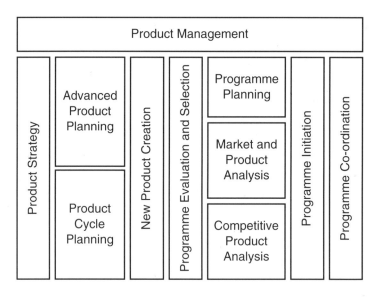

Figure 3.1 The Building Blocks of Product Planning.

Product Strategy

The first activity is the creation of a company's product strategy. This does not have to be a complicated document or statement. Indeed often the simpler it is, the better, but it comes in the same category as the Company Business Idea, the Company Philosophy, and other strategic statements that act as a constant guideline for future action. The simplicity of the wording can bely the enormous amount of effort used to create strategy statements or gain their acceptance. Some short company product strategy statements might read as follows:

- To identify and participate in market niches offering reasonable volumes where the name of the company can add value to the product and where the profit margins are above average.
- To make the best possible product, regardless of cost, for those customers who want and will pay for the best.
- To create new market opportunities ahead of the competition through product innovation combined with efficient design and production cost, rapid time to market, and creative marketing.
- To be a product fast-follower rather than innovator and to ensure that all products, when launched, offer the best standards of customer satisfaction, reliability, quality and are backed up by a customer support organisation second to none.
- To offer acceptable quality products with the lowest price in the segment while aiming at the biggest volume throughput.

The above might be suitable strategic statements for Rover, Daimler Benz, Sony, Volvo and Indesit, respectively. Tony Harrison[1] offers some similar examples from the fast-moving consumer goods industry:

- Heinz strategy in the UK canned soup market is to offer superlative quality and a complete product range at a competitive price, thus making it hard for competitors to enter the market.
- Petfoods strategy in their chosen market is to market a range of products that cover all consumer needs and advertise them heavily to make the cost of competitive entry unacceptably high.
- Reckitt and Colman's strategy is to cultivate niche products in small markets and avoid confrontation with mass marketers such as Unilever and Procter and Gamble.
- Amstrad's strategy is to achieve sensationally low end prices by a combination of low-cost manufacturing and volume selling through high street electrical stores and thus open new markets for what were previously high-cost products with limited sales.

There is an enormous amount of work required from product planning to arrive at such apparently simple statements. The statement has to express the will of top company management, and, indeed, can only be arrived at after careful consultation with the executive board. It must be based on skills and resources the company has or will acquire. It must be accepted by all senior functional management. It must be capable of influencing the way that all the company employees act in conceiving or executing new product programmes but without constraining their creativity or leading them to do the wrong things. It must also be reviewed annually, if appropriate, or at whatever time the planning cycle starts. It must be followed by a further definition of how each product, both current and proposed plays a role in the strategy. It must not be something which constantly changes and thus becomes more of a tactical than a strategic statement.

Since the strategy is about products it must be the first step in the product planning process and not something imposed from above or outside by people with no "product feel". For all employees, and for product planners specifically, it must guide subsequent product research and advanced product planning activities so that time and resources are not wasted on evaluating product ideas and programmes which, while attractive in themselves, do not meet the strategy criteria.

At this point I may be accused of preaching motherhood. But it is amazing how many projects are started and later halted after the spending of considerable resource when an early check against the main strategic criteria would have shown up the main problems. Indeed many companies press blindly on with new product programmes without even an explicit company or product strategy. No wonder that so many new products fail in the marketplace, though lack of a strategy is not by any means the only reason.

Advanced Product Planning

Sometimes this is a separate function within a product planning department, sometimes just a set of responsibilities divided up between the different product teams. However it is organised, those responsible for advanced product planning work should report to, or be the concern of, the head of product planning. This is one of the necessary work elements that must precede the start of any new product programme. It contains the following main elements.

1. Evaluating the new external product technologies and component developments that could be adopted by the company. These could come from

inventors: there is certainly no shortage of innovative ideas coming across the advanced product planner's desk. They might come from the creative capabilities and imagination of people within the company. Advances made by competitors can be another source; input may come from suppliers offering new components or process technologies that could help a company meet competition, reduce costs or improve their products. Lastly, there is always a wide range of published research and application development work on view at shows and exhibitions or presented in learned papers at various technical society symposia. The creative skill of the advanced product planner lies in distilling all the possible developments into alternative scenarios for the company.

2. Allied to external technology are future legislation requirements that sometimes call forth new technology or development work and resources. The advanced product planner's task is to sponsor internal investigation into the impact of proposed legislation, to ensure feedback to legislators if the company is in the habit of trying to influence future legislation and to prepare the company for action if a proposal becomes law.

3. Next is the formulation of a complete technological road map for the company, a task performed in conjunction with advanced engineering and research and development, and which shows how the products of the future will be developed with new features and ideas. This is not planning the details of the individual product programmes so much as determining the technological platform on which the company will base its engineering and its image in the future. To companies such as Sony, Volvo, Mercedes and Phillips, this will be a very important part of forward planning since their reputation and future image objectives are firmly rooted in being among the best in technology. For other companies it will be less important or, perhaps, just less visible if only because future technology aimed at reducing costs can be just as strategically important to an individual company as a high-tech product image. Compare the approach of Fiat with the Tipo, which is aimed at the most highly automated manufacturing processes, with that of Saab, where safety and the Swedish technology incorporated in the product itself are important.

4. The road map must include technological trend forecasting: where are *today's* technologies or current product performance standards going to be in five or ten years' time? It is very important to know, when planning a new product, what standards of performance should be set. Comparing it only to today's market and competition is guaranteed to result in a less than

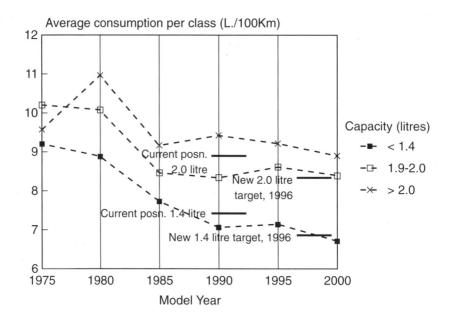

Figure 3.2 Compact Segment, Fuel Consumption Trend Targetting for New Model.

competitive product because market trends result in continuous improvement and competitors are seldom standing still. An example of this kind of fore-casting is shown in Figure 3.2 in relation to the positioning for a new vehicle model. The projected trend shows average fuel consumption improving in the relevant product segment, such that today's average will be totally uncompet-itive within five years. This means that even with a modest objective of remaining at the average level, a company must achieve a significant percentage improvement.

5. The advanced product planner concerns himself not only with what might come, but with what must be done now to prepare for the future. This is something the Japanese do well; it is referred to widely as shelf engineering.

In the dialogue with advanced engineering, outside suppliers and research organisations of the company, it is often necessary to start programmes of work without a specific production end date in mind in order to put suitable developments on the shelf. When proven out, these can then be inserted into new product development programmes and contribute to the advance of the new product over the old without placing the timing, quality or reliability of the new programme at risk. Advanced product planning must provide the justification for such work. In so doing, it provides a focus for the com-pany's advanced engineering and product-based research work. There is a growing realisation among companies investing heavily in this area that all advanced work must be focused on market opportunity, either creating it through technology, or directing technology research to meet perceived market needs and trends. The end result of this work could be a kind of advanced product plan, showing all the advanced programmes to be undertaken. This should also be amplified for each product range by showing how technical and performance characteristics of the products must develop over time. Volvo use this technique to create what they call a *property plan*. Table 3.1 is a simplified extract. It divides the vehicle into its most significant performance or customer perception areas and states the target for the new model year in each area in terms of its competitive position: best in class, upper segment, segment average, or low segment. In the short term, the elements of improvement must be built into a new product programme. However, when the targets are first set by advanced product planning, they usually require some shelf engineering preparation because the new product programme for that year has not yet started.

6. Some companies use an advanced product planning team to start new product programmes before they are taken over by regular teams. This is, for example, desirable if the product is all-new or different from the company's product mainstream. In this case, knowledge of the new market or technology has to be separately acquired and the responsibility fits better with the forward-looking mentality of the advanced product planners. The Ford of Europe product planning organisation of 1984 worked in this way.

Feature	Rating in Segment			
	Best	Upper	Average	Lower
Safety	◄———○			
Corrosion	◄—○			
Performance		◄		
Reliability		◄———○		
Comfort		◄		
Handling		◄		

Key: ○ = Current Model property position
◄ = Target New 1992 model position

Table 3.1 Product Property Targets: model year 1992.

This creative and forward looking quality can be a disadvantage when dealing with a more routine new product such as the replacement of an existing model with an upgrade, where rigorous product planning disciplines must be applied to meet timing, cost and profit criteria right from the project's start. It is desirable to avoid too many responsibility handovers in the product planning process. Better programme consistency is achieved by having one product manager for the programme's whole life. The primary task of advanced product planners, therefore, is to handle product studies and shelf planning as a preliminary sifting of ideas for the business and product plan.

If we return to Akio Morita's statement about the three important creativities for a successful company – technology creativity, product planning creativity and marketing creativity – we can see that advanced product planning sits at the crossroads between the first two of these criteria.

Product Cycle Planning

The product cycle plan is the central evaluation that determines how much new development or refreshment effort is put into each product during its life cycle, when it will be replaced and when the work on the replacement should start.

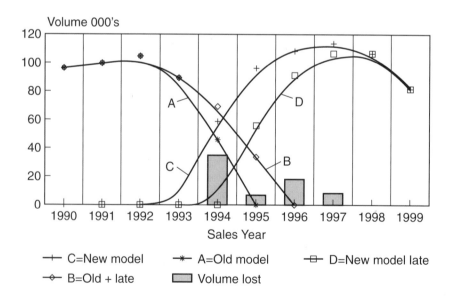

Figure 3.3 Product Life Cycle Planning. Timing of Replacement Model.

Enough has been written about methods of evaluating the new product cycle for a company to be able to plot the likely cycle of all its products with a reasonable degree of detail. Each market has its own characteristics. A study of the historic sales and market penetration pattern of competitors' and one's own products will provide important guidelines. Marketing as well as product planning information should be used for this. The difficult element of cycle planning lies in deciding what should be done to improve or replace the product– and when, since a company can also influence the length and extent of the natural cycle to a certain extent. The techniques associated with the product cycle are covered in Chapter Six but here I would like to deal with some of the more strategic or judgemental aspects.

Figure 3.3 shows a typical product life cycle where sales of an existing product are on the wane (graph A) and where it is planned to be replaced by a new product. Graph C shows the necessary introduction timing for the new model to maintain the total volume at a steady level. The effect is also shown of introducing the replacement product one year later (graphs B and D) a move that reduces overall volume. Delaying the introduction of a new or revised model nearly always loses volume and profit. Studies have shown that control of introduction timing can be the major contributor to lifetime profitability. In many companies, under the heading of tuning the long range plan to reduce resource or capital input, development costs or new product investment is spread forward, resulting in the postponement of planned new product introductions. The usual financial assumption is that the total profit and volume can be slipped bodily forward in time without losing anything. The reality is that competition never stands still. Lost volume is lost for ever.

Two Examples of Life Cycles

Let us now look at two further examples of product life cycles, both taken from the automotive industry where the data are most readily available.

BMW 3-Series. Figure 3.4 shows the volume growth of the BMW 3-Series in the period 1976 to 1987. Throughout the period BMW introduced many new versions of the original model range. Although the company achieved very successful growth, this stemmed from a large amount of product action, expanding and improving the product range. A complete new model range was introduced after an eight year interval. This emphasises that product cycle planning is concerned with influencing the length of the cycle as well as calculating the effect of market forces. This is a key issue for product planners.

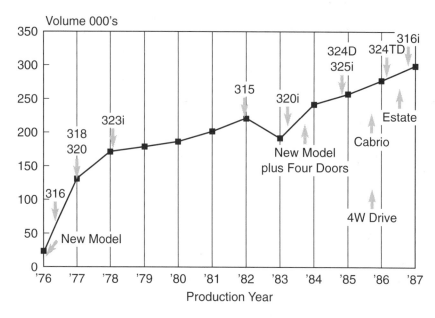

Figure 3.4 Product Life Cycles. BMW 3-Series 1976 to 1987.

Ford and Vauxhall. Another significant life cycle example is provided by the new front wheel drive Vauxhall Cavalier's overtaking, in the UK market, of the Ford Cortina in 1983. The new Cavalier was introduced one year before the new Ford Sierra, the Cortina's replacement. Thus the Cavalier was well-established in the market against the fading Cortina when the Sierra was introduced. It was this factor, rather than the rather controversial styling of the Sierra, which caused Ford its UK market share headaches. (By 1986, however, Ford had recovered its market leadership.)

Interestingly enough, the successor to that first Cavalier has now been in competition against the better established Sierra (which has undergone several worthwhile improvment programmes) for nearly three years. The new Cavalier has regained Vauxhall's lead over the Ford Sierra. The Sierra replacement is not due until 1993. Ford must have decided to slip a full half model cycle behind General Motors and come up with a superior product as a different way of competing because from a pure timing point of view they could not beat the latest Cavalier into production.

Importance of the Product Cycle to Product Planning

Determination of the required product life cycle for each product family and the creation of the product cycle plan is one of the most influential activities of product planning, not least because of its impact on the rest of the company. It acts as a basis for the business plan, lays the foundations for resource needs, capital spending and manufacturing capacity. It also has a big influence on future profitability. The product cycle of existing products is one means of suggesting the need for new product action to the product planner. Several more are covered in the next section.

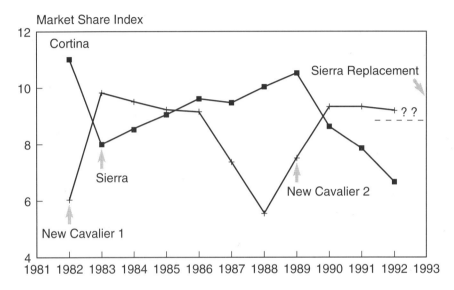

Figure 3.5 Product Cycle Planning. Ford and Vauxhall in the UK Market.

New Product Creation

This involves the evaluation of all possible sources and stimuli for introducing new products in order to create or revise the official company product plan.

The literature on product marketing gives a number of different categories of new product, often divided into "new to the company" and "new to the market". In considering types of new product activity of interest to the product planner, I have tried to define those external and internal pressures that lead the planner, to evaluate the need for product action. Taking this viewpoint, however, does not necessarily cover reasons for creating a new product that may occur in industries which rely not just on pure product or market planning but also technological innovation for the creation of markets and the generation of new products. Under such a heading could come the kind of technological development or innovation as practised by 3M, Sony, Intel or by the major semi-finished product producers in steel, textiles and plastics. Yet, product planning should not be seen as a merely mechanistic process. It should be possible from a professional planning base to arrive at innovative new product ideas and concepts. There are eight categories of new product relevant to product planning.

1. New Products from Life Cycle Timing.
2. Change because of Consumer Dissatisfaction.
3. Pressure of Competition.
4. New Market Niche or Segment.
5. Forced New Product by Legislation.
6. New-to-the-Company Market.
7. Facelifted or Upgraded Products.
8. Newly Created Product.

• *New Product* as a replacement demanded by the timing of the product life cycle of the old one. This assumes that the company is in a stable product area such as automobiles or other durable consumer goods rather than having a portfolio of widely differing products as is the case in the fast-moving consumer goods sector. The significance of the product life cycle is that a new product fitting into more or less the same market spot is required to avoid a profit and volume drop. An example here would be the automotive habit of regular product updates. Volkswagen are on the third version of the Golf, Honda are on the fourth version of the Accord. JCB have launched three completely revised versions of their original tractor-digger-loader machine, the basis of their main volume business. Japanese consumer electronics companies confuse the market by appearing to replace models before they are old!

• *Consumer Resistance or Dissatisfaction* with the current product forces a product change regardless of life cycle considerations. Although this may be considered a risky action in a capital- and development-intensive industry such as consumer durables, it is by no means unknown among Japanese companies and others who have honed their product development skill, efficiency and speed so much that they can recover from the problem rather than soldier on with an unsatisfactory product. As an example, Toyota have, in Japan, launched two new smaller versions of their multi-purpose vehicle, the Previa. The basic model was launched only two years ago, but was not selling well in Japan because it was considered too large.

• *Pressure of Competiton.* Bringing out a new product under pressure from competition can be part of a deliberate fast follower strategy, where a company decides always to let competitors break new ground before coming in themselves with a strong product. It may also indicate that a company's style is to act reactively, often in a panic, because it has no real strategy of its own. Nevertheless, companies ignore the actions of the competition at their peril. This type of action may also be designed in the hunt for a new niche first identified by a competitor (see below) or it may be needed to fill a profit gap caused by a declining share in one of the company's market segments. The fight between Canon and Minolta in 1986 for dominance in the SLR camera market is a good example. Canon's response to Minolta's initial success was to product plan a complete new and advanced product that leapt over the Minolta product's qualities and re-established Canon's market leadership.

● *New Market Niche or Segment.* Developing a new product to capture or create a perceived new market segment or niche within the company's known market area is presently a favoured product strategy approach. Consumer requirements are getting more diverse: operating in new niches is seen as a way of adding both image and value to a company's activities. The unfortunate thing about niches is that they soon become overcrowded unless they are of a size such that only a few companies will want to participate in them. Compare the "new" niche markets of MPV minivans and autofocus cameras (which now have all the big players competing or planning to do so) with the market for hand-built medium-priced open sports cars which Morgan has had virtually to itself in the UK for many years though TVR is now becoming well-established also. The Polaroid Land Camera was marketed in a real niche – protected by patents for many years – which is only slowly being occupied by a limited number of competitors.

Another variant can be to enter a new market segment – new to the company – where the volume base can be expanded, perhaps at economical cost, by marketing a derivative of an existing product. A topical example would be the new Ford Granada Estate, long awaited since the original Granada launch in 1986, but only made available in 1992. From another industry, there are the various models derived from the original European Airbus 310 aircraft, the 320 and 340 aircraft, which all use some carry-over technology, components and manufacturing processes but each of which fills different market sectors and customer needs from their predecessor.

● *Forced New Product by Legislation.* Making a major product change or introducing a new product because of legislation is perhaps a rarer occurrence, especially when considering a complete product rather than the need just to upgrade one. Yet legislation is one of the reasons for the increasing cost and complexity of new products by comparison with ten and twenty years ago. The electric or hybrid electric car, if it succeeds on the west coast of America, currently the focal point for severe emissions concern, will succeed as much because of legislative pressure as consumer demand. The development of many of today's environment and safety features in cars has come about through legislative demand. The clean engine running on lead free fuel and with a catalytic converter is in origin entirely a child of legislation although in recent years consumer pressure has resulted in its more widespread adoption.

In a completely different field, smokeless fuel was one of the first truly "green" products. Lead free household paint was another. Both were occasioned specifically by legislation. There is also a large body of ever changing consumer and construction and use legislation, which does not necessarily create the need for unique new products but which does require constant new product development activity and investment to ensure product compliance.

- *New-to-the Company Market.* Entering a new-to-the-company market in a manner that requires either the re-engineering of an existing product or the creation of a new one is similar in concept to entering a new niche or segment in a known market since the product must be tuned to customer preferences, legislation and operating conditions. However, a new-to-the-company market is always a bigger step, especially if it is a totally new market – geographically or from a product point of view – since other resource capabilities and competences come into play. The company must be capable of competing and succeeding long term in that market. It must acquire the necessary additional competences: technical capability, distribution, financial strength, a good name in that market or the will to develop one.

With the original personal computer, IBM set up a separate team to handle planning and development because the technology and the marketing conditions were so different from their existing business. Recently IBM has announced the spinning off of the personal computer business as a completely autonomous division. With the introduction of the 190 model series in the early 1980s, Daimler Benz moved successfully into the smaller car segment and considerably expanded its volume base, though the process was not without its teething troubles. In the 1980s, Renault tried hard to establish itself in the US car market, buying American Motors and developing new products to suit American tastes. In the end, however, the company had to withdraw.

- *Facelifted or Upgraded Products.* A frequent rationale for a new product programme is the product facelift. This can cover a multitude of forms, from minor cosmetic improvement to a package of changes that leaves much of the product the same but transforms things which have a major benefit for the customer. The facelift by definition contains a proportion of carry-over components and a proportion of new components. I come back to the importance of the carry-over concept to the product planner in Chapter Nine but here it is interesting to note that many apparently new products are really nothing more than very clever facelifts.

The degree of change applied to an upgrade is one of the key decisions facing product planning, as was the case in MG's TD and TF story. When an all-new model is planned to replace an old model, the old model usually has little or no money spent on it in the last years of its life. This can be dangerous as in the case of the Volvo 300 series, which was to be replaced by the all new 400 series in 1988. There was a risk of the new model being late, and so product planning insisted on a fairly major facelift of the 300 series in 1987 to maintain market volume. This was a successful move: the revitalised 300 was able to stay in the market until 1991, providing much needed bottom-end volume support for the more upmarket 400 series. Without that last minute facelift, volumes on the 300 would have declined much more steeply.

Many Japanese cars, accepted by the motoring press and public as new, are based on tried and tested technology and components from the previous model or another in the range. (Notably, they do look new and carry one or two apparently way-out technological innovations.) This is one of the product planner's key skills: to create a package of proven and new technology, of new and old components, of well accepted old and exciting new product ideas, in order to gain maximum customer impact for the new product with the minimum of risk and resource input.

Grundig, the German electrical consumer goods manufacturer, gained market advantage in Europe over Philips with their attractively styled range of television sets even though the underlying chassis technology was not as advanced as Philips'. Conversely, the latest Honda Accord, virtually a brand new car, though successful in North America, was criticised in its home market, Japan, for not looking sufficiently different from the old model. So much so that Honda quickly came up with a facelift for Japan. The styling was completely different but the technology was almost the same beneath the skin.

Much of what is seen in the consumer electronics field, where the speed of introduction of new models is ever-increasing, relies on facelifts or repackaging of existing components and systems.

● *Newly Created Product*. The product planning process tends to be focused on the business of a company as it exists at a point in time and, with its strong planning and checking focus, might be thought of as the antithesis of a creative process that produces truly new products. However, the potential scope of the product planning activity is so broad, from the first germ of a product idea to its targetted, successful introduction into production, that true product creation cannot be ruled out. In the kind of process needed to invent new products, there are four key elements, all of which appear among the product planning building blocks.

1. The need to understand markets and identify what consumers really want from products.
2. The search for technology and systems that will make a company's future products competitive and different.
3. The creation of a planning framework in which a potential new product or idea is subjected to a detailed evaluation. The main considerations are: what must be done to turn it into a reality – the cross functional programme planning analysis – and the product's chances of being successful.
4. Business evaluation and the obtaining of approvals and decisions to implement the programme. The stimulation of actions to make the project a reality.

Many creative new product ideas pass the first and second steps successfully but fail in the marketplace because of inadequate attention to the third and fourth steps. If a company really wishes to focus its efforts on innovation, an effective advanced and product planning process should provide all of the four above elements. "Skunk works" or "tiger team" approaches, employed in the creation of truly new products, are nothing more than intensive multi-disciplinary product planning teams without the rigid systematisation needed for the big main-line product programmes. In other words, the entrepreneurial aspects of product planning are emphasised instead of structured processes. Basic professional competence is still needed.

Programme Evaluation and Selection

This is the evaluation of the impact of alternative new product ideas on the company as a whole and their effect on all involved areas of the company, leading to the creation or amendment of the company's product plan.

Product planning is by nature a cross-functional activity and therefore no other department is so well placed to conduct programme evaluations.

Finance must be involved but can be hampered by their financial view and often lack the "product feel" to understand the assumptions behind the financial numbers. Corporate planning are usually too far from operational reality to handle the task effectively. The big line departments such as engineering, marketing or production should be too focused on their own areas of specialisation to give a company-wide unbiased evaluation. This is the reason why companies without the right kind of product planning knowledge and competence, whatever it is functionally called, have more difficulty in achieving a high success rate in evaluating and starting potentially good product programmes.

In this activity, often the most difficult of all because of the cost-versus-risk balance, I have encountered different approaches in European and Japanese companies. This becomes evident while working with them on product programmes and in examining the results of their actions in the marketplace.

Typically, European and American companies study in great detail which products to proceed with and which to reject. The problem is that resources are limited and there is no totally foolproof way of evaluating one project among many others in order to reach the certainty that it can succeed and therefore should go ahead. Such non-financial techniques as Kepner Tregoe (and similar decision analysis methods) or the various forms of qualitative forecasting can only provide the same sort of guidelines as a good and experienced judge of the business. Attempts at absolute financial judgements using DROI, nett present value, discounted or straight cash-flow analyses or simple variable profit generation comparisons are all used with a greater or lesser degree of success.

The problem is that when alternative potential product programmes are under study, each with a potential substitutional or other effect on other programmes, the multi-project alternatives become very complicated. The product planner, with help from financial analysis has to start scenario-building in which the new alternative programmes are logically grouped together and the total company financial model can be used to try and determine which will be the most profitable. Yet this is not always the solution. Any financial analysis is only as good as its underlying assumptions. A minor change in exchange rate, volume substitution, base model profit, or the failure of a targetted cost reduction can distort the evaluation. It is also a truism of new product programme analysis that the new programmes with the highest resource inputs always seem to generate the highest profits but also offer the highest risk of failure in striving for new and untried targets.

Much needs to be done with the evaluation of uncertain, high resource multi-project combinations before we have a perfect methodology based only on quantitative and financial analysis. What currently must be used is a great deal of senior managerial judgement based on consideration of all factors – qualitative and quantitative. The product planner's task is to assemble the analytical base and to make recommendations to top management. The following is a check-list of what should be done for major programme alternatives.

1. Test all alternatives against the strategic rules for the company and its products, which should already have been clearly established.
2. Identify all measurable criteria related to the programme alternatives.
3. Evaluate the alternatives using an appropriate ranking decision analysis.
4. Create a "do-nothing scenario" in conjunction with marketing to act as a reference point which contains the current product base plus all the already committed new product programmes projected to the end of the planning period.
5. Create scenarios with logical combinations of the new product programme alternatives so that the multi-project resource and timing situation can be evaluated.
6. Evaluate financially, using readily available spreadsheet models, the alternative business plans thus created.
7. Present to the product committee or board.

It is the product planner's task to guide the product committee in reaching the necessary decisions.

In Europe at least, many alternative scenarios need to be evaluated because of resource limitation. Often this leads to a simple approach whereby projects are ranked in terms of priority, not necessarily in terms of profitability. A cut off point is established at the point where key resources are used up. Usually, development capacity or investment is the key. This can mean that potentially attractive and profitable projects are ruled out.

Judging by their proliferation of new products, the Japanese approach seems to be different. In Japan the product research and development resource is only in the short term a limiting factor. The approach is that the development team on the running programme should transfer to the next new model as soon as the engineering and planning of the current programme is complete. Detailed feasibility and profitability calculations must be made on each potential programme, but they also take the view that a product programme desired for strategic or other reasons can be made feasible by correct financial targetting and management action. This is the so-called cost-down approach, which devotes far more time and effort to cost reduction during the life cycle of a programme than in most European companies. In addition, because of their strong drive for efficiency, a constant development resource level can produce an ever-increasing number of new products, so increasing volume and eventually allowing more development resources. A virtuous rather than a vicious circle.

In such circumstances, Japanese companies worry less about choices between competing programmes and concentrate more on developing their overall product strategy usually focused on market share gains, which they do more intensively than companies in Europe, and on executing all their planned projects well. Because, up to now at least, capital for industrial expansion has not been a limiting factor in Japan, this allows growth through bringing in new products until the entire market is covered. Hence efficiency in developing new products is given priority over concern about which ones to do.

Compare the evidence of the Toyota Challenge, a UK advertising campaign run at the end of 1991 with the Ford model range at the same point. Toyota claimed it had something for everyone: five four-door saloon ranges each with estate-car and five-door versions and some with coupe versions, plus three sports cars, two off-road vehicles and one MPV people carrier or Minivan. The other major Japanese manufacturers are not far behind. Ford Europe, however, has only one body variant of the Fiesta. The company introduced the four-door Sierra two years after the five-door and estate models, and has only just managed to unveil the Estate version of the Granada, several years after the original Granada launch. In Europe, Ford has not yet found a way to replace the Capri, despite its status as the original trend setter in that popular coupe market. They are using the Probe model – jointly developed with Mazda – to fill the gap. As yet they do not have a Minivan or people carrier on the market in Europe. Nor do they have a European-produced off-road vehicle.

Since it is not so difficult to think of new product concepts, I am sure Ford of Europe knows what it would like to do. The problem is one of resource limitations and choices. The difference between Japan and Europe must be that Japanese companies, through continuous efficiency improvements, find ways of fulfilling a greater proportion of potential new programmes than major European companies, all of whom are still struggling to bring out models to cover every key segment. A similar situation exists in the camera, video, TV and home entertainment markets. The lean-clean product development machine of the Japanese automotive industry emits a clear message that all European companies must heed, whether in automotive or not in order to keep the flow of new products coming to the market and to remain competitive.

Programme Planning

Planning the detail of new product programmes includes specifications, different model versions, options, markets, positioning and prices and performance standards for all areas of the company.

This represents another core element of the product planner's task. Product requirement planning is a start, but the true product planner must go well beyond the requirements and look at the implications across the company. Product content requirements have to be planned rationally and negotiated with colleagues in other functions as to the effects on capacity, feasibility, achievability, profitability and realism. There are product planning departments that merely state the requirements and leave the decisions on what to do and the implementation to others, but the feasibility analysis is a key professional element of the product planner's task. So is the negotiation of trade-offs between the conflicting requirements and capabilities of other departments. Even in matrix-based or programme management organisations the product planners within the teams should perform this function.

Such is the importance of the requirements laid down at the start of a programme that these must be formally documented and released just like any other element of a product specification. The engineering drawings, CAD models, process standards and the complete bill of material are created and released by engineering at the end of the development programme. Product planning releases come closer to the front end of a programme and are used for guidance and work authority by other departments. Product planning activities must therefore include disciplines for releasing and updating this guideline information as well as for the communication of new information, assumptions and decisions made or acquired during the running progress of the programme. Product planning documentation is described more fully in Chapter Nine.

It is at this point also that the voice of the customer must be brought into the picture. The product plan has been developed to correspond to the needs of the company's strategy and to the requirements and opportunities presented by the market. Now, in developing the product and programme requirements, the customer's needs must be paramount. This must be reflected not only in improvements of today's products but also in forecasted or even created needs in the future. QFD (quality function deployment) is a technique for turning customer requirements into product requirements. Although it is a complex and detailed technique, QFD represents the complete cross-functional product planning process in microcosm: almost every significant part of the product can be planned from customer requirement through to efficient production. In this process, the views of all participating functions have to be taken into account. Trade-offs between conflicting requirements are also a key feature of QFD: again, they are part of the basic product planning task.

Market and Product Analysis

The evaluation of trends in customers' use of, and need for, products and the collection of customers, reactions to existing products is the precursor to creating product requirements for a new programme and, at a different level of detail, an input for product cycle planning. Normally such work would be carried out in a consumer product company by the marketing or market research department. However where product planning exists, it is important that they have direct contact with the customer and access to customer information, present and future. They should also retain direct responsibility for requesting and using the results of product-related research and analysis.

In some companies, the role of the sales and marketing department is oriented to maximising the sale of existing decided projects. This means that marketing acts primarily as a driver of, or a support for, sales activities, rather than spending too much time researching the future market and product needs. Activities such as "long term" market planning – in the period beyond the current products' cycle – can then be performed within the product planning department. This does not mean that marketing loses interest in this aspect of the business. They must buy-off to the market planning forecasts made for each new programme. Today's new product programme provides tomorrow's product for sale. It is perhaps more important that short-term marketing strategies and action on current products taken by sales and marketing must not be at variance with the strategy and positioning of the new product programme.

As an example of this, and referring back to the replacement of the Cortina by the Sierra, Ford came under such intense pressure after the successful new Vauxhall Cavalier launch in 1982 that the sales department requested increases in the average specification levels of the Cortina in the last year of its life to hold up sales levels. This meant that the specifications as well as the costs of the new Sierra had to be increased by the Sierra product planners just before launch in a bid to preserve some product consistency with the displaced Cortina. (It is certainly true that all current UK car specifications are higher, model for model, than for the same cars sold in continental markets. This must in part account for the price differentials which are the subject of so much criticism, study and speculation in the present EC environment.)

There are organisations where market planning is closely allied, within the same division, to product planning. There are also situations where all forward marketing activities are carried out quite satisfactorily by a separate marketing division that works very smoothly with product planning. Each organisation should follow its own preferred route in this matter provided the product planners are fully in touch with the market analysis and feedback and provided the sales and marketing group buys-in to the product strategy and to each new programme at the appropriate stage.

The elements of this task may be broadly divided into customer- or market-related investigations and product-oriented analyses. It is not possible to treat the two elements entirely separately. Both are covered in some detail in Chapter Nine. The need to understand what kind of customers buy the product, why they like or dislike it and how their needs will develop in the future should not be in dispute. It is a major part of product planning work to perform this analysis. There must be an adequate source of information for each different type of enquiry.

With the drive for continuous improvement in product quality, the customer's view of products should be constantly studied. Starting with the points of dissatisfaction with existing products and high scoring features of competition, a picture can be built up of areas for improvement. How does the customer use the products? How does he perceive the products is another important area of rating: it is essential that the image and perception of a product should not diverge too far from its actual state and from where the company is trying to position it. The use of perception maps, trends in product performance and product feature usage and segmentation analysis of products all contribute to answering the four key questions for the product planner.

1. How is my product rated versus competition?
2. Is my product achieving the positioning, image and rating that I want it to?
3. What areas of improvement, both physical and image-related, must I target for the next product?
4. What features and characteristics will give me an edge over my competitors in the next new product?

Market segmentation is a critical analysis tool that breaks products and customer categories into homogeneous groups to facilitate comparison and performance measures. Segmentation analysis is one of the most important tools of the product planner and more time is devoted to it in Chapter Nine because it is not a familiar technique in many technical product industries as it is, for example, in fast-moving consumer goods. An engineering product usually has more individual characteristics than an FMCG product so segmentation and positioning is more complex.

Competitive Product Analysis and Cost Targetting

This can be considered both as a product planning responsibility and a specific technique. The use of competitive product analysis and costing is a technique of product planning. As techniques, testing in use of competitive products and desk analysis of performance, positioning and strategy belong to the general task of market and product analysis mentioned above. There is another way in which a company can study its competitors' products: tear them down to extract the interesting physical details, especially the design, process and cost characteristics. The objective is to find what makes the product so good. This is usually evidenced by its performance and feel, by its sales achievements and by the competitive company's profitability levels. Teardown can provide clues to each of these aspects. This is a major contributor to arriving at an achievable and profitable cost target for a new product. More broadly, product planning must also be the initiator and primary driver of the bottom-up cost targetting activities that occur at the start of each new product programme and operate in a sort of concurrent cost engineering manner because they should involve all functions in the programme.

Top down, starting from market price and calculating the necessary margins for a good financial result, it is relatively easy for the product planner to determine a total target cost for a new product. The bottom-up analysis, part by part, shows how the achievement of this cost target can be guaranteed. The teardown of competitor products is one important contributory factor. Another is close and creative, instead of adversarial, relationships with suppliers, although that is not our subject in this book.

The actual teardown is often carried out by the engineering workshop with the product cost analysis department, part of engineering or finance. I have chosen to put cost targetting in this section and not in the tools and techniques chapter because of the distinction between who provides the basic data and who takes management action as a result of it. All too often the providers of information in companies think they should be the only ones to use or interpret it. This is often the case with cost targetting where teardown and competitive analysis play a significant role.

The setting of cost targets to meet a customer and market-oriented target price and profitability should be a task of product planning because it involves trade-offs between required cost and market and customer value. Achieving individual component or assembly cost targets is a design and process engineering responsibility, together with purchasing. The measurement and analysis of costs, covering material, design and process, is a responsibility of the cost analysis department. Because of this expertise the cost analysts should also play a very significant role in helping the engineers and purchasers achieve their targets.

This is therefore a prime example of the sharing of responsibility which I have referred to several times. This is one of the keys to improving the efficiency of engineering product development processes. Sharing does not mean that the relative roles are unclear but rather that a complete value-adding activity, such as cost targetting, comes about through the interaction and co-operation between two or more departments with each one understanding its role, how it should interact with other departments and that it will share in the knowledge of the end result.

To show the starting points for the cost targetting and teardown process, here is Ford's approach as described to me by Sir Terence Beckett[2]. This description covers the methods used during the early days of product planning at Ford of Britain. It was, and remains, a good approach; one that Japanese businesses use constantly in their cost-down sessions – the drive for continuous improvement in achieving lower product costs – and one that many European companies seem never to have discovered.

'In arriving at a target cost for each part of the car Ford adopted a practice they called 'triangulation'. This meant that they took a comparable part from one of their existing models and one from a competitor's car. They used a mix of parts from different competitors and evaluated the probable cost of the competitive part by using the same manufacturing and process assumptions as the new Ford car so as to compare like with like. This was known as a design cost evaluation. It produced an estimate of the intrinsic cost built into a component. They then fixed the cost and also the weight targets for the component on the new car in relation to the other two examples: hence the term triangulation. From the objectives for size and price and quality of the different parts of the car they made their decisions as to the acceptable and achievable targets. These decisions were taken at cost co-ordination meetings where engineering, manufacturing and purchasing were also present to sign off to the targetting process.'

The focus in the original approach described here was placed on the design cost rather than on cost versus quality, cost versus function and performance, or cost versus manufacturability. Nowadays, the concentration in teardown exercises with competitive products should be to try to estimate the reasons for the total competence of the product across all the departments of the competitor that planned it, designed it, developed it, bought it, and created its manufacturing processes. The key message from the Ford example is that cost targetting is a multi-functional activity, involving detailed analysis of all cost parameters. The process has to be related to improvement based on study of the competition and market requirements as well as internal capabilities. It finishes with the acceptance or buy-off of all functions to agreed cost targets. For these reasons, it is an ideal subject for product planning attention.

Programme Initiation

This involves kicking off new product programmes following a board or product committee decision and clearly communicating targets, studies, assumptions, parameters and decisions to all those in the company with a need to know.

This may not seem like a key activity but it is, in fact, one of the most important responsibilities of product planners at the start of a programme. I develop this idea further in Chapter Five in dealing with the role of product planning within the total new product development process. I have used the description D1 decision stage as the point of programme start. To ensure simultaneous and co-operative working by all departments of the company it is essential to communicate effectively at this point. The product planning release of documentation referred to above is part of this activity. More specific management impetus should also be given by a series of briefing meetings. At the early programme stage there are many alternatives still not worked out and many assumptions that have been made for planning purposes. There will be many things that need specific face-to-face communication and cannot be described in a specification document.

Sir Terence Beckett, in a paper entitled "Design, Product Planning and Prosperity"[3], describes how product requirements were communicated at Ford of Britain before the formation of product planning.

'Until that time product development took place when the managing director got his chief people together and told them: " I want a new car in two years' time, about the size of the Morris Minor. We shall need four hundred per day. The weight will be 1600 lbs. The engine displacement 800 to 1000 cc. The acceleration will be 0-60 in 26 seconds and the touring fuel consumption has to be 40 miles to the gallon. Now I want some styling and engineering ideas from you and we will meet a month from today."

Sir Patrick Hennessy, managing director of Ford at that time, realised that with increasing competition, this occasional direction would not be adequate.

I think it is essential that the chief executive acts in a way to make the customer, product and design of superordinate importance in a company.'

In forming its new product planning department in 1953, Ford clearly realised the importance of both targetting and controlling new product programmes. The company recognised that this was a delegated responsibility from the chief executive and one that definitely needed more initiating detail than the sketchy outline of a new product shown above. The instructions and guidelines issued at the start of a project are a key factor in achieving fast time to market by ensuring that as complete a definition of the path to be followed – and alternatives to be studied – is available.

The initial communication process is a key element in motivating everyone to work together. In the absence of clear communication, people will make their own assumptions and find their own way forward. This is the very antithesis of co-operative parallel working. The tone must be set from the top down, by the managing director and the board, but the content, quality and consistency of cross-company communication on new products must be assured by product planning.

Programme Co-ordination

After the initiation of a new programme comes the task of steering and co-ordinating development of the front end of a new product programme, at least until the programme approval decision.

Here we reach a somewhat controversial point. It concerns the scope of product planning's role and, specifically, the overlapping of the pure product planning role with that of management and control of the progress of a programme. This problem area occurs both in companies already using some form of programme management and in functionally organised companies.

As long as product planners only act as "planners" of what should be done and "advisors", there is no real clash with the large line functions. However, even the programme planning period, which can cover several months or up to two years in a large programme, requires an iterative approach involving negotiations with, and work by, all functions involved. In order to negotiate progress towards an agreed product requirement – what is possible as well as what is needed – the product planner must take an interest in, and possibly also a responsibility for, the progress of the programme up to that point in all the contributing departments: industrial design (styling), design engineering, purchasing, suppliers or design sub-contractors, manufacturing engineering.

Certainly a traditional engineering department seldom has the breadth of view or organisation to manage the multi-functional decisions, trade-offs and analyses that must be made in this phase of the programme. These involve most other company functions as well as the board. It is therefore logical that product planning can also "project manage" this creative phase, at least up to and including the programme approval decision, which is the decision point that starts the implementation of a product programme. An alternative, already referred to, which also cuts across the traditional responsibilities of the big line functions, is the establishment of a programme management team with a programme director appointed at an early stage in the programme. In this case it is usual to cover the necessary product planning actions by putting product planners in place as part of this programme team. This subject is covered more fully in Chapter Seven.

Downstream Product Management

A watchdog role for the product manager should continue at least until the successful production launch. This ensures that someone continues to "own" the product right through the last implementation phase of a programme's life. It also maintains product integrity and helps the achievement of product objectives as well as providing for re-planning should things go wrong.

This is an extension of the last section. If there is no overall programme management activity or if programme managers are concerned mainly with progress towards the objectives and are not responsible for the already defined product content, then product responsibility must remain with product planning through all the evaluations, product tests and sign-offs that lead to a successful programme conclusion. Likewise, any re-planning or re-negotiation of aspects of the product programmme that have fallen off target, or been changed due to an external influence, must be handled by the responsible product manager.

If, however, product planning activities are part of the programme team from the very beginning, the team must be responsible for total programme integrity, including the product.

The Product Committee

Most companies that recognise the importance of new products have a steering body called something like the product planning committee or product policy committee. Presenting new product plans and programmes, reporting on running programmes to the product committee and making recommendations for decision, action or change require a permanent secretariat for the committee.

Since product planning acts on behalf of the board in its daily working, regardless of its reporting level, it is usual for the head of product planning to provide the secretariat of this main company product meeting. This is a critical task because, quite apart from the high level product decision-making involved, slippage of the management decision points can become a major reason for programme delays. The secretariat must therefore become adept at obtaining results from the product committee. There are some common reasons for failure to obtain decisions at the right time.

1. Programmes that are not properly presented. This seems an obvious point, but some approaches to boards with major new projects are performed remarkably badly.
2. Financial release procedures lagging behind the agreed programme decision stages, because the financial decision-making follows a different circuit. This can often be the case in European companies dominated by a focus on short term results.
3. Participating divisions not signing off on each programme decision point because of bad briefing and preparation – or simply because of office politics.
4. Failure by the board to make a decision for its own internal reasons.

Political and presentational skill must be acquired at an early stage by the head of product planning and the individual product managers who present their programmes.

Decision Management

Communicating decisions, progress and revisions on running product programmes to the rest of the company is a key element of integrated product development.

This need arises as a result of working with the product committee and from the day-to-day, product-related decision-making of the product manager. Once again, this is a very important task and one subject to certain pitfalls. This task of communication has been described, somewhat disparagingly, as the "bureaucracy of product planning". Yet it remains a necessary skill and responsibility that calls for some elements of routine rigidity and repeatability. Otherwise, it cannot work.

- Board meeting minutes often have a legal company status and may therefore be produced for other purposes than communicating programme decisions at a level of detail suitable for implementation; therefore, they should not be used for the purpose. Product planning needs its own system of formal decision and revision communication such as suggested in Chapter Nine in the case of product letters.
- There should only be one source of product decisions. The content of such communications must be available both for action and information. They are confidential but that does not mean restricted circulation – and the copying machine working overtime in each receiving department to get the message down to the workers.
- The central issuing authority must behave responsibly and the instructions must be accepted without being converted into a political football. An easy way to create programme confusion is when six directors have attended a product committee meeting and each then holds a separate meeting to communicate his interpretation of the results to his own staff.
- The information release must be at a level and in a format – financial or technical – that the users can immediately take action on. Vague statements allowing for interpretation can also cause lack of cohesion.

Figure 3.6 shows the programme planning elements I have just described. It looks as though product and programme planners have all the weight of responsibility and that the line implementing functions of design engineering, styling, process engineering and purchasing play a minor role. This is not true, nor is it my intention to give that impression, but since the focus in this chapter is on the building blocks of product planning, it inevitably gets more space. In fact, in every new product programme, all functions must work in balance. The "software" of product planning is no good without a committed and highly competent technical and commercial "hardware". Equally, an engineering function that creates products without taking on board the inputs necessary for a customer-oriented approach will produce superb technical products that look in vain for markets. Examples include Concorde (as opposed to the Boeing 747) and the APT (as opposed to the TGV).

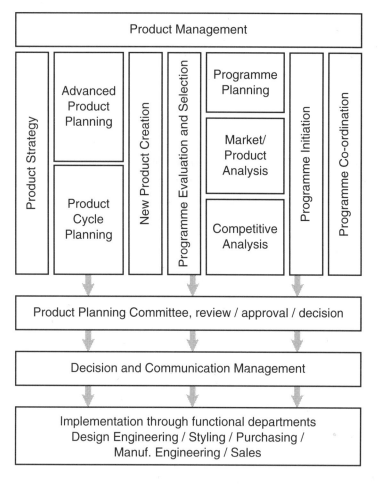

Figure 3.6 Product Planning, Decisions, Communication and Implementation.

CONCLUSION

It is possible to combine the six different kinds of product planning departments described at the beginning with the various building blocks described
in the rest of the chapter. The purpose in describing product planning in this
way was not necessarily to suggest the creation of large functional departments called product planning, especially if these do not already exist. There
is enough current dissatisfaction with, and moves away from, functional
organisations at present. The building blocks must exist somewhere,
however, and, in particular, those that lay the groundwork for new product

programmes need to be formally organised and placed under a board member responsibility. Product planning has a special cross-functional character and the best examples act in a role that is seen not as just "another function" but in a role that is accepted as acting on behalf of the board to provide both strategic and functional guidance to other departments. In this respect, product planning tends to act as if it were part of a matrix. This can be difficult to get across to the traditional line functions. Perhaps with the introduction of more cross-functional teams, the natural role of product planning will fit in more easily. It is a very relevant and necessary discipline for a wide variety of industries. The mere creation of teams will not produce world-beating products; the creation of product planning's key building blocks, however, should do this.

Notes

1. Tony Harrison, *The Product Manager's Handbook*, Kogan Page Ltd, 1989.

2. From discussions with Sir Terence Beckett, May 1992.

3. Sir Terence Beckett, 'Design, Product Planning and Prosperity', paper delivered to the London Business School design management seminar, 1989.

4 PRODUCT PLANNING IN DIFFERENT INDUSTRIES

> There are specific characteristics of business – and, in particular, a number affecting the new product development process – that make the need for some form of product planning expertise more likely. The principal characteristics are analysed. The analysis is applied to a variety of industries and product types. Product planning is an appropriate discipline for many industries beyond the automotive sector. These range from computers to bakery plants to toys and games.
>
> A key element of successful product planning, regardless of industry type, is the willingness of all functions to work together.

The need for a separate identifiable product planning activity has arisen from the growing complexity of business and the increasing scarcity of large scale businesses controlled by a single individual. One of Alfred Sloan's contributions to the modern management process was his recognition of the different organisational needs of complex businesses. Sloan opened up the path to decentralisation and professional management thinking. As soon as a business becomes too complex for the owner or chief executive to control the implementation of all his own product ideas, product planning of some kind must be considered.

THE NEED FOR PLANNING

Every business, of whatever kind, must do some planning of its products or services in order to exist. Almost all the building blocks for product planning should be in use somewhere in the organisation. However, a fully structured and formalised product planning organisation – what I described in Chapter Three as "normal" product planning – is not necessarily required by every type of company or industry. Yet it is possible to identify broad categories of business where such a properly organised product planning approach is needed.

Companies whose activities conform to several of the conditions defined in Table 4.1 are bound to formalise and structure their planning and implementing processes. Otherwise, their new product process will become unmanageable, driven often by the subjective views of senior management, or, equally dangerous, by an internal, sometimes technically-based and engineering-led view of what the product should be. The third unsatisfactory option sees marketing asking for what the successful competitors have got.

Many companies also over-emphasise the implementation aspects of product programmes that start before being adequately planned only to be adjusted as they go along. This is a favoured tendency in product development. It may deliver a product at the end, but certainly not one that meets competitive cost, time or profit criteria.

The establishment of a product planning function should be aimed at eliminating this kind of haphazard product introduction process.

Product planning is not necessarily a consequence of each of the conditions in Table 4.1 individually, but it is required when several are present together. Even if product planning does not exist as a formal part of the organisation, then a full range of efficient techniques for planning the product in a multi-disciplinary manner becomes the only way to cope with the complexity of a business where combinations of these characteristics exist.

---

1. Lead times from first concept to production are long relative to the life cycle of the product.

2. The product has a multi-customer or mass market application.

3. There is strong competition in the market in new product innovation and/or rapid technology change.

4. There are high project development costs committed before results can be measured.

5. The product requires high expenditure on dedicated product tooling and facilities and the cost of late corrections is high.

6. The project development and implemetation requires the co-ordinated interaction of many of a company's operational departments.

7. The new product combines several new technologies in its design or manufacture.

Table 4.1 Business Characteristics of the Product Development Process

1. *If lead times from first concept to production are long, at least relative to the life cycle of the product.* The long lead time between the taking of major product decisions and their implementation – and therefore the visibility of success or failure – is a key factor here also, even where the product itself is not complex.

A product programme that takes a long time to implement, relative to its life in the market, and which involves a complex series of actions, must be well thought out before the start and well co-ordinated in its introduction process. It is not only programmes that are long in absolute terms which fall into this category. A new computer product currently can be conceived and introduced in a matter of months, using the slickest techniques of concurrent product development, but such is the competitive and technological pressure in the electronic products market that the corresponding product life cycles are often measured in months.

Starting a programme that has not been well thought through will increase the total time to production start by increasing the likelihood of one or more corrective development loops or target adjustments in the downstream programme. These are expensive in terms of resources and time. Bad decisions made upstream will not be found out until the start of production or even after customer use. The cost of correcting this kind of mistake is enormous. These business characteristics put a premium on the quality of the initial concept work, planning and decision-making in product programmes.

2. If the product has a strong multi-customer application and thus is not a bespoke product, where the requirements are defined by a single customer. Similar conditions are present in a product destined for a mass consumer market.

An industrial product, one sold by one company to another for its own use, industrialisation or commercialisation, can be developed for one single customer or for a market containing a number of customers. A single customer can define the product he wants, often as the project proceeds. The product development effort of the developer and producer is devoted to executing the project to order. Developing products for a variety of customers introduces product complexity and variety, as well as uncertainty as to alternative product routes to follow and the need for trade-offs. Usually the lead time for developing a new industrial component or system to be sold to OEMs is longer than the lead time for the OEMs own product development cycle. This puts the onus on the supplier of the product or system to anticipate not only the needs of the direct OEM customer but also the OEM's own customers' needs. A very high degree of uncertainty and risk presents itself in this equation.

An engineering product sold to consumers – a consumer durable – has to be created to suit a mass market where no one customer or homogeneous group of customers can be asked to define the product need. Hence the product has to be varied to suit the variety of tastes in the market or standardised to capture a big share of the market's high volume centre while ignoring peripheral variety. Either way, the product must meet market needs. The variegated approach for maximum market coverage risks a too high development cost and product proliferation in production. The standardised approach may be slightly off target and fail because of its very inflexibility.

3. *If there exists in the market a high level of competition in new product generation – perhaps combined with a rapid rate of technology change.*

This characteristic requires continuous careful study of the competition and the market to be aware of where both are heading. Active surveying and acquisition of relevant technology and shelf engineering is needed to prepare that technology to fit into new product programmes at the appropriate time. Creativity in synthesising these two fields of study distinguishes successful companies like Sony, Honda and BMW. Yet shelf engineering is, in itself, difficult to address because it involves allocating (usually scarce) resources to future product needs or technology acquisition rather than to bringing current new product programmes to production.

The risk of not doing good research into new products, markets and the competition is to be wiped out by more customer-oriented products. The risk of doing the right things too late is that the competition and the market will have moved on. The risk of not performing shelf engineering can result in an absence of the right technology improvements on time. In that case, they have to be developed during the course of the new product programme itself. This always lowers quality and reliability levels or increases time to market. There is also the problem of the opportunity cost attributable to shelf engineering the wrong things.

4. *If the product requires a high level of project development cost to be committed before results can be measured.*

The product development investments required to produce all types of products are constantly increasing because of legislation, available technology and materials and the need for greater consumer choice. In relation to the production costs of mass production or multi-customer products, the ratio is changing dramatically because all the pressure is to reduce manufactured costs and selling prices.

Complex products entail high development costs before the results can be seen in terms of either the start of production or the customer's decision to buy. Company economics dictate the more efficient use of resources. Product development is a major resource and so there is pressure to produce the same, or better, results with smaller resource inputs.

Some industries can minimise risk by having large pre-committed customers. Others can test-market before committing the major part of the complete programme development. Many engineering companies can do neither. They must rely on the excellence of their preparation and execution of new product programmes.

5. *If the product requires dedicated product or facility expenditure where the lead times and costs for corrections or new directions are high once the expenditure has been committed.*

Dedicated production facilities for a product imply some form of repeat or volume production. Lower production costs per unit are often obtained by raising investment in new production technology. For this, and other, reasons the investment costs for a given volume of product tend to increase.

These production facilities may be owned and controlled by the OEM itself, the owner of the product, or by an outside supplier or sub-contractor. The decision process is the same and requires early and correct decision-making regarding the size and configuration of the product, its material and assembly method or the volume and variety to be produced. The production facilities and product tooling are completed only after the product development is finished, but all of these decisions must be made at the start of product development. Thus the risk of dedicated facilities and product tooling is that, as with the product itself, mistakes take a long time to be discovered and become costly to correct.

6. *If the creation of the new product requires the co-ordinated interaction of most of the main operational departments in a company.*

Many new product programmes can be executed without this. Complete product development or the production of a new product can be sub-contracted to another company. Likewise, making a product that is marketed by someone else cuts out large amounts of cross-functional interaction and decision-making. But where a new product programme does involve many functions, there are always compromises between the competing requirements of each function.

Programme implementation can follow a relay race pattern with each department handing its work and the programme responsibility over to his neighbour.

The modern approach to integrated new product development, however, includes cross-functional co-ordination of some kind, but the chief executive cannot devote time to resolving every inter-divisional dispute on every company project. Hence some other means of achieving efficient multi-disciplinary working must be developed.

7. *If the product combines several technologies in its design or manufacture.*

Products combining several technologies suggest: high investment to prepare or research those suitable technologies; high investment in skilled manpower to manipulate the technologies into the required product programmes; and a high level of dedicated research and production facilities.

Most products combine more than one technology. Some contain a small number, such as a plastic injection moulding or a coil of steel. Others are more complex, as in the case of consumer electronics or white goods. Still others are very complex: power stations, chemical plants, aircraft or motor vehicles. Complexity of technology *per se* does not require anything other than competence in product research, engineering design, assembly, construction and project management. On the other hand, technical choices that can affect product cost and can create a risk of unreliability or that can lead to customer dissatisfaction, need decision inputs and trade-offs other than the purely technical.

COMPARISON FOR DIFFERENT INDUSTRIES AND PRODUCT TYPES

If we now apply this characterisation to different types of product, identifying which of the seven factors are present in the product development process, we can begin to see what may be required in the way of either a structured approach to a "normal" product planning activity, or merely the performing of some elements of the total product planning portfolio. Table 4.2 summarises this for a number of widely dissimilar products and the importance of the main characteristics to the different products or industries is outlined.

A Motor Vehicle Sold to the Public. In our chart, a motor vehicle product development programme contains characteristics 1,2,3,4,5,6,7. Clearly, since all seven characteristics are present, it is no coincidence that product planning as a formal organisational entity first started in the automotive industry and that the various product planning techniques are most widely used there. The approach of the first and second chapters was to show why product planning arose in the automotive industry and the contribution made by its various skills and techniques. As we progress further, in this chapter, it will be seen that the presence of all seven business characteristics it is not necessary for the full range of product planning techniques to be useful.

Product	Business Characteristic						
	1	2	3	4	5	6	7
Motor Vehicle	X	X	X	X	X	X	X
Personal Computer	X	X	X	X	X	X	X
Chemical Plant	X			X	X		X
Warplane/Ship	X			X	X	X	X
Civil Aircraft	X	X	X	X	X	X	X
Engine Component	X			X	X		
Woollen Garment	X	X	X	X	X		X
Air Compressor	X	X		X	X	X	X
Bren Gun/Helicopter	X	X	X	X	X	X	X
Speculative House		X	X				X
White Goods	X	X	X	X	X	X	X
Toys and Games		X	X	X	X		
A Bakery Plant		X	X	X		X	X

Table 4.2 The Seven Business Characteristics of Product Planning as Applied to Different Industries and Product Types

A Personal Computer. This product has characteristics 1,2,3,4,5,6,7. Lead times and life cycles can be very short. The number of different technologies is limited compared to a car, truck or van. Yet, the creation of a new computer or piece of electronic equipment is no less complex. Competitive drive in the marketplace and the short reaction time available to correct mistakes is so critical that product planning should be a necessary discipline. It must also be true that the shorter the product life cycle – because of competition or technology development – the greater the emphasis on doing the right things first time around.

Computer equipment companies have been amongst the first in Europe and North America to adopt the more efficient techniques of concurrent new product development. Digital Equipment Corporation, for example, is claiming quite dramatic improvements. Time to market, it says, has been reduced by up to 50 per cent. The number of parts in products has been slashed by 50 per cent and levels of measured quality and reliability have been improved by a factor greater than ten. Total life cycle programme profits on one particular new product improved by $21 million. Within the multi-disciplinary teams that Digital create to implement their programmes, product planning must be one of the main activities to achieve these improvements combined with enhanced customer satisfaction.

A Major Chemical Plant. A chemical plant has characteristics 1,4,5,7. The creation of a new chemical plant design will be based, presumably, on a technological evolution or development from the last one. The plant design company is unlikely to design from scratch a new "range" of chemical plants or even a single new plant until receiving such a request from a potential customer. The new plant will also be based on a precisely-defined set of customer requirements. The new plant will, however, require some new process research or the adoption of new process sub-systems that have recently come on the market.

Under these circumstances, there is little need for the main product planning activities in the creation of a chemical plant project. But there is definitely a need for a high level of project planning to cope with the complexity of its design and construction. To the extent that such a plant will contain standardised or proprietory components or sub-systems supplied by subcontractors, these should already have been "product planned" by their suppliers, so as to be available in time to meet the plant construction schedule. The same goes for any complex process plant built to order. If the required sub-systems are not shelf engineered at the time of the initial planning work, then they are too late. Although the plant is a product in its own right, it is also a system and requires a more system- and technology-oriented planning process than a total product focus.

A Military Aircraft or Ship, Commissioned by a Single Customer. Such products would have characteristics 1,4,5,6,7. As with the chemical plant, product development and production would be carried out as a sub-contracting job, with the customer or user supplying the customer and application input. The main performance and use parameters of the product would be specified by the customer. The product developer performs mainly a technical and project development and management task. In the defence industries, contracts have often been awarded and carried out under a cost-plus approach where the front end creative input and the performance aspects of the developer's product development activities have low emphasis.

In this case there is the additional factor that the customer – the defence agency – should itself have done its product planning homework for the complete product before finalising the order. Product responsibility lies with the buyer and not the developer or producer. The object being bought is a product in its own right. In fact, the customer should keep a product planning and programme management organisation operative starting before the quotation or tender request and it should continue to function right through the development programme. How else can he know what he is buying? Study of the public news about defence projects that very often fail to meet time, cost or technological objectives leads to the conclusion that much more product and programme planning should be instigated at the customer end, especially in the planning phases. How many product planning types are there in the Ministry of Defence or the Defence Procurement Agency?

With the increased emphasis on technological planning, shelf engineering and simultaneous product development throughout the engineering industries, there must be more consciousness of this kind of technique in the defence sector. It is interesting to see that part of the preliminary planning for the European Fighter Aircraft (EFA) project involved creating a flying platform prototype on which some very key new systems and concepts could be tried out before committing to the final production design. This is shelf engineering at its best. By all accounts, it was a very costly up-front action, not found acceptable by all parties within the EFA project, but it will save time, cost and uncertainty downstream. The mere fact that the EFA is a multi-customer programme brings into play the need for some developers to take on board aspects of product planning.

The difficulty with this kind of consortium product is that each customer will have its own "product planners" with their own performance requirements. To avoid developing a separate product for each customer, some overall system and product option analysis and planning for the whole programme is desirable. As of this writing, in November 1992, this seems to be happening as defence agencies in each country try to balance their technical and operational needs with their financial capabilities. Some very careful product planning configuration work must be performed to accommodate all the different product and system needs into a rationalised airframe package so that the programme costs and time scale are kept under control.

Civil Aircraft. A civil aircraft programme would include characteristics 1,2,3,4,5,6,7. As opposed to the military aircraft example, the product owner and product developer of a civil aircraft are likely to be one and the same organisation, perhaps Boeing, Saab-Fairchild or Airbus Industries. The potential users of the aircraft, the airlines, are their customer group.

Civil aircraft production is another clear candidate for product planning because the risk levels at the point of committing development and production resources are high. Although the customer needs will have been carefully targetted and built into the design and even despite tentative commitments, the programme outlay is enormous by comparison with the proportion of the required return that can be guaranteed. This is why governments are often asked for up-front funds to support the development of new civil airframes or major systems such as engines.

The lead time between major decisions and the ability to see the need for corrections is also long, although in the aircraft industry to make quite major changes after the start of running production is easier to justify. This is because of the favourable ratio between the cost of the change and the cost of a single product so that different phases of the aircraft production programme can be organised with different product characteristics for different customers or with the addition of new systems. Each aircraft can be, to an extent, bespoke, even if the base concept, development and tooling investment must remain common.

A Piston for an Internal Combustion Engine. A piston or other component for an internal combustion engine has only three of the characteristics: 1,4,5. In this case the "product" is almost wholly determined by the single customer, the manufacturer of the engine. Product planning by the piston or component manufacturer is therefore inappropriate. In this case, technology research and planning and ensuring that he has the most efficient processes available to make the component are the key factors for the supplier. Without the existence of the customer's product, in which the component operates, the component has no life of its own. This is true of all bespoke components supplied to OEMs. Shelf engineering of basic piston technology in advance of a customer's call for it is also one of the most crucial success factors.

There are many supplier products, both proprietary and specially designed, that would require product planning if they contained more of the seven relevant business characteristics and particularly if they could be seen as operating products in their own right and not just as a product or system supplied to an OEM for inclusion in a larger product. A diesel engine made by a proprietary supplier such as Perkins and Cummins and sold to a truck or excavator manufacturer is both a component and an operating product in its own right. So is an electric motor range sold to industrial plant manufacturers. At Perkins and Cummins the direct OEM customer, needs must be researched as well as the needs of the OEM's own customers, the users of their engines. Decisions on their new products have to be made before the OEM's new products are developed. Almost all aspects of the product planning task should be used by suppliers of such components.

A Range of Woollen Garments. A new line of woollens for, say, Marks and Spencer could involve six of the seven characteristics: 1,2,3,4,5,7. On the face of it Marks and Spencer need product planning. So far as I know, they do not have it. However, since all Marks and Spencer products are bought-in, the product planning process must be carried out by the very wide-ranging buying activity. The power of Marks and Spencer's buyers and their influence over the activities of suppliers is well known.

They use their suppliers' capabilities to develop or create products, start-ing from customer or market requirements. They lay down specification and quality standards and prescribe – even have created – specific manufacturing methods to ensure production of the right product at the right quality and price levels. This describes exactly the process that a proper product plan-ning department should follow, regardless of how the department is named or to whom it reports. The fact that all product is supplied and perhaps also developed or engineered by outside manufacturers makes no difference to the need of the product owner, in this case Marks and Spencer, to do the product planning work.

A Portable Air Compressor. A compressor product programme involves characteristics 1,2,4,5,6,7. Product planning is necessary here because of the multi-customer situation, development lead time and up-front development costs. A compressor or any other item of mobile industrial, construction or agricultural equipment has much the same characteristics as a motor car or commercial vehicle in its product creation processes.

A Bren Gun Helicopter. A smaller item of military equipment with multiple customers such as a light helicopter or a bren gun boasts all seven character-istics. Unlike a military item created for a single large customer, a multi-customer market immediately necessitates product planning by the devel-oper and producer who takes the risk and makes the investment and product development expenditure before any customers are committed. The condi-tions here are almost exactly the same as for a manufacturer of civil aircraft.

Housing Constructed on a Speculative Basis. An architect-designed housing scheme built speculatively involves characteristics 2,3,7. This is an inter-esting situation. One may look upon the architect as product planner and stylist rolled into one. Indeed, in the engineering industry many industrial designers see their role as including a major element of product planning. The architect of this housing scheme, were he employed by the house builder, should certainly be involved in lots of product planning issues concerning the viability of the overall project. An outside architect would be less involved because he would produce a design to order.

The components that an architect uses to create his product, however, are largely pre-designed and supplied by outside firms. Thus architecture is mainly a synthesis of other people's components, at least when looked at from a product development point of view. The cost achievement for the house builder is therefore a matter of specification and buying skill in finding materials and components at the correct price-quality balance. Up-front product development cost and risk is minimal in this case, and the customer's needs in the product are assumed to have been incorporated by the architect. However, in speculative house building, expensive land must be bought first. From there, the trade-off between product requirements, laid down by the architect and the market and business opportunity determined by the company management, decide the final form of the programme.

Since housing demand can be satisfied by a wide variety of supplier sizes – from a local one-man housebuilder to a national house-building contractor – it is probable that only the larger companies need some form of product planning. This is not because the product development itself is complex or risky but because of the necessary investment in land and marketing expense before success can be seen. There is also the fact that at least one version of the product must be created and manufactured to act as a sales aid.

This has already been proposed for engineers, so perhaps architects in training also need exposure to product planning tools and techniques to enhance their ability to do their jobs well.

White or Brown Goods. The development of TVs, dishwashers, stereos, vacuum cleaners, involves all the numbered characteristics. These products should follow exactly the same development path as a computer or motor vehicle. In fact, they fall into the same general market classification of durable consumer goods. I give some view of the product planning practices in non-automotive durable consumer goods companies in a later chapter, but here I would note that, in Europe, there seems to be far less formalised product planning in these industries than this analysis suggests is needed. The multi-customer situation, the competition for ever-new (or new-looking) products, the technological drive to create new and improved products, the need for dedicated product development teams and high volume, cost-effective factories all point to a high risk, high investment climate in which management would benefit from effective product planning organisation. Product planning is a recognised discipline or process in all Japanese consumer electronic companies. We have already seen the importance of the product planning creativity in Akio Morita's eyes. In the organisation examples offered in Chapter Six, the completely different approaches to the product creation process of two durable consumer goods companies – Philips and Electrolux – are contrasted.

Toys and Games. These products involve four of the seven characteristics: 2,3,4,5. From dolls to space men, from computer to board games, from plastic cars to Meccano, the amount of product planning in the toy industry, must be significant. For in addition to the characteristics mentioned above, long development lead times (1) and the need for combination of new technologies (7) can also be present. Another that would vary depending on the design of the product is dedicated manufacturing costs (5).

Toy companies must dream of finding a long-life product like Monopoly. In reality, however, many successful toys and games are short-lived. Most toys – including many unsuccessful ones – cost a great deal of product development time and marketing expense to launch. Except for computer or electronic toys, the technology, as such, is probably less important than an understanding of the markets, the creation of new product ideas and their speedy execution using all the necessary resources within and outside the company. This requires considerable up-front investment of development, market research and pre-promotion effort. The risks are high. In an industry with these conditions, the bulk of the companies' internal activities are probably product planning-oriented if only because production is often entirely subcontracted to outside firms. In such cases the marketing director, or perhaps the technical director, also takes care of the product planning activities. There is certainly a strong need for them. Large toy and game companies should have a separate product planning manager and a product planning process.

A Bakery Plant. A piece of industrial process plant such as a bakery could involve characteristics 2,3,4,6,7. Although bakery plants are sold to the major food manufacturers from a menu of pre-designed systems and processes, there will always be a bespoke element to suit the particular configuration of the customer's factory, his product or his other particular requirements. Often, new elements will be designed to meet his needs as part of the contract quotation that places a premium on speed and accuracy.

The plant will not be test-operated until it is installed and commissioned on the customer's site. Naturally, all of the individual systems and unit machines that go to make up the main plant must have been proven in some way before on-site installation. Speed of delivery and the working quality of the machine must be a competitive element in winning orders.

Many in the contracting plant industry probably see themselves as bespoke product makers that keep some systems and machines ready on the shelf. They must rely on technically competent sales engineers who can design the plant with customers. Fancy footwork by their engineering and manufacturing departments probably helps to produce the customising work on time, in order to secure enough orders. However, from the brief analysis of the key business drivers above, the conclusion must be that the competitiveness of such companies would be considerably enhanced by having a properly established advanced product planning and product management organisation covering each of the company's main product categories. As with a military aircraft manufacturer, the situation of having several large customers, each with his own peculiar requirements, should not make it impossible to product plan virtually a complete range of system options from which customers can choose. Speed of quotation, contract and delivery and advance knowledge of cost and investment implications must make it worth the effort.

THE KEY DRIVERS FOR PRODUCT PLANNING

We have seen sufficient examples to draw some central conclusions. The potential need for product planning skills exists in any company. The presence of all seven business charactersistics is not necessary to make this the case. However, some characteristics underline the need more than others. Product planning becomes highly desirable in such cases.

- Where the primary external driver for product planning comes from the multi-customer or mass market situation.
- Where a second and related driver is the presence of strong competition.
- Where an important internal driver is the need to co-ordinate and combine the requirements and work of several disciplines.
- Risk management aspects are probably the most significant. The combination of a competitive market situation with long lead-times and/or high development and tooling costs creates a situation that cries out for effective planning and management well ahead of visible results.

The minimisation of risk is an important overall factor. Product planning must reduce risk in a new programme. There is also the positive task of identifying, more effectively than competition, those products that customers will buy and those that a company can effectively develop and produce. The combined task balances risk with the possibility of significant profits and market growth. This is a truly entrepreneurial challange. It underlines how, in complex companies and industries, the product planner has taken on a part of the old entrepreneurial role. This is done on behalf of, and not in the place of, top management.

It is by no means clear that all companies needing product planning have it. Indeed, "product" responsibility is often claimed by engineering departments – with or without dialogue or interface with the sales and marketing department. A product planning function may be located in marketing. But this concentrates attention, more often than not, on product requirements planning. Such a set-up can have little influence in fulfilling the real product planning task, which is the balancing of all the competing requirements for the new product into a feasible whole.

There is a belief that responsibility for creating new products should lie with engineers and that a company with a good engineering department needs nothing more. The industry and product segments I have described are almost all engineering industries. I hope it has been clearly demonstrated that product planning disciplines are needed over and above the kind of engineering and process excellence that remains, admittedly, a vital input to the new product creation process.

Many successful product planners have engineering qualifications and experience. It is not my intention to suggest the creation of a parallel force in engineering product companies. I shall return in Chapter Eleven to the relationships, good and bad, between traditionally-organised engineering or technical departments and product planning. The creative conflict supposed to derive from this relationship is crucial to the effective running of a competitive new product creation process. Unfortunately, the conflicts often outweigh the creativity. There remains one key question for top management. How to have the best of both worlds?

STEPS TO IMPROVE PRODUCT CREATION EFFECTIVENESS

Any organisation wishing to improve its product creation process efficiency should consider two points.

1. The need for an effective product planning activity should be accepted, whether embodied in a single new department of that name or simply as a process, with the various elements of the product planning mix and activities grouped around the existing organisation. If the latter path is chosen an effective cross-functional working atmosphere must support all product programmes.

2. The traditional product creation departments of industrial design, engi-

neering, marketing and manufacturing should accept that a part of what they have considered their responsibility has been removed. In return, they receive a better input of precisely defined and customer-oriented terms of reference for new projects. They also benefit from increased ability to concentrate on their core business. For technical departments this means designing and manufacturing with quality, speed and cost-effectiveness. In the case of marketing this involves finding out what the customer really wants now and in the future, while concentrating on selling current products.

There is room for more product planning activity in many types of engineering or technical product industries. The new product development process in those industries will gain in efficiency, speed, focus and will result in a more successful portfolio of new products.

Already, many companies that have for some time enjoyed the benefits of a strong product planning organisation are beginning to move into another phase of organisational development. Product planning activities are being developed in the direction of business planning concepts that embrace more than just the pure product. Product planning is also evolving into programme management as the cross-functional negotiating skills of product planners become the core of programme teams. There planners are able to concentrate on initial programme planning, decision-making and the effective implementation. It is impossible to think about the development of product planning activities without also considering the implications of cross-functional working and more effective ways of product programme implementation. The development and wider adoption of effective programme management and business planning practices is so important that the whole of Chapters Seven and Eight is devoted to them. Admittedly, this goes slightly beyond the scope of a pure exposition of product planning. The three disciplines are, however, very tightly bound together. Rather than consider them as overlapping or competing activities, we should consider them as natural partners within companies that wish to achieve a quantum leap in integrated product development performance. One form will often evolve out of another over time as companies learn to take advantage of what the first of those disciplines, product planning, has to offer. This is precisely the process we shall see at work in some of the organisation examples that make up Chapter Six.

5 PRODUCT PLANNING'S ROLE IN THE NEW PRODUCT DEVELOPMENT PROCESS

Product planning plays a significant part in the whole process of developing and introducing new products. The stage by stage process of creating a business and product plan, of starting a new product activity and of programme planning is described. This illustrates the role of a product planning department in driving and managing the different decision stages and emphasises the essential principles for achieving quality, efficiency and success in the processes leading to the launch of profitable new products.

To assist understanding of the place of product planning in an organisation, one needs to envisage the total process of developing new products. What follows is a description of a typical step by step process as used over the past twenty years in Europe and North America by companies that have brought at least the top level of their new product development process under control. There is no blueprint. Each company will, of necessity, have its own version of the process, whether formalised or informal, adapted to suit its house style, its products and stage of organisational development.

The process is capable of constant refinement and improvement. To compete with the lean-clean product development machines of the Japanese and best practice Western companies, no company should regard its established process as static. More importantly, companies not already operating such a widely accepted and understood process should start to develop one immediately.

There are two key reasons for having an agreed product creation process. First, to ensure that top management is able to see the risks of investing resources and, ultimately, capital in a product programme. Second, so that operational management have a stage by stage process framework in which to work, with each stage bringing an increasing level of commitment and involvement. In order to understand these two key issues I offer first a very high level overview of the process, followed by a more detailed explanation that concentrates on the role and involvement of product planning.

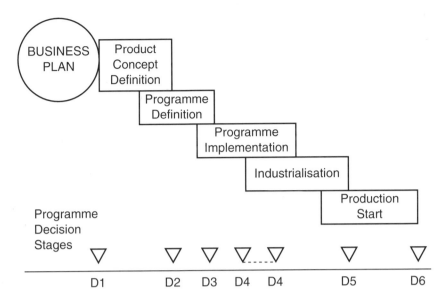

Figure 5.1 Decisions in the New Product Development Process.

OVERVIEW OF THE COMPLETE PROCESS

If we adopt an overall view, the process emerges as shown in Figure 5.1. Each programme goes through a formalised series of decisions. The depth of decision and commitment grows at each stage. For simplicity here I have used the terminology D1, D2, D3, D4, D5 and D6 to refer to the start of different project phases. In many companies, these stages are given significant names such as Product Study phase, Programme Approval, Engineering Sign-off, Job One.

The Business Plan Stage: pre-D1

The business plan stage should precede any official project start (D1). In the creation of a business plan or strategic plan, concentration is laid upon the new issues, external and internal, facing the company. Decisions are taken as to what new projects should be added to the total plan. That is to say: the already existing, and partly implemented, projects and action plans form the basis for the new plan; in each cycle – which can be yearly or twice yearly in a faster moving environment – new elements and corrections are added. This connection between already decided, current actions and new project decisions as part of the new business plan process is important in linking a company's planning and operational activities. It is emphasised with more explanation and examples in Chapter Eight.

D1

After approval as part of an overall business plan, individual programmes must each start by going through D1. This move will be determined in timing by the required product introduction date and the total lead time required to fulfil the programme. D1 constitutes a formal decision by the board or other authorising body to start the project. More decision stages and check points can be used for larger complex programmes and fewer for simple product upgrades, but decision stages are important to assess degrees of risk and ensure that all participating departments buy-in to each new programme stage before the decision is taken to proceed to the next stage.

From D1 to D2

The decisions at points D1 and D2, although important, are only taken to move the project on to the next stage. They should not mean that a decision is taken to implement the project as a whole; only to start it (D1) or to approve its basic product details (D2). D2 is often called Product Study Approval or something similar, since at this point, the product concept must be fully worked out. The starting of a project at D1 must nevertheless be seen as involving a serious intention to proceed with the project if the check-points along the way remain favourable. Resources are allocated to move to D2 at the D1 decision point. The same goes for the project between D2 and D3. It is an important tenet of good product planning that decisions must not be made late. It is also important that decisions are not made too early. The reasons for this follow.

1. If the implementing parts of the company are told that a decision to implement the project fully has been made at D1 or D2 they will always behave differently than if they know they must concentrate all efforts on getting successfully just to the next decision stage. Getting there success-fully involves performing certain actions and achieving a measurable amount of progress on the product programme and so even the planning stages of a programme must be executed with high quality. It is only at deci-sion stage D3, Programme Approval, that a final implementation approval should be given to the project when a high level of programme feasibility and confidence has been established.

2. A decision made too early will be based on inadequate information and, without the sequenced decision stages, management and participating divi-sions will lack the chance to assess adequately the level of project risk.

3. A too-early decision may be actioned later than its actual decision date, by which time circumstances may have changed and the decision will have to be modified. The results are needless uncertainty, further evaluation loops and wasted time.

4. A decision made and acted upon too early – that means earlier than the technical timing requirements of the specific element – is also more likely to result in programme changes downstream.

D3

Decision stage D3 is often called Programme Approval. This describes its function well. At this point commitment is made to full scale prototyping, supplier commitment and preparation for manufacturing facilities and tooling. Here, the balance of the programme, usually its largest part in expenditure terms, is approved. It is also important, at or about this point, to trigger the major financial releases since these commitments will bring in the heaviest parts of the external programme expenditure. (Naturally, at each stage of decision, including D1 and D2, the company must be prepared to commit the necessary resources, including some tooling if needed, to move the project on to its next stage and preserve its overall timing.) This is particularly important in view of the most up-to-date approach to implementing new programmes, with many activities proceeding in parallel, which inevitably leads to more effort and more expenditure, including tooling, in the early part of a programme.

This whole "D" decision approach is a risk management process in which the level of certainty increases with the progress of a programme. So does the level of financial outlay and financial commitment. These are not necessarily the same things. Most important of all, however, the costs of cancelling or correcting bad decisions or finding that new market input changes a major element of the programme increase dramatically with time.

Hence a very large part of this new product development decision process, which might seem to some people to be rather unwieldly, is aimed at increasing management confidence and minimising risk at each stage. Another aim is to ensure that the later implementation of the programme can proceed as swiftly, and with as much quality, as possible so that the programme deliverables are fully realised.

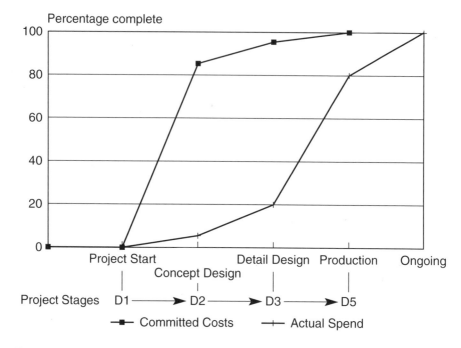

Figure 5.2 Programme Costs: Commitment Versus Outlay.

Source: Digital Equipment Corp.

Figure 5.2 illustrates the validity of the careful step by step programme decision process. As a project proceeds, the actual spend curve rises quite slowly
initially. At D2 only some five per cent of the programme cost has been
spent – but up to 85 per cent may have been committed. At programme
approval (D3) still only 20 per cent has been spent, but up to 95 per cent
may be committed. This does not even mean commitment in a contractual
sense to outside suppliers, but rather that because all the major programme
decisions and parameters are fixed, the eventual costs for the programme's
total life, both internal and external, are committed. This includes also such
elements as commitment to achievable profit margins, although many
companies institute profit improvement actions half-way through a new
product development when things go wrong. The problem is that the room
for manoeuvre is limited at this point because of product, design and process
decisions made earlier on.

D4

Decision stage D4 is a quality and reliability check point; more properly, we
might call it a sign-off point prior to fuller involvement of production tooling

and facilities. This may not occur as a single point in the process. It might spread over a number of weeks for different parts of the programme that involve different departmental sign-offs. Yet it has an important role to play in giving all participating departments a chance to sign off on the project and proceed to the last phase; Productionisation, Job One and Sales Start. D4 is a point often not considered or not properly achieved under time pressure to get a product to market. However, its value as a formal part of the planning process is that all the actions leading towards finalisation of the specification, design release, tooling and quality status and the finishing of product testing should be focused here and not on the production start date. If changes are still being made to get the product right up to, and beyond, Job One, then the project is already out of control from the point of view of quality and profitability. The D4 point provides a means of improving this situation. Many companies, including automotive, are beginning to concentrate on hitting this point by tying to it, for example, the completion of the last, fully representative prototypes or some similar significant programme event.

D5 and D6

D5, the actual production start, needs no explanation or comment. D6, the achievement of full production, is the point at which all programme objectives are seen to have been achieved. The following elements of a programme cannot be perceived at production start but are an integral part of finishing a project. They are three of the main determinants of maximised profitability. D6 is, therefore, a means of checking progress in these three areas.

1. Time to reach full production from first production: so-called ramp-up time. This is a critical target to ensure the earliest full utilisation of heavy capital expenditure.

2. Launching of all market versions and customer variants included in the initial launch plan. This is the time beyond which there are no further product arguments from sales not to achieve the target volumes.

3. Reducing start-up costs during launch to targetted cost levels. These costs will include prices from suppliers, man hours per unit of production, scrap and rework rates, quality standards, machine utilisation efficiencies, the effective running of logistic systems. This is the most crucial period for ensuring the life cycle profitability of a new product, since although no company can hit full programme efficiency from the very first production unit, profitable companies *do* take least time to ramp-up and to hit target cost and efficiency levels.

D6 is also used as an audit point by some companies that wish to look back at, and draw lessons from, the success or otherwise of the project. Others concentrate on D6 as the culmination of a project, to which everyone in the company contributes before going on to their next task. This view is perhaps particularly appropriate to programmes with long lead times where the feedback and learning process from one project into another must be continuous rather than waiting until a particular project's end. In the electronics industry, product cycles can be short and many smaller projects pass through the same organisation at the same time. Here the need for project feedback after the D6 point and performance benchmarking to sustain continuous improvement in succeeding projects is very necessary. This learning and improvement process applies equally to product planning at the front end and to technical aspects of the programme execution.

THE CONTENT OF EACH PROGRAMME PHASE AND THE INVOLVEMENT OF PRODUCT PLANNING

So far I have given an overview of each stage of the process without describing enough to demonstrate the main actions appropriate to individual stages or the specific interaction and contribution of product planning. For the process to be used as a quality tool to minimise risk, it is necessary also to define the deliverables at the end of each phase that support the decision making, act as a quality yardstick and form the information and decision base for the next phase. The checklists described here are used at management level as part of the risk and quality aspects of the decisions. They also provide a contents structure for documentation prepared by product planning to sponsor the decision.

The Business Plan and Product Cycle Plan Phase

Action to refresh forward planning decisions and to create a new business plan is a company-wide process that should take place at least once – and preferably twice – a year. It is based on a systematic look at the total new product activity, including running and yet-to-be started projects and all the other opportunities, pressures and constraints, internal and external, that the company faces. Product cycle plan studies pinpoint products due for replacement or revision and define for the first time the outline terms of reference for the work programmes necessary to create the new product. From this input, which is usually formally reviewed at board level, will emerge decisions on the timing, targets, content and preliminary resource allocation for any new projects to be added to the plan. Additionally, an audit will adjust already running projects in the light of new company insights.

This multi-project review can only take place in the context of a total business plan because within each running project the cross-functional or "umbrella view" of the company is impossible. One of the arguments against a total project- or business unit-based company organisation, where management focuses on the needs and progress of individual business projects, is that the "umbrella view" of certain key company-wide factors such as resource utilisation, product image and technology standards tends to get lost. Hence there must always be some company-wide activities which provide necessary co-ordination and overview. The business planning function, if it exists separately, will provide a financial expression of all the planned actions in the business plan. Product planning, with its responsibility for the creation and control of the product cycle plan, takes the major role in initiating the business plan process by defining what should be its content and its underlying targets and assumptions.

Business planning in this context should not be confused with corporate or long-range planning. These activities are separate but often parallel activities to the creation of the business plan. They deal with general corporate strategic issues, such as diversification, refinancing, acquisitions or restructuring, but are not focused on product projects in the same way. Where they exist side by side, business planning and its long-range cousin come together to provide guidelines for the new budget year.

At the end of the business plan cycle, the following information should have been generated on each proposed new product programme. This information should be contained in the business plan, acting as a reference to start a programme at the appropriate time and as the first quality and risk check point:

Checklist for Programme Start

1. The need for, and the origin of, the project: market need, strategic requirements, legislation, product cycle plan that forecasts the need for replacement of existing products.
2. The market strategy, positioning, pricing and volume estimates and description of the target customers.
3. An outline of the basis of the product design, and the derivation of the main systems and technology, newly developed or carryover.

4. A preliminary statement of the main product targets.
5. A description and first costing of the project: resources, investment, cost objectives.
6. Timing of the project related to the main activity milestones, decisions and financial releases.
7. A manufacturing and supplier plan outline including new processes, capacity required, manpower, make/buy implications.
8. Project feasibility and profitability.

For programmes entering the business plan for the first time, these data will be based on an informed product and business planning desk study with some internal technological research, advanced engineering and styling input. Even at this stage, consultation with manufacturing and purchasing is also desirable. The external study work on customer, market and legislation needs should also have been evaluated and researched for the first time. Thus the work from product planning must be well-defined and based on factual investigation long before a programme reaches the timing point of the D1 decision, when it must start in earnest.

The above will suffice to introduce the business planning phase of the total process and the product planning role that resides within it. Chapter Eight is devoted solely to the rationale for, and the creation of, a business plan. I have already covered the detailed workings of product planning in this phase in dealing with the building blocks of the product planning activity.

The Product Study Phase: D1 to D2

At the D1 decision point, the point at which a programme really starts, all involved departments focus on a single market need or product concept for the first time. Product planning should take the initiative to kick off the stage by preparing for the D1 decision and defining the start points for the programme.

The starting points and objectives for this phase are the summary description and targets of the project contained in the business plan. As a further check on quality, it is desirable to update any key base figures that influence the project but have changed since the business plan period. Such figures could include economics, base volumes and assumptions regarding competition or legislation. Lastly, an agreed detailed work plan to take the project from D1 to D2 should be created together with an appropriate budget.

The D1 decision will be made by the product planning committee or the board and should be communicated by a formal document that sets out the programme elements contained in the business plan and the other assumptions, investigations, alternatives and actions by all company departments that form the target for the D1 to D2 stage. This information will be created by product planning, after negotiation with colleagues. It will be issued in the form of a preliminary programme description. This is referred to, in companies which use the idea, by many titles: the Red Book, Yellow Book, Design Brief, Product Brief and so on. I much prefer to use the literal title of Programme Description because this documentation should be concerned with the whole programme objective and action plan – not just the design or the product content.

Between D1 and D2 product planning should also discuss and optimise results of the additional study work by all participating departments to create a firm product requirement specification. This period, like the D2 to D3 phase, will require many high level trade-offs between conflicting requirements within the overall programme. Good co-operative work and good decisions taken here will enhance the effectiveness and speed of the downstream implementation.

In addition, this is the phase where heavy emphasis must be applied to evaluation of overall project feasibility: the cancellation or re-directing of projects after D1, and certainly after D2, is expensive and damaging to company morale.

Product planning bears a very important responsibility in ensuring that consistent and timely communication of terms of reference, new information and decisions permeate through the company to everyone involved at an appropriate level of detail. Product Decision Letters are used for this purpose in many companies. They give authority to such updates and revisions – of which more later. The first versions of the programme description document, created and issued by product planning at the start of the programme, must be kept up to date by an effective programme communication process. Linked programme information and planning systems help to avoid excessive paperwork.

This need for consistent communication is often underestimated by product planners – but even more so by the receivers of product planning communications. To be effective, product planning guidelines must descend to the kind of technical and commercial detail that may be perceived as interference with other departments' traditional responsibilities. However, in my experience, the need for cross-functional decision making and communication is best fulfilled by an independent department. The lessons of the past show that technical departments are not good cross-company decision-makers and communicators.

Another frequent complaint from the line functional areas can involve bad communication on programme or product definition issues. Thus it is difficult for product planning departments to "win" here. All the same, good communication should be their first priority and scoring political points the second.

Prior to the D1 decision there must be discussion about how the programme will be controlled and managed. This may occur through the product manager in product planning, through the appointment of a more independent programme manager or director, or by the creation of a separate programme team. These issues are addressed in Chapter Seven when discussing the relationships of product planning with programme management. It does not matter whether your plans involve a full scale programme team or simply a loose matrix form of programme organisation; someone must "own" the programme from the very beginning. They must act as the focal point for decisions, analysis and communication. Because at this stage the concentration is on what should the product be, this task works well if handled by product planning.

At the end of the phase, a concrete product definition must be provided to allow the technical departments and purchasing to begin to make their own long lead time decisions and commitments. There may still be alternative aspects left open for further study, provided that all critical lead time aspects are respected. For example, in a new car programme, all major product dimension and major specification items should be clarified but some minor options, such as the precise configuration of the interior design or a complete definition of the markets involved, may be left open. However, because many product and technical decisions are taken during the next phase, it is essential to firm up the product requirements as much as possible and to handle the evaluation of still open alternatives so as not to cause downstream problems.

Programme Quality Check-list at D2

To achieve a quality level appropriate to the end of this stage in the process, the following information and progress should be presented to, and confirmed by, management as a preparation for decision D2:

1. Confirmation and update of all data in D1.
2. Representative product models for clinic purposes if the product can benefit from market research at this stage.
3. Initial styling or industrial design work with the possible choice of a theme or a definition of main alternatives.

4. Some preliminary external research results, especially concerning new conceptual aspects of the product. Alternatively, the sifting of concept alternatives.

5. Packaging studies and decisions leading to a complete physical layout of the product and a description of the main customer interfaces.

6. Detailed requirement specifications for the product's performance.

7. Customer profile and requirement statement.

8. Choice of all the principal technical solutions or alternatives required to achieve the product objectives, including an agreement that they can be developed in time to meet the product introduction requirements. This does not mean detailed design but, rather, agreement by the design and process group on a design outline including all systems and major components.

9. CAD and CAM simulations of the main system areas and other key product performance elements. The maximum amount of performance simulation should be performed on the proposed product configuration.

10. An advanced parts list (APL) to support the above.

11. A preliminary manufacturing, capacity, process and make/buy plan.

12. A preliminary cost-target based on the APL, the product requirement specification and the principal technical and make/buy solutions.

13. A more detailed time, activity and resource plan than appeared in the business plan, including a detailed workplan for getting from D2 to D3.

14. Preliminary discussions with long lead time suppliers. Discussions should include a search for "black-box" or "grey-box" solutions – complete supplier responsibility for design and production, or principal responsibility with OEM overview – for those components and systems that will be sourced outside.

On this last point, supplier involvement has historically been left to a much later stage. The past few years however, have seen a change of heart. Relationships between OEMs and their suppliers have moved away from the old adversarial style. Participation is often invited in an earlier phase of a project. Commitment to specific suppliers is occasionally earlier. Quite apart from leading to better OEM-supplier relations, this move has been necessary to achieve shorter lead times for engineering work and tooling and is part of a wider move to parallel working and so-called simultaneous engineering. It has also been triggered by the start of manufacturing in North America and Europe by Japanese firms in a wide variety of industries. Japanese-style supplier policies have been introduced into these new environments. The benefits of the Japanese supplier relationship model, which makes the maximum early use of a supplier's input, are well understood, but the move from adversarial to co-operative supplier relationships will not be an easy one for all European firms.

The Programme Development Phase: D2 to D3

The checklist of information and commitment levels that results from the D1 to D2 phase acts as the input to kick off the D2 to D3 phase. This is nothing more than an intensification of the first phase, with the emphasis on hardening up the degree of technical, financial and commercial certainty. The same departments will be involved but there will be much greater relative involvement from the design and process technical areas, purchasing and suppliers. There will be a full programme of external research – with product models and rough prototypes or photographs and even computer simulations. This phase is the last opportunity before Programme Approval (D3) to check major details with customer groups or the distribution network. Thus it is very important to allow time and funds to produce good quality product models for market research. In fact, many see this phase as a predominantly design engineering phase. But this is a mistake. The voice of the customer should still be listened to in order to support the creation of all the product features and details. Quality Function Deployment (QFD), if used, should be heavily worked in this phase; this is a technique for translating customer requirements into product specifications and manufacturing processes in an optimal way. A planning technique is used to identify the logical relationships within which the product can eventually be designed: more is explained in Chapter Nine. However, cross-functional discussion, planning and evaluating methodologies are a feature of this stage of a product programme. These represent leading edge techniques that should be more widely adopted as part of the improvement in new product creation efficiency.

The traditional way to create new products is to design something and try it, then re-design and try again when it doesn't work. The leading edge approach means not designing or testing anything until the proposed new product programme has been thoroughly studied, thought through, and simulated on computer if relevant. By then, it should be effectively created as a totality in the minds, and on the desks, of the people who will eventually implement it. This preparation adds time, and some cost, to the front end of the process but it can pay back major returns during subsequent implementation in terms of faster time to market, fewer mistakes and repeats, better adaptability of the product to process and logistic systems and many other benefits.

To achieve this cohesion, other departments such as purchasing and process engineering must also have sufficient budget, resources and time to make their own decisions and so make their contribution to the programme. As already mentioned, these departments traditionally started their detailed involvement much later in a programme's life than is now agreed as necessary. This means that traditional budgetary yardsticks may not allow them sufficient room to make their vital upstream contribution adequately.

Cost targetting is also a very important aspect of this phase because after the design concepts and supplier and process inputs are frozen the cost aspects are also largely determined. Prior to the programme approval decision, product planning should also engage in the final study of aspects confirming or influencing the programme's feasibility and viability.

Commitments for D3: Programme Approval

Product planning will usually also co-ordinate this phase including final product committee presentations and decisions. However, in order to ensure a high quality programme approval decision at D3, the product manager has to put in a tremendous amount of work to obtain the commitment of all the functional directors who must share in the implementation and thus accept their part of the programme commitment. The problems of getting all functions to buy-in to a new programme are common in a conventional functional organisation. It is precisely the problem of getting that commitment at the right time, and to the right degree, that has caused the move in some companies towards matrix or full programme management-based organisation structures.

In a company that has separate and effective programme or project management structure, the commitment process can be slightly different. Here, the "strong" programme or project director is usually the one to make that commitment based on buying the resource and the performance from the functional areas. It doesn't matter who does it, but it must be done.

The end result of this phase must be successful programme approval, (D3). Next, it is full speed ahead to the implementation phase without looking back and without questioning one's direction or revising previous decisions. All the main elements of the programme should be known and all decisions or major assumptions should have been made and communicated to those with a need to know. This is the point of highest quality in the planning phase of a programme but since not everything should be left until the last moment, the whole phase D1 to D3 should focus on quality aspects. Management should allocate sufficient resources to each participating department to allow their fullest contribution as well as enough of their own time to participate in those parts of the programme which they feel require their input. Changes of direction due to late management input is a well-known European phenomenon and, however well-meaning or "justified", this phenomenon should be avoided. Hence management should also allocate sufficient of their own resources and time at the early pre-D3 phase to put the necessary input into the programme.

Timing Discipline in D3 Decision-Making

It is vital that product planning should devote all its efforts in the run-up to D3 to removing any obstacles to an efficient and timely decision. These come in a number of guises.

1. Failing to gain the confidence of top management in the period leading up to programme approval. A good piece of advice: never to go to a board or product planning committee with a key decision only once. Mention it and describe some of the key issues in earlier meetings when the pressure to make the decision is not pronounced. Committee members are notoriously more amenable to new information and ideas when the decision deadline gun is not pressed to their heads. Prepare the ground with position papers, briefing meetings for small groups of top management or else rehearse the presentation with them a month earlier. Make sure that they understand the timing and commitment structure of the process being followed.

One of the surest ways to delay a project is to go past decision point D3 without getting management approval, because the whole company is poised awaiting a go signal that involves heavy budget expenditure and probably external commitments, both physical and financial. An alternative to rehearsing the presentation a month earlier, which is not always possible due to last minute information or the simple pressures on top management's time, is to rehearse with senior representatives of each committee member a few days before the meeting proper. They can then brief their respective bosses on key issues or disagreements.

2. Failing to get the commitment of one or more of the functional heads who must implement the project. In some smaller companies this and the previous point could cover the same individuals.

This commitment process can often be made more difficult by organisational peculiarities that split normally homogeneous operational departments into two: for example, separate advanced and product engineering or manufacturing planning and process design. Whatever the structure involved, no hiatus can be allowed between the upstream "planners" and the downstream "implementers". Consultation should start at least half way between points D2 and D3. In companies with split responsibilities, some of the upstream technical and project planning people can be moved downstream with the project if problems with the transfer of knowledge are anticipated.

Coping with Handovers

Roy Axe was head of advanced design at Rover and, as such, he was responsible for taking programmes up to programme approval and then handing over to the programme implementing departments. His guidelines for smooth transitions from the "planning phase" to the "implementation phase" which he described to me were as follows.

- Bring downstream technical people – doers not managers – into the upstream phase to start on a new project and let them go through with the project. Handover is not needed with them: they act as missionaries for colleagues who come later into the project.
- Move parts of the "upstream team", including the managers, downstream with the project after D3 if this is seen to help a specific project.
- Upstream engineering section managers should stay in touch after the handover. This helps avoid the "not invented here" syndrome when downstream corrections are discussed.
- Start early in involving the downstream managers who will have to implement the project.
- Make it clear to the whole company that what is handed over is primary responsibility but not involvement. Styling, for example, must stay strongly in control of the visual elements of the product throughout the industrialisation process. Product management authority over the product itself continues through to production and beyond. The advanced technology decisions made at the beginning of a programme should stay valid right to the end.
- Faults and mistakes found after handover should be dealt with openly – but mainly by the downstream team as part of the implementation. They must be seen as company project problems and not as "someone else's" problems. This may require motivational training to overcome certain inbred types of unco-operative attitudes.
- Rover has a long running quality training programme for employees at all levels. One of its objectives is to encourage multi-disciplinary groups to work together to solve problems and to improve continuously. This creates a

co-operative working atmosphere within projects and within the company as a whole.

- Last, and most difficult, but worth thinking about, the project budgets are not handled by the functional managers themselves but by project-responsible programme directors.

It is interesting to note that with their latest 1992 organisation, Rover Group has gone even beyond the concept described above of a forward programmes group handing over at the D3 decision point to dedicated product development programme teams. They now operate a structure where the different product groups – Land Rover, Large Cars, Small and Medium Cars and Powertrain – covering both current operations and new programmes, are separate business units. New product programmes are still originated in the forward programmes group, but the programme manager for each major new programme is appointed at the very beginning and reports initially to the head of forward programmes and then transfers over at programme approval, with his complete programme team, to report to the managing director of the relevant product business unit.

The Need for Continuous Improvement

This phased decision-making and detailed planning at the start of a programme is something that will be familiar to many who have worked in major manufacturing companies. I can also imagine that some managers not familiar with it will consider it a somewhat idealised description.

There are, however, many companies in cars, consumer electronics or computer equipment that are actually operating their new programmes in the manner outlined and reaping the results in the quality of their new product introduction performance and increasing competitiveness. The European engineering products industry should not only reach this "idealised" description of programme planning but go further to improve its product development processes to compete with world class standards.

Today's by-word for new product development excellence is continuous improvement. Companies already reaching towards the most modern and efficient ideas are reporting measurable improvements in lead times, part number reductions and lower lifetime programme costs – as in the case of the Digital Equipment Company. Most of them, encouraged by their success, are aiming for even greater improvements in the next new programme and the next and so on. Indeed, the establishment and acceptance of the kind of process I describe is only a first step. Continuous evaluation and improvement of this process must then take place to shorten lead times, reduce implementation costs, increase customer satisfaction and raise product quality, while reducing product costs and complexity. Therefore it is essential for each company to develop, communicate widely and have accepted its own version of the process as a basis for the continuous improvement.

A Japanese Example

The following example shows how new thinking and new attitudes must be adopted within the new product creation process. The episode revolves around a negotiation with a Japanese automotive company to start up a major joint manufacturing venture in Europe.

After negotiating for several months we had already reached the beginning of version four of our joint feasibility study before getting into the D2 point in my process chart. The feasibility study was a very detailed plan to implement two new ranges of products in a largely rebuilt manufacturing facility. Each version of the study went deeper into the commercial, technical and resource implications. Teams of manufacturing, purchasing, styling, engineering, product planning and finance personnel from both sides participated from the early stages of the negotiation. Thus the quality of the information and study that had gone into the business planning and early product concept studies was already of a higher quality than some companies have in preparation for D3. However, no actual project engineering had been performed, only shelf engineering of the major suspension and drivetrain units and planning of the project details. The initial planning however, was achieved with considerable engineering, process and purchase department involvement.

At the point of transition between phase three of the feasibility study and phase four, a senior member of the Japanese team made a speech along the following lines. "So far in the phase three feasibility study, we have made many assumptions to arrive at the current stage. Now we go over to phase four. We wish to strengthen those assumptions. Therefore the whole project must be gone through in more detail and the assumptions made much more certain." The point was repeated several times with emphasis placed on communicating the fact that, while we were still dealing with assumptions, these had to be of a much higher quality than in the previous negotiating rounds. A timing plan was also presented for the provision of the new, harder information. It caused us all much concern.

We were quite worried by the further degree of detail and certainty requested. Timing was tight, if only because our normal planning process did not provide for such detailed information and decisions so early. Although we still considered them as decisions, the fine distinction between decision and assumption only became clear later. Our own board was also concerned that we should not change any of our previous "decisions" already written into the feasibility study in order not to go back on earlier commitments and so disturb what was seen as a very firm Japanese decision-making process. They did not want to cause problems in the negotiations by appearing to change their minds.

The reality was different. The Japanese statement about assumptions was just that: check your assumptions, they were saying, and make them more firm. Increase your level of commitment to those assumptions by the quality of your work. They did not see this as the final decision process but only as a preparation for future decisions. Indeed, they showed willingness later in the programme to change their own previous assumptions for their own reasons or at our request, right up to the final decision point on each major issue. Thus the concentration on assumptions as a preparation for future decisions followed the guideline I described earlier: no decision should be taken too early but the best quality information and therefore assumptions should be developed right up to the decision point.

The actual Japanese joint venture programme decision was made about the time of my D2 decision point. The level of programme knowledge and confidence was higher in many areas than proposed in the D1 to D3 scheme above. Overall project feasibility was more deeply studied, and the parallel work of all participating company functions from the outset meant that the consistency of the data was greater. The level of technical planning was higher despite the fact that our Japanese colleagues had done little actual new design work on the product itself apart from a lot of product planning, checking and feasibility work using the carryover product as a basis. In addition, there were new shelf engineered systems such as powertrains already available for the new product. They were also prepared to make the necessary information releases, such as information to suppliers, to support the longest lead time programme activities. Had it not been for specific timing problems within the study phase, they would have been preparing to take a "D3" type of decision six months earlier.

Planning as a Basis for Implementation

This may all seem very intellectual, even "airy fairy" to the down-to-earth European manager but it is important to understand three things from this, all of which should be clearly built into any product planning process:

1. The Japanese do handle new product programmes in this intellectual or conceptual way. They also attend to all the practical details.
2. The development of new product programmes is a complicated business requiring a high degree of intelligence in planning and implementation.
3. The Japanese can progress a long way into projects without physical working just by the quality of product planning preparation as well as the assumption and decision making they put in.

The following phrase was first coined some years ago by a friend, Alan Martin, at that time an automotive consultant with Arthur D. Little, but now business strategy director for the Rover Group. It describes perfectly my perception of the Japanese. It also describes the secret to successful new product creation.

Plan superbly then run like hell.

The iteration and checking process throughout the early decision phases facilitates a good decision, and ensures a high quality implementation phase. It also minimises the actual hard product and process engineering work commitment before the button is pushed for D3 programme approval by concentrating on the "soft" product and programme decisions. Thereafter the programme implementation phase has a firm rationale in allowing the speediest and most trouble-free progress. I have no doubt that European companies will have to target ever tighter time and activity schedules for the D1 to D3 process to remain competitive but the quality of work done in that phase must also improve.

The lesson to be learnt from working with the Japanese is not so much the need to copy their work methods and procedures but more to follow their philosophy of constantly trying to do things better, cheaper, quicker, with fewer resources, yet never missing out the really important things: getting it right first in your mind before you commit and never forgetting the customer.

Quality Checklist for Programme Approval

The main elements of information and project progress that should be available to management by the D3 decision are as follows.

1. Confirmation or updating of all data presented at D2. By this time, probably, management will regard the D1 and D2 data as targets. The last time that any significant deviations should be presented is at D3 when the feasibility of the project must be finally demonstrated. Even then, full justification will be needed.

2. A detailed engineering package for the product with long lead time releases already made, certainly for prototypes, and no major technical issues left unsolved, or without a back-up.

3. As much as possible of the product evaluated and described or designed using two- and three-dimensional CAE models.

4. All long lead suppliers should be chosen. For other suppliers, as a minimum, the details of the process type should be defined for all major bought-out components so that competing suppliers who can supply an identically performing product can be decided later.

5. A fully detailed process plan for the whole project including preliminary design of all new layouts and plant and full participation with the design engineers and suppliers on tooling and assembly design.

6. A fully representative model of what the product should look like outside and, if relevant, inside. This should have been agreed by management and accepted by "representatives of the customer" – the sales organisation, distributors, or direct customers themselves through market research and clinics.

7. By now, depending on the type of product involved, workhorse prototypes could be in use. These could be based on conversions of current products or "lash-ups" that have the purpose of testing out individual systems or product concepts which the engineers need to check out before making final representative prototype decisions. These are not conventional prototypes: they do not have to be visually representative, but are potentially a great time saver.

8. A complete product specification describing, from the customer and market point of view the features, options, performance and quality levels expected of the product.

9. An agreed cost target related to market value and price and compared to competitors for every part or sub-group of the product. Often, at this stage, costing is seen as nothing more than a cost estimating department report. However, by D3 it should be a detailed cost plan that every responsible part of the organisation, including suppliers, is committed to.

10. A detailed parts list or lists showing the engineering and manufacturing view of the product; at its simplest level, the same parts or sub-assemblies but in different order or grouped differently. This is one of the most important programme control tools. It should be made available as early as possible in a programme to all participating departments with a clear definition of who is tasked with maintaining it.

11. The full results of a series of market investigations demonstrating the validity of the product in the eyes of the market and the customer.

12. A preliminary view of the market introduction plan with prices per market, option off-takes, launch quantities, marketing expenditure by major categories and other key elements of the marketing mix.

13. A fully detailed implementation plan for the project including all major timing milestones, work planning, organisation and responsibilities, financial release dates, all of which must correspond to the budget and tooling estimates contained within the financial analysis.

14. A financial analysis of the project showing results in different forms: sensitivities of the project to varying external and internal factors; profitability of individual parts of the project if it contains more than one product; effect of the project on the rest of the company or division's results; alternative means of financing, if appropriate.

15. Long lead time funding for supplier tooling or commitment to other subcontractors should be approved.

The process from business plan to D3 consists of a series of iteration loops. Essentially the same project information is evaluated during each loop but with a higher degree of confidence each time based on a greater degree of marketing, technical and physical work or results. The value of the iteration is to firm up programme elements and increase the confidence of the management team and participating departments so that the rapid implementation will be as fault free as possible. It is also aimed at avoiding the need for questioning, or worse, revising the programme parameters downstream.

The main workflow and content of the process for the main functional participants in the pre-D1 to D3 phases are as shown in Figure 5.3.

The Programme Implementation Phase: D3 to D6

After D3 the project begins implementation phase. "Running like hell" should be the order of the day. Prototypes will be built, evaluated and tested, orders will be placed with suppliers of both tools and production equipment. Production release drawings will be prepared, some before prototype work is finished. The next major milestone will be product sign off: D4. I have already indicated that D4 can be a series of points covering all the main sign-offs on different aspects of the programme, signalling the end of certain of the functional work phases.

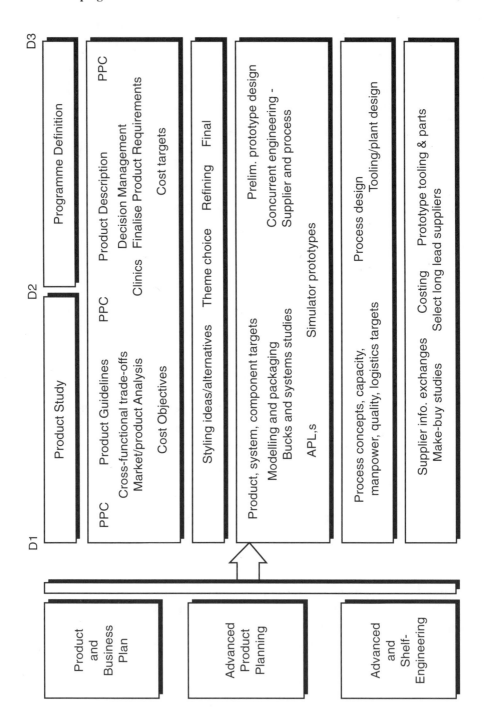

Figure 5.3 The New Product Development Process. D1 to D3 Phase Key Events.

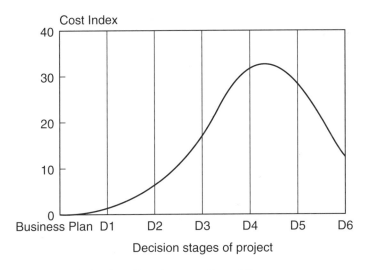

Figure 5.4 Typical Product Development Spend Pattern.

After this point, the main engineering work on the programme should be completed and the next phase, D4 to D5 production, should primarily involve production, process engineering, sales and marketing, purchasing and logistics personnel handling the last details of the launch with suppliers.

The task of product planning will decline substantially in this phase. The bulk of the team should be upstream working on the next or next-but-one new product. The product manager is the mainstay of the remaining product planning effort during this later programme stage, responsible for maintaining product consistency right through the production launch and ramp-up. There are often key last minute product issues that need a decision or necessary updates of detailed product market definitions to assist release and capacity planning both in-house and at suppliers. The product manager is also involved in assisting marketing to prepare the launch presentations, briefings and material.

The pattern of product development expenditure in a new programme shows the relative intensity of resource input during the different phases. In Figure 5.4, the product development spend follows what may be called a typical European pattern. It starts slowly, reaches its peak after programme approval and continues into, and often beyond, the launch date. There is an old saying, not beloved of engineers, that in every project there comes a time when it is necessary to shoot the engineers and start production. Of course, this is pointless if the product is not yet ready, but perhaps the saying could be understood as an encouragement to everyone working on the prog-

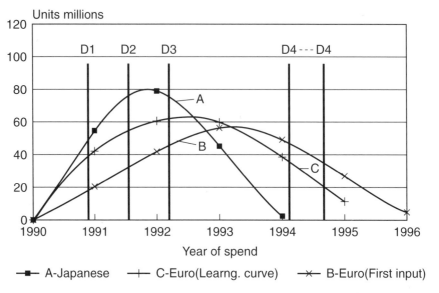

Figure 5.5 Product Development Cost Comparison: Example from a European-Japanese joint venture.

ramme to pay heed to two other, more modern, sayings that bear on the same subject. The first: "Do more early." The second: "Do it right first time." As a result, engineering is finished well before production.

Figure 5.5 shows the shape of two early estimates of the product development spend curves, excluding manufacturing and process expenditure, for the joint Japanese-European project mentioned above. One curve originates with the European company for their part of the project, the other with the Japanese company. Project start time was identical, tooling release and production start was planned in the same period for both companies and both products had more or less the same product content.

What is interesting is not so much a comparison of the size of absolute figures but the shape and timing of the curves. The "do more early" concept is evidently at work in the Japanese curve (A) as is the "do it right first time" approach since after the end of the engineering there are still eighteen months of the project left and yet the main body of product development expenditure has come to an end. The European pattern (B) was based on a work pattern which followed past experience, not untypical in European product programmes, and it assumed that engineering must continue after sign-off should have taken place. Typically, this occurs because of the large amount of last-minute engineering and correction attributable to ill-conceived products or the inclusion of risky, non-shelf engineered technologies.

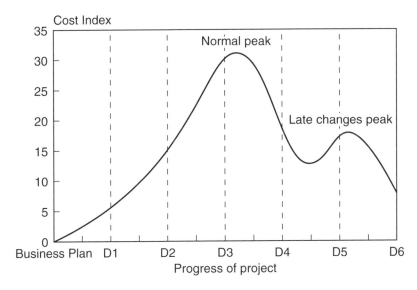

Figure 5.6 Product Development Spend Pattern: Example of Late Changes.

In subsequent planning rounds, the European group made great efforts at the front end of the programme to bring the quality of their planning and development work and the related development spend pattern much closer to the Japanese. This is illustrated in curve C, which resulted from their putting in place actions at the front end of the programme that minimised the need for downstream change. This involved a steep learning curve for the whole organisation.

I have also heard other companies describing their own experience with development cost curve shapes as shown in Figure 5.6. Note the extra peak after D4. This indicates an intensification of the total engineering spend to get a product right in the last stages of a project.

The Machine that Changed the World[1] contains a table based on the research of Clark, Fujimoto and Chew into the methods of European, American and Japanese automotive firms. This is reproduced here as Table 5.1 showing statistics for new product development efficiency. I have highlighted the five factors that govern the amount of change and disruption around the product release and launch.

These figures do not show a complete absence of Japanese development activity after release but they do indicate that the Japanese spend less on last minute changes than their European and American competitors and that the disruptive effect on production and quality is less significant.

The task of product planning is to contribute as much as possible to the desired outcome and spend pattern timing by doing good work upstream.

	Japanese Producers	American Producers	European Volume Producers	European Specialist Producers
Average Engineering Hours per New Car (millions)	1.7	3.1	2.9	3.1
Average Development Time per New Car (in months)	46.2	60.4	57.3	59.9
Number of Employees in Project Team	485	903	904	
Number of Body Types per New Car	2.3	1.7	2.7	1.3
Average Ratio of Shared Parts	18%	38%	28%	30%
Supplier Share of Engineering	51%	14%	37%	32%
Engineering Change Costs as Share of Total Die Cost	**10–20%**	**30–50%**	**10–30%**	
Ratio of Delayed Products	**1 in 6**	**1 in 2**	**1 in 3**	
Die Development Time (months)	13.8	25.0	28.0	
Prototype Lead Time (months)	6.2	12.4	10.9	
Time from Production Start to First Sales (months)	**1**	**4**	**2**	
Return to Normal Productivity After New Model (months)	**4**	**5**	**12**	
Return to Normal Quality After New Model (months)	**1.4**	**11**	**12**	

Table 5.1 Product Development Performance by Regional Auto Industries, mid-1980s

Source: Kim B. Clark, Takahiro Fujimoto, and W. Bruce Chew, "Product Development in the World Auto Industry," *Brookings Papers on Economic Activity*, No. 3, 1987; and Takahiro Fujimoto, "Organizations for Effective Product Development: The Case of the Global Motor Industry," Ph. D. Thesis, Harvard Business School, 1989, Tables 7.1, 7.4, and 7.8

Early and accurate product and market information and input, management acceptance of the programme details, early commitment of colleague departments and realistic but demanding planning targets: these are definite contributions of a competent product planning organisation – the kind of input that cannot easily be made by any other functional department acting within its normal area of responsibility. The cross-functional working practice of product planning should be a major contributing factor to success. Effective planning of the product as well as effective engineering is the only way to achieve this aspect of programme efficiency. There are many good product planning organisations, as illustrated in Chapter Six, that add much value to the whole process.

The D4 Decision Point: Sign-Off

I said earlier that D4 may be spread over a period because it involves the agreement of participating functions that the product as designed and tooled meets its intended objectives. A number of different sign-offs are usually involved. The production process and equipment, as designed and tooled, must be capable of making the product to the right quality standards: thus there is a need for process as well as product sign-off. Starting with the engineering sign-off, the end of the D4 period arrives after the initial production line try-out where the product is built for the first time off production tools. This is then followed by a fuller pre-production series.

In this area, each company must establish its own particular ground rules according to the type of product and manufacturing facilities involved. A general list of all activities to be completed by this stage would be too long to be included here. However, in view of the responsibility and concern of product planning for the product itself, the timing of introduction and the performance of the product in the market, there are aspects of the sign-off processes that should be emphasised.

The traditional point in a new product programme driving all main activities is job one, start of production. However, as already indicated, there are earlier necessary check-points at which work must be finished well before the job one date if the job one quality and subsequent ramp-up to full volume is to be achieved. This means that functional departments or groupings of activity within a programme must focus on these earlier check-points and accord them the same importance as the job one itself. The definition of the various D4 points as major milestones in a programme shows when the different groupings of activity should be completed. Four activity groups are particularly relevant.

1. *Engineering sign-off.* Has engineering completed its task of producing a product to the required specification and form, a product that behaves and performs in the manner planned? Some companies are beginning to refer to this as Engineering Job One.

2. *The product quality check.* Does it radiate exactly the quality levels needed to be competitive: both perceived quality and execution quality?

3. *The reliability check.* Reliability is not the same as quality. Have enough tests or predictive analyses been done to ensure that niggling early life failures have been eliminated and that the reliability will be maintained through the expected life of the product?

4. *The stability of stages in the process and their ability to produce a stable product.* This contributes to good product quality and reliability and leads to control of manufacturing costs during the ramp-up phase and the run-up to planned capacity levels. The main elements of the process should be passed off using off-tools product components to assure compatibility between released product and designed processes.

These sign-off elements are cross-related. D4 can only be completed after some line build try-out since manufacturing excellence is as much a contributor to reliability as design.

Although the D5 and D6 points are very important in the total achievement of a programme's objectives, the role of the main body of product planning is minimal, and, as indicated earlier, the planners will already, by this stage, have their eyes on the next major new product. Therefore it is not necessary to enlarge any further on these phases of the new product development process.

There are many good textbooks that focus on the complete new product process including the critical roles of engineering, manufacturing engineering and purchasing in creating and releasing the products with the maximum of speed and minimum of resources. *The Machine that Changed the World*[1] and *Product Development Performance*[2] contain excellent examples, based on benchmarking and wide research of different best product development practices. This chapter has concentrated on higher level aspects of the process: initiating and guiding the content of programmes, creating understanding with company management and providing a framework by which the programme "owner" can steer. Product planning plays a major role at this level of the new product process because it acts for the board, because of its cross-functional working methodology and because of its responsibility for defining a feasible and customer-oriented product.

These are four key concerns for product planning in this task.

1. Establishing the significance of different decision stages and other critical programme milestones.
2. Managing specific checkpoints through which the programme must pass.
3. Obtaining at the appropriate stages the decisions of management and the buy-in of all contributing functions.

4. Providing their own input as preparation for the formative start phase – D1 to D3 – of all new programmes and as support and authority for the progress of the programme thereafter.

The next chapter shows the wide variety of organisational forms in which different companies perform the planning and implementation of new products. The examples offer a wide selection of solutions to the planning, implementing and cross-functional needs of the product creation process.

Notes

1. Jones, Womack and Roos, *The Machine that Changed the World*, Figure 5.1, page 118, Macmillan Publishing Company, 1989.

2. Clark and Fujimoto, *Product Development Performance*, Harvard Business School Press, 1991.

6 PRODUCT PLANNING'S ORGANISATIONAL FORMS

> **A critical examination of different styles of product planning and product development organisation. Product planning already has been described both as a process of planning the product and, in some companies, as a specific organisational unit. Five different product planning organisations are described. They show the key determinants of effectiveness and the planners' relationships with the other parts of product development organisations. Automotive and non-automotive companies are included as well as a fast-moving consumer goods companies.**
>
> **At the end of the chapter, for reference, some typical job profiles within product planning are catalogued.**

We have already seen that there are potentially many different ways of organising for product planning. Each company has to find the combination of activities that suits both its type of business and the operating style and capabilities of the company. Looking at how different companies have set up their product planning organisations underlines this. No two organisations are the same. It is also true that, as with other parts of the organisation, a product planning department or structure, once formed, can evolve and change to meet new needs and challenges.

Ford of Europe, for example, went through three principal stages in the development of its product planning organisation as the company began to convert its product planning expertise into a form that could also exert better control over the implementation of product programmes.

CHRYSLER UNITED KINGDOM

Our first example, Chrysler United Kingdom, shows the organisation as it existed in 1971, but this is used as the first example because, in fact, the structure is a fairly typical product planning organisation which is still valid today and represents an ideal model for the creation of a new product planning function.

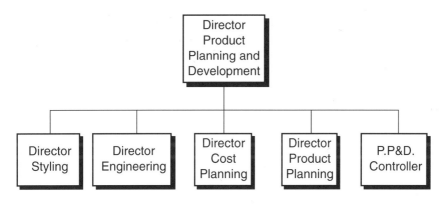

Figure 6.1 Chrysler United Kingdom 1969 to 1971: Product Planning and Development

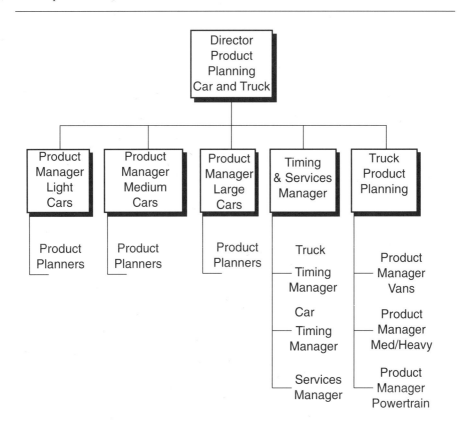

Figure 6.2 Chrysler United Kingdom Product Planning.

Originally, product planning at Chrystler United Kingdom formed part of the product planning and development division, headed by a board member. Although the original Ford of Britain product planning staff had reported direct to the chief executive, by the 1960s, product planning was usually seen as part of the product development activities of a company. Since cross-functional co-operation worked well at Chrysler, product planning's multi-functional role was easily accepted.

In other organisations, the links between product planning (reporting to the product development organisation) and other divisions (especially manu-facturing and supply) have not been good enough to allow a true "honest broker" role for product planning. This is particularly so where planners had to operate more as a tool of the product development boss than as a truly independent, cross-functional department.

Product planning reported into the director, product planning and devel-opment along with the directors of engineering, styling, product cost plan-ning and the product development controller.

Within the product planning organisation shown in Figure 6.2, each segment of the product range was headed up by a product manager. A product manager had complete responsibility for a product range in current production or for the product aspects of a new programme. A number of product planners reported to him.

This organisation into product teams is traditional, but Chrysler had already moved a step further towards better control of product programmes. The company described its product managers as programme managers. This was a first attempt to recognise the company-wide task both of planning and of co-ordinating implementation – at least to a certain stage in the imple-mentation process. The different types of programme manager are covered in Chapter Seven; in the Chrysler example, the programme manager was definitely of the "weak" variety. This was an early effort to get programme co-ordination by consent, rather than with a direct change of control and resource responsibilities away from the line functions.

In this organisation there was no separate advanced product planning department, the theory being that the complete product spectrum – from short to long term – was to be covered by programme managers who were expected to see to their own advanced product planning. In practice, this did not work well because of the conflict between detailed concentration on the new programme in hand, the urgent short term product actions needed, and the time needed to look ahead at alternative future product strategies and product technical developments. This kind of division of effort led to the emergence, at a later date and in other companies, of sections with titles such as Business Planning, Product Cycle Planning or Business Strategy. These took care of the evaluation of follow-up strategy and the initial creation of new programmes. Advanced product planning departments with a strong technical orientation were also created. These consisted of engineers and product planners involved in technological and legislative forecasting and planning as well as management of shelf engineering product research programmes destined for inclusion in future products. Examples are given in the sections on Ford of Europe and Volvo Holland.

To the extent that these forward-looking activities existed in Chrysler, they were carried out by the manager of product planning with the programme managers' help and in conjunction with some advanced engineering activity.

One unusual element of this organisation is the combination under one director of both car and truck product planning. Product planning timing and services was shared between the two but in the rest of the company the respective car and truck engineering, sales and manufacturing organisations were still quite separate. This made the task of running this two-headed product planning department somewhat schizophrenic.

The head of any product planning function had a company task to perform in addition to running his department. This task was connected first to the top management of the company; the product planning committee that was set up to review and make decisions on all forward product strategy and new product projects. The head of product planning was usually the co-ordinator and secretary of this committee: it met every four to six weeks, and the presentations and papers were usually prepared by his staff. He therefore had to propose fully worked out strategies and action programmes to this committee. It was through this medium that he was able to retain a nominal link to the chief executive. He also had to be seen as a cross-functional referee.

In this respect, at Chrysler, the head of product planning worked with colleagues inside his own division and with other divisions, from whom he had to obtain a commitment first to the overall product strategy and product plan and then to individual product programmes and projects at various approval stages. The head of any product planning activity should ideally be able to concentrate on a homogeneous company operation and decision making structure: with Chrysler's double responsibility for cars and trucks, this concentration was more difficult.

An effective but expensive solution could have been to have individual heads of car and truck product planning reporting to the director with timing and other ancillary support functions placed alongside.

This would have given the specialised car and truck managers the task of obtaining colleagues' approval of the various elements of the plans. This could have resulted in a possible reluctance from colleagues in other divisions, on the same organisational level as the director of product planning, to commit their divisions to his two manager lieutenants. This is not a minor point and has been a key reason for the failure of some pioneering product planning, project management or programme managers to secure commitments and therefore action from colleagues who considered themselves superior in terms of status or reporting level.

Any organisation that has the task of guiding others must report at the right level. Otherwise its effectiveness will depend on simple force of personality – not real authority.

Superiority has nothing to do with social status and everything to do with willingness to accept instruction. In a company that tries to operate management by consent, strong line functions always win the day where consent is difficult to achieve. Alternatively, the highest organ in the company, the board or product committee, can be brought in to mediate on every disagreement. This eventually also leads to an impossible situation. Many times product or programme managers have been heard to say: "I am sick of constantly having to present other people's problems to the PPC for decision or resolution". The reporting levels of product or programme managers seems to be one of the secrets of success in multi-disciplinary projects.

The function of timing within product planning in the Chrysler organisation was interesting. In some companies timing is not even accepted as a discipline. In others, it is handled as part of the engineering function and based mainly on engineering actions and concerns. Timing is, however, one of the most critical activities for success in new product development. The timing department for product planning in Chrysler UK provided a planning and control service for the whole company up to a point close to D4 when a manufacturing launch timing group took over. This system worked well. The manufacturing launch timing group also ensured, in the upstream part of the programmes, that manufacturing input was obtained. The existence of the two timing departments meant that timing discipline was accepted company-wide – and at a senior level.

The product and programme planning organisation at Chrysler worked well, not least because all the component parts of the product development function, engineering, styling, cost planning, controller and product planning knew their role in the process and were intent on working co-operatively. This was also true to a large extent of colleagues in other divisions such as purchasing, manufacturing and marketing. The complexity of the product was less than it is today. Competition was also less fierce, but acceptance of product planning as a cross-functional department was pivotal to the efficiency of the product creation process. This is a characteristic still being sought in many companies today.

ALTERNATIVE AUTOMOTIVE ORGANISATION MODELS

Let us now look at five more recently-formed organisations involving product planning where the scope, relationships and responsibilities have been further developed. Changes in organisation occur to overcome perceived operational problems in the total new product development process or just to suit certain companies' management styles. All organisations must evolve, however, to suit the circumstances of the moment.

The first example comes from the Ford of Europe organisation before and after its reorganisation in 1985 and as it stands at the time of writing.

These are not meant to be perfect descriptions of the Ford organisation in every detail at each time point, and there may have been other interim steps of organisational change between 1984 and today. What is shown, however, is the main content of three phases of organisation through which Ford of Europe passed. A classical development emerges: from the traditional, functionally-based organisation to a more integrated and team-based approach.

Ford of Europe: 1984

Figure 6.3 shows the product planning organisation and the main elements of engineering – all reporting up to the vice president of product development.

This was an organisation very similar in its working method to Chrysler UK. One different feature made timing a separate department reporting to the vice president product development – as has always been the case at Ford. This ensured an independent view of timing within the product development division. The timing department also had, as at Chrysler, a company-wide role of reporting programme progress at executive committee level and resolving inter-divisional timing problems.

Product planning itself consisted of five main activities:

1. Product strategy and planning, which looked after the overall product cycle plan and the various elements of future product requirements and technical objectives.

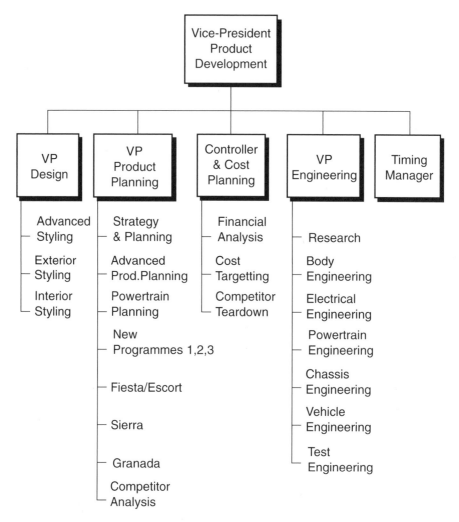

Figure 6.3 Ford of Europe 1984: Product Development Organisation.

2. An advanced product planning group that handled the early creative planning phase of each major new programme up to the D3 point – called programme approval at Ford.

3. Powertrain product planning formed a separate team, because engine and gearbox product cycles were different from car model cycles themselves and major enough to justify separate attention.

4. A product manager and product team that took over each major new product programme from the advanced group after programme approval and through to production.

5. Product managers and teams for the models in current production.

This structure had the advantage of allowing Ford to develop the detail of new programmes with separate new teams while the current teams concentrated on running production models and making the necessary minor improvements to keep models competitive.

The product strategy and planning group looked far ahead to anticipate new technological and market developments and to review the total Ford product and business plan on a multi-project basis. Product cycle planning was a major part of this department's task, as were many of the assumptions and decisions that went to make up the total company business plan.

Relationship to Engineering

Here also is shown an overview of the engineering department structure, designed to assist understanding of the relationship between engineering and product planning. Apart from some changes in emphasis and in scale, this was similar to the Chrysler UK engineering organisation that existed alongside the Chrysler product planning organisation. The point is that it was still very much a functional engineering organisation with its own built-in planning and control elements. It was responsible for maintaining its own relationships with the other functional areas outside product development such as manufacturing, purchasing and sales and marketing. Hence the pressures for action on this engineering organisation came not only from the product programmes driven by product planning and timing but also from requests, usually shorter term and equally urgent, for short term product change or improvement action from other divisions.

One notable operational feature of this organisation was that product development problems, disagreements and other issues within each programme could only be resolved by the vice president product development or the product committee. Theoretically, the product teams within product planning had responsibility for creating and driving the programmes forward, and this was described by Sir Terence Beckett as one of guiding principles for the establishment of product planning in the first place. However, by 1984, reporting in to the product development division of Ford Europe instead of the chief executive, as when they were first set up in the 1950s, they were probably not always sufficiently strong or independent to override the will of the line engineering heads. Similarly, they would have found it difficult to change the will of the heads of other functions beyond product development where conflicts arose.

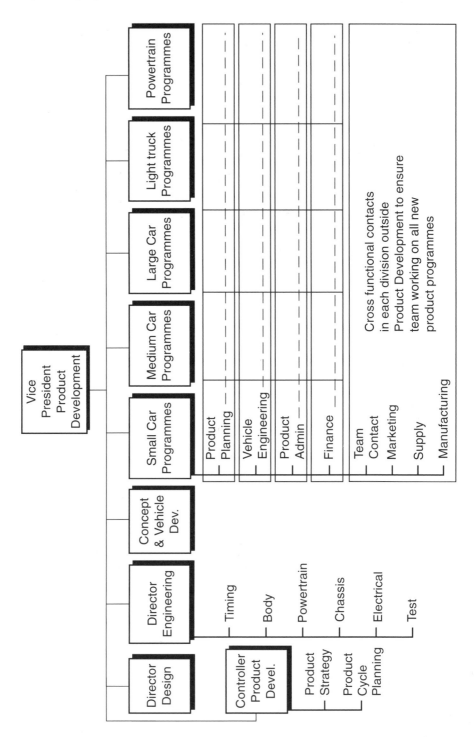

Figure 6.4 Ford of Europe post-1985: Programme Office Organisation.

Problems between the product development division and, say, manufacturing, which the product managers could not resolve, could only be settled by the product committee, chaired by the president. This must have been one of the reasons for changing the organisation after 1985: the president of an international company such as Ford Europe does not have the personal time to resolve every minor product programme dispute. Nor can the vice president of each division handle all problems on all programmes either within his own division or with his colleagues in other divisions. On the other hand, the requirements of meeting the programme objectives should be paramount. Somehow, problems have to be resolved.

Another of the motivations for the organisational change of 1985 (shown in Figure 6.4) was to stop too much resource being applied to unstructured short term product change and to try to perform a better and faster job on new projects with these same resources. By doing more at an early stage in a new product programme, the need for late changes should have been reduced and the quality of the implemented programme increased. At the same time the continued product development spend at the tail end of the programme would be reduced if a better job were done upstream. However it is not just a matter of saying what is needed. The organisation must be structured to achieve the desired motivation and move towards a "do it right first time" approach to see the real downstream benefits. The strengthening of these product management and control activities was one of the key factors which led to the 1985 re-organisation.

Ford of Europe after 1985

Four elements in the new, post-1985, Ford organisation, shown in Figures 6.4 and 6.5, were designed to improve the quality of the total new product development process.

1. Product planning evolved from a single department into a number of programme teams. These were headed by a "strong" programme manager who now had a more complete cross-functional responsibility to deliver a programme at job one. Each team was made up of a combination of product planners and the former vehicle engineering organisation of engineering which was responsible for the engineering integrity of the complete vehicle. Thus all programme definition and project planning activities were centralised, per programme, from the very beginning. Some other programme control responsibilities were also given to these teams – including financial analysis, budget control and product administration – in addition to all the

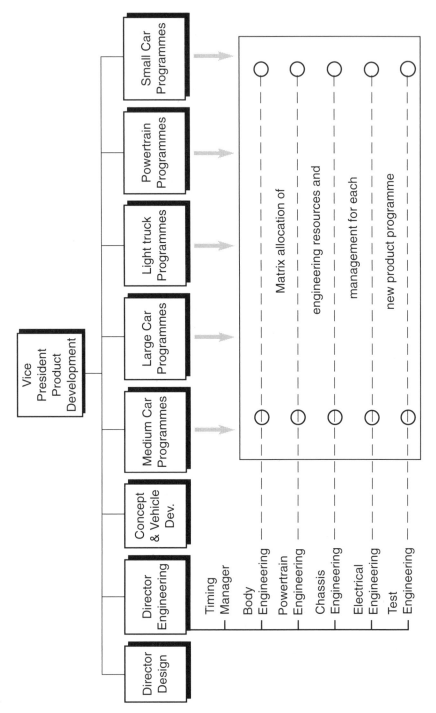

Figure 6.5 Ford of Europe post 1985: Engineering to Programmes Relationship

old advanced product planning functions aimed at planning the details from the very beginning of a programme.

These teams were larger than the old product planning teams and they had much broader responsibilities and "clout". Thus they could get better control of the programme planning and implementation, which was the main object of the exercise. Timing was still centralised within product development, however. The management of the engineering resource and technology was still under the control of the engineering departmental managers. Yet the head of each of the new programme teams was more senior than the old product team heads of product planning. Therefore, they had more authority to make programme decisions and to keep other divisions in line. They reported one step higher in the organisation. They also had responsibility for the product range or product segment as a whole and not just for new projects as and when these were handed over to them. They themselves had to initiate the product action to keep their product segment in good shape.

2. Product strategy and product cycle planning were split from product planning and became a separate department reporting to the product development controller. This was not illogical because product planning as a single entity no longer existed. All strategies and cycle plans eventually had to be evaluated in financial terms and incorporated in the overall business plan. However, it also moved responsibility for the product cycle planning activity away from both the programme teams and marketing and made it necessary for the product development controller to develop these insights. An alternative would have been to let it report directly to the vice president product development so as to put it on a par with the new programme managers. Certainly product and business strategy and product cycle planning are key activities and if they are badly done, in terms of timing or product content, no amount of good programme management will correct the conceptual mistakes. In this organisation, strategy planning was the only part that had a central overview of the product.

A more effective approach could have been to keep strategy planning reporting at the same level as the new programme managers. This would also have allowed a more product-oriented multi-project view of the company's future needs. Dividing any activity into multi-disciplinary teams per individual product family can mean that the cross-company view of that functional aspect could be weakened. It would have been preferable to keep an integrated product cycle planning and product strategy activity, closely allied to product planning and programme management activities.

3. Each division outside of product development had to appoint a co-ordinator or even a group of participants as a contact for, or member of, each programme team. This wasn't quite a complete matrix approach but it must have helped to involve other divisions in programmes on an early and regular basis. A team feeling could thus be generated within and outside the product development function. An active functional contact of this kind can produce more co-operative and parallel working than if the links to the programmes are not formalised. The level of representation in each division remains unclear, but it must have been high enough to secure divisional commitment to programme actions and decisions when necessary.

4. The functional specialist engineering departments lost some of their autonomy and had to accept programme priorities and decisions to a greater degree than before since vehicle planning activities – the creation of engineering work packages for the total vehicle as required by the product description – now belonged to the programme teams instead of being part of engineering. The programme budgets were also under the teams' control. However, the engineering managers still retained a clear task for the implementation of the programme, providing through their functional departments the resource for each programme and ensuring the technical integrity of the work done in specialist areas such as body engineering, chassis, electrical and so on. The advanced engineering task was also still attached to each specialist area.

In looking at these changes, one is inclined to wonder whether the new programme directors should not have reported directly to the board. This would have meant that they also had real authority over the manufacturing, purchasing and marketing aspects of their programmes and perhaps could have brought representatives of those functions directly into their teams. Certainly, in the light of today's views about continuous improvement of the product development process and integrated, parallel working, manufacturing and purchase involvement has got to exist from the first glimmer of an idea about a new programme. Yet it is also true that organisational change within a company must proceed in steps appropriate to the degree of development of that company and to the readiness of the board and the people in the organisation to change. No doubt this played a role also in what may be considered an interim organisational step for Ford.

There are, alas, especially in British industry, too many examples of sweeping organisational change arising from external pressures or simply the megalomania of a new boss. In such cases, companies' "racial memory" of the key aspects of their business is obliterated by the extent or insensitivity of the changes. All organisational development must always keep one

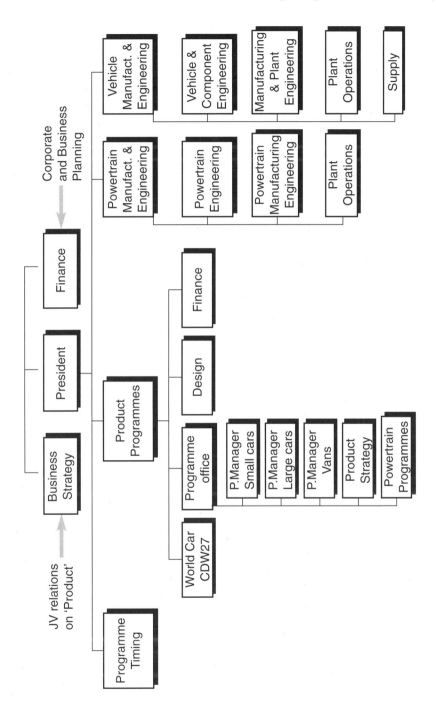

Figure 6.6 Ford of Europe 1990 to 1992: Programmes and Product Development.

foot firmly planted in the best of what the company previously could do, had learnt and believed in.

Ford of Europe: 1990-1992

A third step in the development of Ford's product and programme planning activities took place around 1989/90. It constituted a further attempt to bring closer together the traditionally strong and separate divisions of product development and manufacturing. This move was motivated, at least in part, by Ford's adoption of Simultaneous Engineering (SE) by which the design and development, process engineering, purchasing and supplier input are brought together as early as possible in a new model programme. Ford has made many public statements about its commitment to this way of developing new products.

The organisation, shown in Figure 6.6, boasted some new features.

1. Product development and manufacturing, including purchasing and supply, were placed together in one organisation instead of having separate vice presidents, each reporting to the president of the company.

2. Two new organisational units were formed, covering powertrain (engine and gearbox) and vehicle (stamping, body and assembly) manufacturing and engineering operations. Each group was responsible for the total design engineering, process engineering and manufacturing operations for a major homogeneous part of the vehicle.

3. The powertrain group initially contained the programme office and the programme directors but these were later split off and a separate post of vice president programmes was created with the same reporting level as the other two vice presidents. Reporting directly to the vice president of product programmes was one programme director with responsibility for a single large product programme with world-wide implications – the CDW27 programme – involving both US and Europe. The other programme managers who covered product programmes with a mainly Ford of Europe involvement were grouped under a second-level director of programmes reporting to the VP who also had responsibility for product cycle planning, advanced product planning and product strategy. These formerly reported to the product development controller. Design (styling) and programme finance also reported directly to the vice president of product programmes.

4. Supply for all bought-in material remained attached, as a single unit, to the vice president of the vehicle manufacturing group.

5. Timing, both for individual departments and for central management reporting, was centralised into one group, reporting to the president, since timing was still seen as one of the key drivers of programme success.

6. Business planning, including some competitive product and strategy activities, was part of the organisation of the finance vice president. There was also a central strategy vice president who covered company business strategy and relations, even on product programmes, with other Ford partners, such as Volkswagen and Mazda. Both these vice presidents reported to the company chairman, at the same level as the president.

Possible Further Developments

It is very easy to sit outside such an organisation and say that it should be different in this or another way. One can never fully know the subtleties of company history or fully appreciate the many hours of negotiation and compromise that lead to the formation of a settled structure. From looking at the experiences of other companies who have struggled with the same issues of product programme effectiveness, it does seem that three improvements could be suggested to enhance success in planning and developing new products.

1. First, there is the problem of the rather literal interpretation that seems to have been applied to simultaneous engineering. The main move of the new organisation was to put design and manufacturing engineering together. Simultaneous engineering should not be seen as a purely engineering activity but as the working together of all the key functions that can and should contribute to a new product programme from its earliest stages. The reasons for this have been covered adequately in other chapters but this organisation seems to have formed yet another grouping of departments without a guarantee of real team working that involves not just product development, process engineering and manufacturing but also product and business planning, purchasing, logistics, marketing and service. Truly simultaneous "engineering" – for which a more appropriate title would be Concurrent Product Development – must embrace much more than the engineering that lies at its heart.

2. The Ford of Europe purchasing and supply organisation reports to the vice president of vehicle manufacturing – too low down the organisation for a department responsible for about sixty-five percent of a complete vehicle's cost. This is not a direct "product planning" point, but the presence of an active purchase organisation with suppliers capable and willing to contribute as early as possible in a new programme is a necessary part of the effective product planning process.

My experience of working as the commercial head of two different auto-motive suppliers shows that OEMs are not always willing to take on board the technical and product brainpower offered by supplier companies as an input to initial new product programmes. More often than not, such information is evaluated without effective feedback because the old image of the OEM-supplier relationship is still predominant. The OEM felt that he had to make his own decision and did not see the need for really open participation with suppliers.

To overcome any tendency to preserve these old ways of working and to focus on the actions necessary to do things differently in the area of supplier relations – which I know Ford, along with most other automotive OEMs, is striving for – the purchasing and supply function should report at the same level as the powertrain and vehicle manufacturing vice presidents.

3. The last point relates to the grouping and reporting levels of the various departments responsible for "product", especially at the formative, creative end of new product programmes. Strategy has its own separate VP including relationships with other product partners. Business planning includes competitive product analysis and reports to finance. Product cycle planning activities are in the programmes office, but one level down from the VP and some programme managers also report at this level.

The main purpose of this book is to explain and promote the value of an integrated and organised approach to the complete product planning process. It can be suggested, therefore, that this Ford organisation structure will not be so efficient at conceiving and planning new product programmes.
Referring back to the building blocks of product planning, the 1992 Ford Europe organisation has so dissipated the various product planning building blocks around the organisation that they will have difficulties in working in an integrated way.

The programme office organisation forms a good platform for further development but it would be preferable to have all programme managers or directors reporting directly to the VP with an equally senior advanced or strategy planning manager reporting to the VP who has sole responsibility within the company to create the product strategy and plan the front end of all major new product programmes. In this he would be working with the existing programme teams, with other divisions, with suppliers and external partners. In addition, he would co-ordinate relationships with the other product-responsible Ford companies and, in particular, Ford US. Thus, new product programmes would start well and the programme directors, with the necessary cross-functional team members, would be well placed to take over and successfully implement the programmes in the shortest time possible: to "plan the programmes superbly, then run like hell to implement them!"

My suggestion effectively involves reverting to one of the elements of the pre-1985 organisation where all product, business strategy and advanced product planning activities were the responsibility of the head of product planning. This only goes to show that in any new organisation there is often a large element of shuffling of the old building blocks under a new management and control structure in the effort to obtain more effective working of the whole system, rather than the creation of anything fundamentally new.

Volvo Holland: 1988-1991

The Volvo Car Holland organisation, set up in 1988, incorporated many new ideas that the Dutch arm of Volvo had studied in the field of work quality, employee motivation and the more efficient control of new product development. Not the least of these ideas, and one that had a great influence on operational results, was to devolve responsibility to individual directors of departments so that they could feel responsible and be accountable for the complete performance of their departments.

Three Organisation Sectors

Figure 6.7 shows the overall organisation, with three main sectors (Advanced Operations, Technical Operations and Commercial Operations) all reporting in to the board and headed by a board member. Each director controlling a major department within these three sectors was responsible for his own performance, both in day-to-day operations and in the implementation of programmes. He had his own budget controller as well as his own personnel and systems staff.

New product programmes originated in advanced operations through business and product planning who obtained approval to the company business plan as part of the annual planning cycle and initiated the front end of each new product programme authorised by the plan. Advanced engineering and styling played a major role in each new project, creating a full engineering, process and styling definition by the D3 decision point. Advanced operations implemented and controlled the programme up to the D3 decision point, after which there was a formal handover to technical operations and eventually from them to commercial operations.

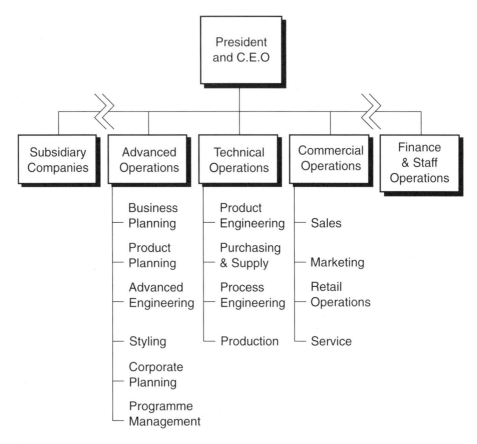

Figure 6.7 Volvo Holland: Car Division, 1988.

Structure of Advanced Operations

The detail of the advanced operations and business planning structure is shown in Figure 6.8. This organisation structure displays some unusual features.

1. Business planning included product planning, market planning, manufacturing planning, timing, financial planning (for projects only). This allowed a completely integrated plan for each new programme to be developed for the whole company which was capable of being implemented successfully in all aspects; customer needs, time to market, product acceptance, resource capability (taking account also of all other programmes), technical and process feasibility and profitability. The sign-off point for the business planning activities as a whole was D3. This worked well as an integrated high

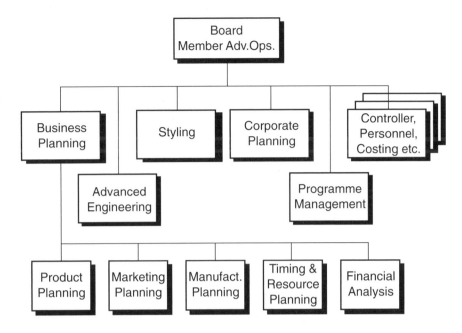

Figure 6.8 Volvo Holland: Organisation of Advanced Operations.

quality planning team but some friction resulted from overlapping responsibilities with other functional areas containing manufacturing, marketing and financial planning departments that were supposed to focus on shorter term or operational issues. A feature of life in business planning was the constant need to negotiate with other departments. In itself, this was no bad thing but there were perhaps too many shared responsibilities to ensure the most efficient programme implementation process.

2. Advanced engineering operated in a different organisational sector from product engineering. This meant that an enormous handover of decisions, technical information and project responsibility took place at D3, the point at which virtually the whole of the technical and design content should have been decided. This created a large duplication of effort in programmes at a time when rapid implementation was necessary. The reasoning – to give each functional director the chance to accept, commit to and be responsible for his own task – was laudable. But too many "relay-race" style handovers were involved. Inter-sectoral politics also intervened.

3. The function of programme management also belonged to advanced operations although its responsibilities were to overview and control the programme progress from the D1 point through to successful implementa-

tion in production, right through the activities of technical operations and commercial operations. This was a requirement from the board and programme management effectively worked for the board. The idea was not to run programmes at detailed level, but to act on behalf of the board to see that nothing fell between the cracks at the interfaces between major departments – so-called "boundary control".

This organisational model allowed the board an independent overview of project progress but had two main problems. First, a conflict with the responsibilities of business planning which also had the cross-functional task of bringing each programme successfully to D3 before handing over to technical operations. The question of who really owned the programme had not been thought through properly.

Second, in a problem that corresponds with the earlier comments about the post-1985 Ford Europe organisation, programme management should have reported directly to the board rather than one of the sector heads. This would have preserved independence from the three operational sectors. As it was they were sometimes seen as belonging to advanced operations and sometimes in their company-wide role and so were not always able to counteract, where necessary, the will of line functional departments.

4. The manufacturing engineering staff were partly in advanced engineering, sitting alongside their design colleagues, and partly in a separate department, process engineering, which formed part of technical operations. This had the benefit of bringing manufacturing considerations into new product programmes very early on. It also added in more technical handovers at the critical D3 point.

Business and Product Planning

Within the business planning department, the product planning organisation was as shown in Figure 6.9. The product planning organisation shown here is a fairly conventional one – with three exceptions.

1. The advanced product planning group had the additional task of technological planning. This involved plotting technical and legislative trends so as to produce parameters within which each new programme had to be designed. In view of Volvo's reputation for safety, reliability, durability and other aspects of technical excellence this was a key role. It meant that product planning directed the company in advanced work on product technology. The function had to preserve very close links with Volvo Car Corporation in Sweden, which controlled overall product standards.

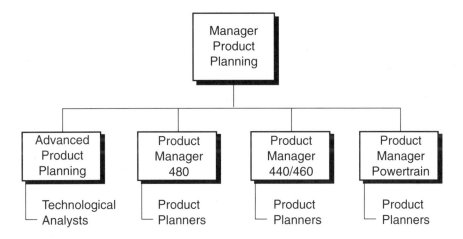

Figure 6.9 Volvo Holland: Organisation of Product Planning.

Technological planning in other companies is a task that can belong to research and development, to advanced engineering, or to a separate technical standards office. Having it as part of product planning meant that its work could be focused more on what the market and the company needed in its future products for each car segment, rather than on what was interesting mainly from a technical standpoint.

2. The product managers had an extra role of "owning" the total programme, and not just the product aspects, between the business plan phase (pre-D1) and the D3 decision point. Thus they were responsible for the overall progress of a programme up to D3. Their role also included a specific responsibility for obtaining management approvals and, therefore, the need to obtain commitments from other functions and to prepare management summary documentation and presentations for each approval stage. This was the only way that business planning could economically fulfil its task of bringing a fully feasible and agreed programme to the D3 stage. Creating project managers in business planning, separately from product management, would have been wasteful and confusing. The product planning task, properly performed in the D1 to D3 phase, as has been emphasised before, contains a large element of project management because the decisions being made to create the programme are almost all product-based in some way or another.

The problem within this structure was the too low reporting level of the product managers and the confusion of roles with the programme managers, from the separate programme management department, who also reported at the same level. At Ford and, to an extent, at Chrysler UK, the potentially overlapping roles of product and programme management were recognised by only having one responsible organisation.

3. The product managers also had the task of co-ordinating, within business planning, the inputs from marketing planning and manufacturing planning, timing and resource planning and advanced product planning in order to ensure that the programme was well balanced and consistent in all its component parts. In a normal product planning organisation this is a task the product planner should try to perform with his colleagues in other divisions, acting in his "honest broker" role. In the Volvo organisation, his task, in one respect, was easier because he was dealing with direct colleagues in the same department. On the other hand, because of the need for other divisions to buy-off on the programme at each decision stage, he had to know that the content of his colleagues' work in marketing, manufacturing planning and timing was accepted by their divisional opposite numbers. Once again, product planners and the other members of business planning had to spend much time building bridges between themselves and other functional areas of the company.

Conclusion

In summary, this organisation was an attempt to combine the best aspects of integrated front end programme creation and planning, individual functional responsibility and quality of output. The loose matrix form of organisation was necessary to ensure the company-wide implementation of new programmes. It was, however, the working of the matrix that needed a great deal of attention because of the clash with the strong functional department responsibilities. The front end planning with a multi-functional team worked well and the integration of design and process engineering early in a programme was a big benefit. Yet the multiplicity of handovers as the programmes proceeded downstream through the implementing departments was a big handicap.

ORGANISATIONS IN OTHER INDUSTRIES

I would now like to turn from the automotive industry and comment briefly on product planning and product management organisations in other industries.

Corporate Level Product Planning

Our first example might be called corporate product planning. This comes from a manufacturer of mobile industrial equipment where the board wanted

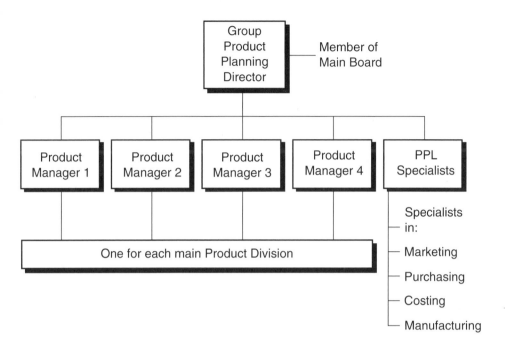

Figure 6.10 Industrial Equipment Industry: Corporate Product Planning.

more control of a variety of divisions and factories located throughout Europe and set up a new department named group product planning with a board member as its head. The following structure and work method was proposed with an organisation as seen in Figure 6.10.

The new department consisted of five elements: a product manager for each main product line or product group (four in all) and a group of specialists with experience in other disciplines, such as manufacturing, marketing, engineering, purchasing and finance. In this respect, its coverage was similar to business planning at Volvo. Its operating responsibilities were somewhat different, however, not least because there were a number of separate operating companies in the group based throughout Europe, each with quite different products.

Principles of Operation

The new department was intended to operate according to four key principles.

1. The board wanted to introduce multi-disciplinary new product development processes. It saw the creation of product planning as a major step in this direction and seemed prepared to give the group product planning director more authority for product within the group than the operational managers who designed, produced and sold the products of this company, which at the time operated five different factories in three European countries. The group product planning director was to be a board member.

2. All product development proposals from whatever source had to be screened by product planning before discussion at board level.

3. Product planning was also to be responsible for reporting progress on already running programmes. This was to include profit progress as well as time, technical and cost target achievements.

4. After the initial screening of current new product activity, the most important task was the creation of a product strategy and improvement plans for each major operational area of the company.

Thus the new group department was to concentrate on advanced product planning work as well as product cycle and product strategy planning. The detailed development of product programmes was still to be carried out by the line engineering, marketing and manufacturing functions in each operating division. They could each submit to product planning their own ideas for product improvement proposals.

However, the recognition that programmes were to be run as multi-functional activities, together with the monitoring responsibility, indicates that this new group product planning organisation was also performing part of the programme management role and that it would probably develop further in that direction once the basic strategies for each operating company and product family had been defined and approved. This was clear from the expressed intention to ask engineering and product planning together to develop plans for improving the manufacturing efficiency and profitability of the company's major UK facility, a task that went well beyond the scope of traditional line product planning or engineering departments.

For a company just starting out with product planning and trying to derive benefits from the most recent management thinking on efficient product development, this seemed to be an effective approach. The top level board commitment and the recognition, right from the start, that group product planning was to be a major cross-functional department, were important elements. The authority to be the only presenter of strategy and product programmes and reports to the board was important for the status and operating effectiveness of product planning. The expectation that the work of product planning would be to create profitable programmes in all aspects, rather than just advising on the product, pointed to maximum utilisation of the informed overview that a good product planner must have of the total company implications of his work.

After the successful launch of such a new department, a later change of emphasis and structure could have incorporated elements of business planning and programme management. This would recognise that management wanted to take a further step forward in terms of efficient product development as well as profitability in manufacturing operations through the creation of this new arm of the board.

Product Management in Fast-Moving Consumer Goods

To provide a balance in this account between engineering-based and other industries, the following section covers the fast-moving consumer goods sector. The extract and figures come from Trevor Sowrey's, *The Generation of Ideas for New Products*[1].

This shows alternative new product organisations that are quite different from the automotive and engineering organisations described above.

Product management features much more often in consumer goods companies than in formalised product planning structures. Marketing also plays a much more significant role in product development: product managers are usually part of marketing and concern themselves with all elements of the marketing mix as well as providing much support for sales of current products. Product ranges themselves are also more varied and thus a heavy concentration of technical resources to create and implement a single new product programme is less common.

Product Managers

'Placing responsibility for development with the product management team in the marketing department is a popular way of handling new products in the UK. It has been used by Lever Brothers, Lyons Bakery, Whitbread, Fisons, Van den Berghs, Pedigree Petfoods and many other well known companies.

A product manager for a number of existing brands may in addition have responsibility for the development of new products in similar markets to his existing brands ... On the other hand, responsibility may be functionally divided so that there are product managers handling existing brands and others handling product development...

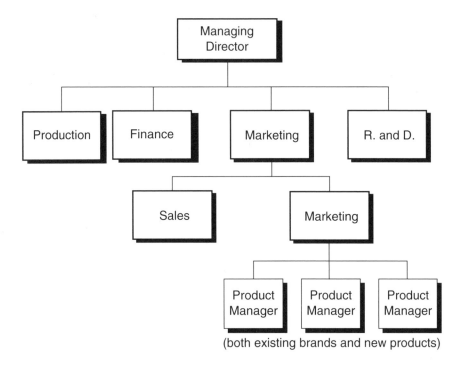

Figure 6.11 Consumer Goods Product Development: Product Managers.

Source: The Generation of Ideas for New Products (3.3a) Trevor Sowrey

The major limitation with both forms of organisation is the inevitable danger that development activities will be neglected. Certainly, when one individual is responsible for both existing brands and development, not enough attention may be paid to the search for new products because of the demands in terms of both time and money from existing brands, which are the profit makers. In this respect it can well be argued that new product development is not a part-time job in the sense that current brands come first when both they and development activities are handled by one person... Dividing the brand group functionally into existing product and new product personnel attempts to get away from this dichotomy and remove the worst of its possible effects.'

Figure 6.11 shows a typical product management structure.

New Product or Diversification Department

'It is but a short step in organisational terms from new product managers to a functionally-based new products department. Like the product management system, many well known companies have used this type of organisation.

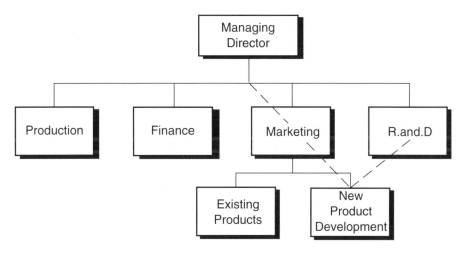

Figure 6.12 Consumer Goods Product Development: New Products Department

Source: The Generation of Ideas for New Products. (3.4) Trevor Sowrey

These have included Cadbury-Typhoo, Findus, Johnson and Johnson, Quaker, United Biscuits and K P Foods. But there are variations in the structure as shown in Figure 6.12, with responsibility in the majority being to the marketing director, in others to the managing director and in some to a new product or R and D director... In some cases it may exist purely in an advisory staff function with emphasis perhaps on co-ordination as the major responsibility. But one common thread, whatever different form the structure may take, is that the department is separated from the day-to-day responsibilities of making a profit and can concentrate on development.

The logical extension of the new products department is the diversification department, which is structured as a department separate from the marketing department and existing as a parallel organisation... The top executive of the department is a board director responsible to the managing director and equal in status to the marketing director. As a result a complete separation occurs between the current operation and development... Also the corporate planning function could come within this sphere. In addition to its own marketing section the department would have its own R and D separate from the central R and D and a specialist negotiating section responsible for the purchase of co-packed products and for acquisition negotiations.

Moreover, the department can adopt a balanced attitude towards development, beginning with the establishment of corporate objectives and long term plans and then proceeding to implement these plans,

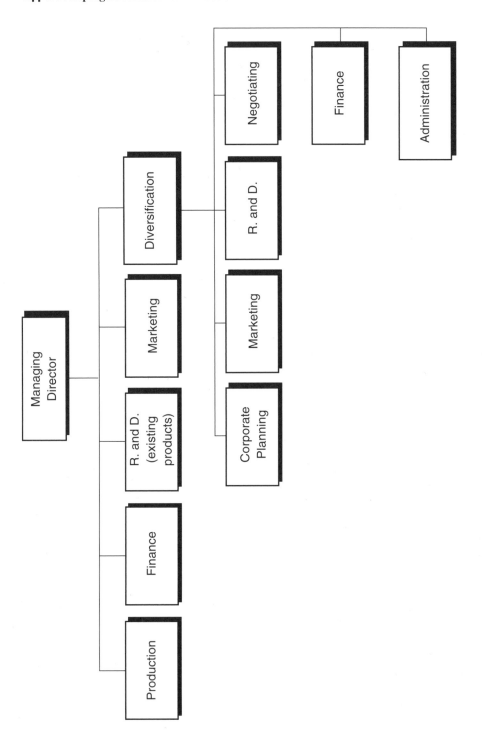

Figure 6.13 Consumer Goods Product Development: Diversification Department.

Source: The Generation of Ideas for New Products (3.5) Trevor Sowrey.

through the wide spectrum of new product development, market development and acquisitions. As a result the company can adopt a fully planned approach rather than dealing with future needs in an *ad hoc* and sporadic fashion. (Figure 6.13).

Few companies in the UK have ever adopted any form of diversification department, probably because of the resources required, but H J Heinz has been a notable exception.'

The differences between the creation of new engineering products and fast-moving consumer products can be summarised as follows.

1. The product manager must generally spend much more time supporting and stimulating the sale of current products than is the practice with industrial or engineering products. Thus the concentration is on packaging, advertising, pricing and promotion rather than just future product improvement actions and needs.

2. Research and development seems to be a less significant and less complex function than in engineering industries and so the management of such programmes is given less prominence than the search for new product ideas – both internally and externally. Research and development is also elsewhere described as being very concerned with current production quality control rather than with looking ahead for new technologies or products.

3. The nearest entities to a separate product planning department in fast-moving consumer goods are new products departments and diversification departments. The latter generally boasts a high reporting level as well as the ability to perform its own product research and product market planning, but it is interesting to note that few companies in fast-moving consumer goods adopt this form of new product creation process.

4. To supplement the product manager or new products department structure, some FMCG companies have a new products committee to act as the multi-functional arbiter of new product ideas and the overseer of their implementation. This mirrors practice in some engineering companies.

The White Goods Industry: Electrolux UK, 1992

The next example of a new product creation organisation comes from the white goods industry. Electrolux UK is part of the Swedish white goods and electronics multi-national which makes four categories of product: Refrigeration, Washing, Cooking and Floorcare. The organisation of the planning

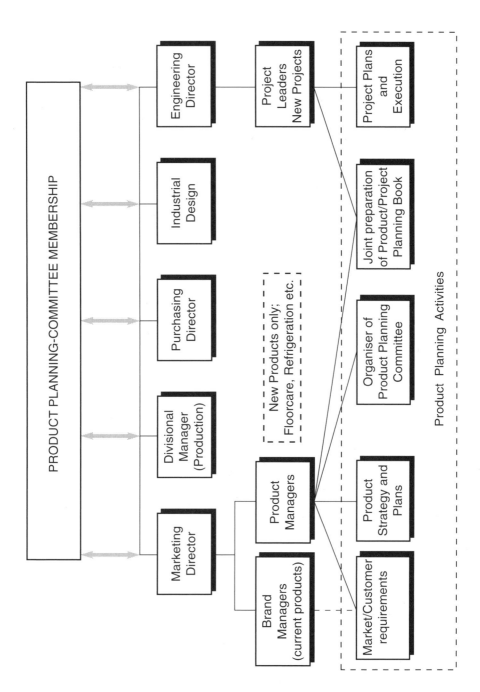

Figure 6.14 Electrolux UK: The Planning of New Products.

and execution of new product programmes is interesting because it combines features familiar from automotive and engineering processes with an organisational structure much more akin to that of a fast-moving consumer goods company. Product management and product development in the floorcare division is shown in Figure 6.14.

Steering by a Product Planning Committee

The arrangements for planning, approving and monitoring the introduction of new products are handled by a product planning committee.

The secretariat of the PPC is provided by the product manager of the floorcare division who is responsible for proposing and getting the committee's approval for the product strategy and plan for the product range. The product managers are part of the marketing organisation. Product managers are also responsible, in conjunction with the product engineering project leader, for creating and issuing the project book that describes the activities and costs required throughout the company to implement the new project. This is done by negotiating with, and getting approval from, each functional area that must contribute work or resources to the project. Informal cross-functional team meetings are called to finalise this process.

The engineering project leader is responsible for implementing the project throughout the company and for ensuring that simultaneous engineering activities, bringing in the manufacturing and supplier participation, are properly carried out. Every two weeks a meeting to monitor the project progress is attended by all participants in the "team".

The company has a four to five year product life cycle with minor improvement and facelift action in between. Electrolux believes that its customers will not accept anything shorter, but the company has shortened its product development cycles by six months to one year by going over to integrated computer-aided engineering systems, among other things. This gives them the opportunity, with the same level of resources, to start new projects nearer to the market requirement date, to try more adventurous and complex new projects or to increase the number of new product projects. Alternatively they can reduce their total spend on new product development without reducing the number of new products.

The PPC meets every month and has the task of approving new product projects and monitoring the implementation of already approved projects. Four times a year, the PPC meeting is joined by the Electrolux Swedish technical and marketing directors to ensure that product policy stays in line with corporate objectives and to monitor the details of projects with an international importance.

Co-operative Working

Electrolux has no formalised new product introduction process or documentation but because this is a successful company, presumably equipped with a stable organisation structure and manning, the informal process works well. For example, project meetings are called *ad hoc* and there seems to be no need for official team or matrix working structures.

Electrolux is the market leader in most of its product segments and the company intends to remain ahead through excellence in new product creation. Electrolux feels that its leadership is firmly based on the quality of its products and the company is confident that it will stay that way.

The company seems to manage the complex product planning process of defining consumer product requirements and achieving technological, engineering and production execution in a quite informal way. This can only be because multi-disciplinary working is accepted as the norm. Managers put company and project needs first and department and self second. This means, in turn, that the "weak" programme management process through the product manager and project leader structure works well and does not require heavy intervention from the PPC.

If it did not work in this way, using a product planning committee as the principal means of ensuring cross-functional co-operative working on complex engineering programmes and of resolving inter-divisional product programme disagreements would be very inefficient.

The Consumer Electronics Industry: Philips NV, Eindhoven, Holland

Background

Philips has been in the news lately on account of a restructuring programme that touches all divisions. One element of the restructuring to receive much comment has been the perceived need to move away from the old technology-led business idea to a situation in which the customer is king and where competitive thrust must be based on regularly updated and renewed new products.

Nowhere is this more apparent than in the consumer electronics division, which operates in the thick of a technological revolution, and has been subject to heavy competition from Far Eastern manufacturers. The market is also constantly adjusting itself, with companies withdrawing from whole sectors and rival new products appearing and then fading as one achieves ascendancy. There is a proliferation of "new" products – mainly facelifts of old products with some minor new technology added.

The Organisation of Product Planning

Against this background, it is interesting to see the new product organisation and strategic approach utilised by Philips.

Philips has had a product planning organisation since the 1970s but it is only in the past few years, with the change in corporate objectives and the need to be more competitive in order to remain a major player in the industry, that the following complete structure has been set in place. The overall organisation scheme of product planning in the consumer electronics division is shown in Figure 6.15.

The division has five business units, each of which has a director responsible for product planning and strategy as well as directors of the operational and commercial units. Several product planning managers report to each product planning director. They are responsible for the creative end of all new product initiatives.

Programme Development and Control

Each new product programme is taken to the beginning of the implementation stage by the product planning manager. It is then carried through implementation by a product manager located close to the factory where the product will be manufactured. The product manager also reports to the director of product planning and strategy for the business group.

The rationale for this split responsibility, which involves quite a complicated programme handover, is that Philips is a large company with many different manufacturing, engineering laboratory and production locations. At the front end of a programme, the product planner must work closely with the technical and marketing teams while paying adequate attention to the process, manufacturing and suppliers' needs. Hence he is usually located close to the technological groups. The product manager, on the other hand, with his responsibility for implementation, benefits from being located at the manufacturing plant, close also to purchasing and connected to the sales companies. Nevertheless, he has to abide by the product content of the programme that has been approved.

Overall Policy Co-ordination

The product policy council is responsible for overall selection, technological drive, customer focus, positioning and integrity in the product packages delivered by the business units. The council's organisation is shown in

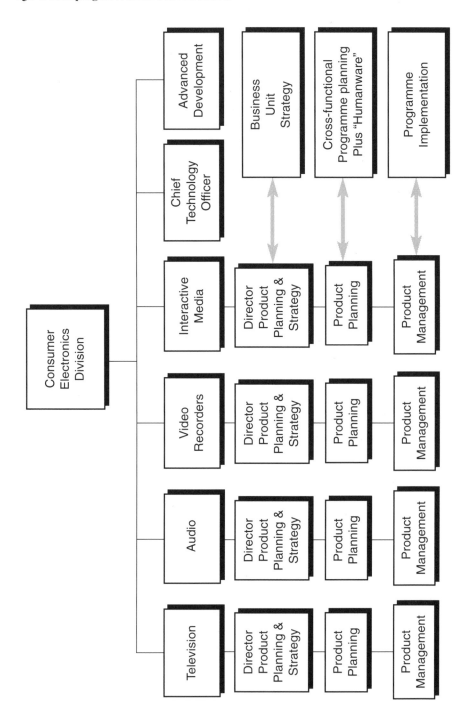

Figure 6.15 Philips Consumer Electronics: Product Plannning Structure.

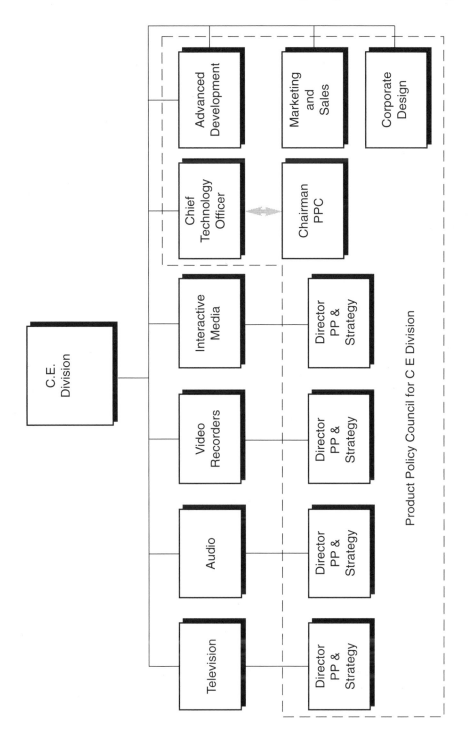

Figure 6.16 Phillips Consumer Electronics: Product Policy Council.

Figure 6.16. Its members are the five directors of product planning and strategy from the five business units plus the division heads of corporate design and sales and marketing. The chief technical officer of the consumer electronics division is chairman. The secretariat, or organising body, of the product policy council reports to the chief technical officer.

The council applies boundary control between the competing requirements of the business units and allocates scarce resources. It also strives for an integrated external image and consistency, market-to-market, for the whole division. One example of its work is the recently launched "Philips Collection", a package of consumer electronics products from different business units that puts over a consistent, up-market Philips product and technology image.

Conclusion

Philips has a very clear idea of what it expects from the product creation process. The company's experience emphasises some other important aspects of product planning.

1. The business units are responsible for creating and managing their own programmes. The PPC keeps an overview.

2. Philips uses a formalised new product introduction process to minimise risk in new programmes, to secure consistency of decision making and to ensure that problems in programmes can be corrected quickly. The process varies between the different business units and places much emphasis on humanware, user involvement and technological aspects.

3. Having product planning at the centre of the new product creation activity ensures that trade-offs between competing programme requirements are decided by personnel with a company-wide view and professional "ownership" of the product. Product planning is thus seen both as an important process and as a professional work force whose value-added comprises the multi-disciplinary decision making and co-ordination necessary to ensure success in a complex process.

4. Currently, a product planning manager's background and experience is mainly in design engineering or software. However, the previous technical bias of products is moving towards humanware – what the customer really wants – from all points of view. Philips even suggests that future product planners could be social scientists rather than technical experts. The technologies required for new products may well come "off the shelf", having been pre-developed by the technologists. Product planning must also

provide an input to this shelf planning from its customer and cross-functional viewpoint.

5. The company's sales and marketing organisation is split regionally. Product planning is expected to know all about the world-wide products within the product divisions and to understand sufficient about the different market requirements. By contrast, the sales companies are expected to know everything about their market territories but also to appreciate how new products are developed. Thus new products, balanced to the total needs of the company, can be introduced and sold successfully. Incidentally, some product managers are located in the sales companies where specific regional product needs exist.

Philips seems to have combined product planning and programme management quite effectively in a single structure.

A FINAL POINT ON ORGANISATIONS

In studying these actual examples of different product planning and product development organisation in different companies and industrial sectors, we can begin to see many of the considerations that lead a company towards a specific organisational model and how each type of organisation can be effective. There is no blueprint for success. There are only options and some principles which should be adhered to. It is also clear that the stage of development, as well as the structure and style of a company, can influence the kind of product planning and decision making structure that is chosen. This should therefore develop and evolve over time to meet new conditions. Even if a company decides not to go for a formalised, wide-ranging product planning organisation, it is important to ensure that all the significant building blocks are included somewhere in the company structure. If not, some important pieces of the foundations for effective new product development will be missing.

APPENDIX TO CHAPTER SIX

To complete the picture of the organisation and working of a "normal" product planning department, the following section lays out some ideas on the principal responsibilities of the main managers within product planning. Included are the potential responsibilities of a head of product planning, a product manager, a timing manager and an advanced product planning manager.

These outlines are not prescriptive. There is no one method or solution. They will serve, however, as thought starters for anyone looking to start up some aspect of product planning.

They are necessarily much shortened versions of the job descriptions with which managers traditionally guide their activities. I have tried to summarise, however, the essence of each job. The rest would then be adapted to the specific conditions in each company. Indeed the fashion today is to operate without formal job descriptions. These are seen as stifling individual creativity and limiting co-operative working. The summaries that follow, therefore, may also be seen as a general indication of the activity profile of the different job assignments rather than a rigid framework.

PRODUCT PLANNING JOB DESCRIPTIONS

Head of Product Planning

Primary Purpose of Position: To study market and company requirements and to develop an overall product strategy and plan for ten years hence. To create, using his specialist staff, the details of individual product programmes required to fulfil the plan. This should result in optimal use of company resources and profit generation.

Main Tasks:

1. Advanced product, market and technological studies.
2. Evaluation of the competitive situation of current products.
3. Obtaining input and commitment from heads of other functions as regards proposed product programmes.
4. Obtaining management approval and/or guidance regarding both overall and individual plans.
5. Communicating approved studies, plans, programmes and decisions to all the involved departments of the company in order to ensure correct and consistent action.

Product Manager

Primary Purpose of Position: To manage the future profitability and success of his assigned product lines by the creation and co-ordination of detailed new product renewal or improvement plans through study of all relevant factors, internal and external.

Main Tasks:

1. To gather all market and product data relating to the performance of his current products in the market and the wishes of his target customer groups.
2. To present, and obtain approval for, feasible proposals for improving his product line. These plans should correspond to customer needs.
3. To ensure that all company-wide implications of these proposals are evaluated with involved functional areas.
4. To preserve the consistency and integrity of the product aspects of his assigned product line throughout its life and to maximise the planned profits over the whole life cycle.
5. To manage product trade-off decisions between conflicting functional requirements.

Timing Manager

Primary purpose of Position: To negotiate and publish effective timing plans for each new product or study programme. These should concentrate on key decision points, major programme milestones and the interfaces between the participating company departments.

Main Tasks:

1. Optimise the timing structure for each new programme by negotiating with all departments.
2. Monitor achievements against overall company timing objectives and discuss corrective action where appropriate.
3. Set out a company-wide approach to time planning and monitoring.
4. Set up systems for controlling and reporting on timing for each product programme. Create a database of timing knowledge so as to improve each new product programme from a timing point of view.

Advanced Product Planning Manager

Primary Purpose of Position: To make studies, recommendations and decisions as to the future configuration, form, performance or technical content of yet-to-be-decided new product programmes or product renewals for all market segments in which the company operates or plans to operate.

Main Tasks:

1. Study technical and legislative trends and recommend items for advanced or shelf engineering work.
2. Set or update customer-related technical performance standards for new products.
3. Act as an advanced product manager for new product projects in the advanced study or product creation phase – before D1.
4. Investigate the potential for complete new product or product system concepts by working with outside agencies, suppliers, government agencies, technical support schemes and so on.

Notes

1. Trevor Sowrey, *The Generation of Ideas for New Products*, Kogan Page Ltd 1987.

7 PROGRAMME MANAGEMENT

Because of the strong relationship between planning the product and implementing the plan effectively, an overlap exists between certain product planning activities and the management of programmes. Programme management is a specific organisational concept for the successful cross-functional implementation of product development programmes. It is widely used in Japan and is being adopted more and more in Europe and America. Programme management's goal is to protect the image and integrity of a new product throughout the programme life. The strategic orientation, main principles, responsibilities and organisational forms of programme management are described so that its relationship with product planning can be understood.

So far, programme management as a function has received a number of mentions alongside product planning. By now, there may be some confusion between these two organisational roles. This is not surprising: there is a strong overlap between some of the functions described as product planning and some of the functions practised by some companies as programme management. In addition, as already mentioned in Chapter One, programme management grew out of product planning with the realisation that a good product planning job was a good and necessary preparation for good product and programme management and implementation.

In this chapter the main characteristics of programme management are described so that the differences and similarities with product planning can be better appreciated. The two functions should not be seen as substitutional or overlapping. They can exist side by side as at Volvo and Electrolux. They can also be performed together in the same department or in sister organisations reporting to the same boss – as in Ford of Europe and Philips, respectively.

Programme management can be seen as just an implementation task or as a task that embraces the total new product development process, from the first glimmer of a new product idea, through to successful implementation into production. In this latter task it must embrace many activities that can also be performed by product planning.

The terms programme management and project management are also used almost interchangeably to refer to similar activities. So it is as well to begin with a definition.

THE PROGRAMME AND THE PROJECT

These two words are often used to mean the same thing but there is an important difference of meaning, especially as this relates to the functions of project and programme managers. The job of a project manager is different from that of a programme manager. The project manager function has been around for a long time in engineering generally, and particularly in the plant construction, civil engineering and military equipment industries. It is also used in many other non-engineering contexts. It describes someone who manages both his own staff and other people who perform complex interdisciplinary tasks to achieve a specific end result: a project.

In a project, the emphasis is on the activities themselves and the resources and measures necessary to complete the project: time, cost, investment, technology, quantity or quality of output. A programme, on the other hand, focuses not just on these measures and activities but also on the life cycle costs, opportunities and profit potential of the new product. Thus the end result is not measured at the finish of development and start of production, but by the potential of that product throughout its life. The objective of the project manager is to reach the end of the project activity with all his original tasks and targets fulfilled. The programme manager, in addition, must maximise customer satisfaction and profitability throughout the product's life. The product in this context constitutes the output of the programme. The difference in emphasis is significant – especially when considering a programme manager's proper span of influence and control.

We can perhaps therefore define a programme as a stream of activity designed to create a new product or service such that after the launching of the product or service there is a continuing production activity whereby the product or service is reproduced for a defined period of time and meets specified volume, performance and profit criteria. A programme covers the complete life cycle of a new product and a programme manager must ensure, during the development phase, that the product is optimised throughout its life cycle.

A project can then be described as a stream of activities aimed at bringing to fruition a single desired objective – perhaps a new or modified product, a new organisation form, co-operation with an outside firm, a new customer initiative or an employee motivation action. A project is therefore executed to produce a desired end result, be it a large activity or a small activity or a subset of a large one. Thus a project manager's task is limited to the activities required to complete the project creation and implementation phases without any concern for what happens after the project is commissioned. Put another way, the project manager concentrates more on the physical progress activities and less on the business aspects surrounding the whole product life cycle.

The two jobs can also exist side by side. Within a total programme some activities may be split off and handled as projects. This may be necessary for operational purposes because of the particularly complex nature of the whole programme. A programme handled in a matrix form, for example, will require each functional department head to manage the activities assigned to his department. He may require a departmental project manager to help him in this task. Several project numbers may be allocated to parts of the programme for budgetary and expenditure control purposes that may have little to do with the management of the programme itself. The manager of any of these individual projects is performing a task on behalf of the programme. His responsibilities support those of the programme manager.

It would be wrong to say that a programme manager's job is bigger than a project manager's. There have been some huge projects in the civil engineering and process industries such as oil or chemical or hydro-electric schemes. The difference of emphasis grants a much more creative, business-orientated and even entrepreneurial flavour to the tasks of a programme manager. This is because he has to focus on the product that emerges at the end of the programme and not merely on programme activities as an end in themselves.

THE NEED FOR PROGRAMME MANAGEMENT

With all the competitive and business pressures for world-class performance in the product creation process, the old ways of implementing programmes are no longer good enough. The modern approach involves multi-disciplinary teams or groups of specialists, working in parallel rather than sequentially. There are four particular aspects of this approach that necessitate the appointment of a programme manager.

1. Someone must "own" the programme. Otherwise it cannot be managed in all its necessary aspects to a successful conclusion. Managing complex prog-

rammes by committee, or with one of the functional departments "taking the lead" has been shown not to work effectively. Independent, strong, functional departments working smoothly together without an external managing agency: such a situation occurs only in the most remarkable of companies.

2. A programme is a company-wide activity and is therefore the end responsibility of the board or executive committee. However, no board can generate the integrated control and supervision needed for a major programme without delegating the task to someone like a programme manager or to a programme team, which should preferably report directly to the board and not to the head of one of the large functional departments.

3. The old style "over the wall" or sequential product development approach has been discredited because it served the interests neither of the company nor of its customers. The idea of having a single senior executive in charge of a programme is to serve both sets of interests and to create a mentality within the programme that will optimise the total result. This requires difficult trade-off decisions between competing functional requirements and a balanced end result. Only a top level manager, supported fully by the board, can achieve this.

4. If a company opts to implement a new product programme by gathering the necessary resources into one organisation, the appointment of a manager to run the activity and manage the resources is an obvious necessity. If the choice is to leave the implementation team working for their line bosses, but to assign them to activities concerned with the new product, then it is essential that the management of their time and technical output be co-ordinated by someone with a complete view of the programme.

PRINCIPAL ACTIVITIES OF A PROGRAMME MANAGER

The job of a programme manager has a number of key elements, some of which have already been referred to in Chapter Three as part of the extended scope of product planning. A programme manager who works in a matrix organisation makes use of the resources from the line functions to fulfil the programme task. In this, however, he needs the help of a permanent core staff that usually consists of product planning, timing and financial control experts, perhaps with the inclusion of some personnel responsible for setting overall technical performance standards for the complete product. The job of a separate programme management team is still more broadly based. It must gather together functional responsibilities from all the necessary departments, not just from product planning and finance. In such a situation the programme manager becomes almost a general manager for product development in his own right. The responsibilities for programme implementation within traditional functional departments are wholly erased.

The following are the tasks and competences of a programme manager who takes charge of a programme from the very start and is therefore responsible for the creative input as well as the implementation.

1. *Setting the Tone*: The programme manager sets the tone and character of the product and programme execution. He ensures that the quality and image of the programme remain consistent throughout its life. This is akin to, but much broader than, the product manager's task and must, in addition to customer-oriented product requirements, embrace working methods, technical standards, systems, management style, relations with every key member working on the programme, decision making and communication practices and, above all, adherence to the intrinsic goals of the programme.

2. *Creating the Programme Content*: The programme manager leads the process at the very beginning of the programme when the detailed objectives are negotiated. Although some higher level objectives and constraints relating to the programme should have been handed down from the board or derived from the business planning process, the translation of these into the necessary commitments from all relevant parties is a major negotiating and management task. This has already been described in Chapter Three as the heart of the product planning task. This emphasises the need for product planning people to be part of the programme team.

3. *Results Orientation and Trade-offs*: A programme manager must be able to drive a programme in a results-oriented manner without getting bogged down in the details of how each section of a team performs its tasks. Results orientation means focusing on what the programme has to deliver at the start of its life and throughout its life in the marketplace. It is often necessary to spend more money in order to make more money. Sometimes a part of the programme may be sacrificed for the greater good of the whole. Many studies have shown, for example, that time to market is one of the crucial drivers of lifetime programme profits. This is reflected in Table 7.1.

It is clear from this that delay in entering the market gives by far the largest relative drop in financial return. Delay sacrifices volume for ever rather than merely sliding the whole programme and its profitability forward

A sensitivity calculation on the profitability of a typical car or truck product programme shows the following range of deterioration in returns due to reduced performance in key programme parameters:

Area of programme loss	Reduction in IRR (Internal Rate of Return)
1. Reducing volume by 10%	7 to 8%
2. Capital expenditure overrun by 25%	8 to 10%
3. R and D expenditure overrun by 25%	12%
4. Delayed introduction:	
a. 6% of programme life	25%
b. 20% of development time	

It is clear from the above that a delay in entering the market gives by far the largest relative drop in financial return. Conversely it suggests that it may be worth spending extra capital or R & D money in order to achieve earlier introduction or to pick up a timing slippage.

Table 7.1 Sensitivity Calculation on Key Programme Parameters

in time. Unfortunately, investment in development and manufacturing facilities remains fixed in time and so the delayed realisation of the programme profits has a more significant effect. It must be worthwhile, if necessary, for the programme manager to spend a little more in development costs or capital to preserve his programme timing. Such typical trade-offs on major parameters within a programme are best managed from a centralised programme management position.

During the execution of a programme, the correction of off-target situations is a constant concern. Managers must foster a target-oriented attitude. To quote a senior product planning and development director in the automotive industry on the subject of changes in a product programme: "Any fool can solve a product problem by spending more money on it. I want to see some solutions that cost no more or even save money".

Thus the programme manager must do what is best for the programme as a whole and especially for a product's lifetime profitability by establishing a creative, problem solving mentality in the programme. Naturally, this need not be done as abruptly as in the above example.

4. *Commitment to Programme Priorities*: Whether he has only a small co-ordinating team reporting to him or controls directly the bulk of the programme resources, a primary task is to create a working team or matrix organ-

isation in which the personal aspirations and functional requirements of members can be met without prejudicing programme needs. In Europe, the function and the boss tend to get first priority. Japanese companies handle these complexities more easily, sometimes working effectively in a loose matrix format without needing even a strong central programme leader.

The mere fact of a company subscribing to the programme management concept and appointing a manager to a particular programme is certainly no guarantee that people will work together. For this reason, many companies in Europe force the issue by creating completely separate teams as a way of ensuring a change in priorities and allegiance. Whatever the organisation model chosen, the skills of the programme manager in leadership and team building are as important as his technical competence and broad experience in the product development process.

5. *Interface Management*: As described in Chapter Five, the new product development process involves the joint working of many different functional specialisations. The point at which things tend to go off track occurs at the interfaces between different functional activities or major stages in the process. Thus interface management is an important task of the programme manager: this consists not just of people management but also the ability to manage a programme step by step, decision by decision, release by release and sign-off by sign-off. For this reason, timing and programme planning activities are often assigned as responsibilities within the manager's team even if the main functional departments continue to work separately in a matrix format. Timing and programme planning create the framework or map for the whole programme. Having this framework is essential, as is the ability of the programme manager to "orienteer" with it – usually on the run.

6. *Working Styles of Programme Managers*: The working style of the programme manager is very important. Different types of programme management exist, which are described below, but the effectiveness of its manager depends on fixed characteristics.

Starting with the customer end, he should set out to check for himself the mood and requirements of the market to supplement the analysed data with which he is presented. This can mean visiting trade shows, distributors or direct customers (especially when dealing with industrial products) and also sitting in on consumer market research sessions.

He will attend or chair many important programme progress meetings but his best work is often done in informal dialogue with people working on different aspects of the programme. He must therefore be able to handle the multi-functional management relationships easily by communicating in terms familiar to the different functions: styling, technical, commercial, production, supplier. Different languages and national management styles can also be very relevant as companies and programmes become more European or global in nature.

A good manager learns to walk around the drawing and industrial design offices, holding informal sessions with the people creating the programme details. This means he is in touch with what is going on and is able to influence the direction and character of key aspects of the programme without getting heavy-handed or bureaucratic. Appraisers and testers of any new product must also share the programme manager's view of the product otherwise they will evaluate against their own criteria which may not represent the customer's needs. As with the stylists or the engineers sitting at their screens, a subtle communication process is needed to maintain product image and character.

7. *Integrated Working Practices*: To achieve programme harmony and consistency also requires attention to what may be called administrative matters. Actions taken in different parts of the company to implement the programme must be consistent with one another in terms of quality, time and character. This is a function of communication of both the original programme content and objectives and a co-ordinated decision making and disseminating process. Two trains running on rails side by side travel in parallel but passengers on either train can remain quite unaware of each another and communicate only with difficulty. The integrated product development process that a programme manager sets out to control must allow constant cross-functional communication and interchange of status, knowledge and creativity. In part, such administrative consistency is related to budgetary control and, especially in a full matrix organisation, it is desirable for the programme manager to control the complete programme budget. Thus a financial balance within the executing activities can also be maintained.

WHEN IS A MANAGER APPOINTED?

As described in Chapter Five, a new product programme passes through six stages, even if they are not all formally recognised in each company.

The Six Programme Stages

1. *The business plan or strategy stage:* when it is decided in principle to produce a new product at a certain date in the future. At this point, the main strategic objectives for the project are formulated.

2. *The product study stage (after D1):* when the alternative approaches to meet the product objectives are evaluated. Normally the formal start of programme activities.

3. *The programme definition phase (after D2):* defines exactly what should be in the programme for all activities, not just product.

4. *The programme implementation phase:* the point at which the company makes a hard commitment to the programme. This point is D3 or programme approval.

5. *The programme industrialisation phase*: this begins part way through phase four with serious commitments to production facilities, tooling and equipment. Many commitments are, in fact, made earlier to achieve fast introduction timing but they all come together in phase five. This phase ends in production start.

6. The effective end of most programme managers' activities comes after the ramp-up to full production volumes and the achievement of planned cost and efficiency levels at D6.

A programme manager can be appointed as early as the beginning of phase one – before D1, the official programme start. In this case he must be a good creator as well as an implementer. Companies which adopt this approach usually add to the programme team some members of creative and planning departments to ensure good planning of the programme's character and content. Additional staff might include a product manager or product planners, marketing analysts, technical product specialists, timing analysts, manufacturing planners, budget or financial analysts.

In companies with good business or product planning departments, which are capable of managing the start-up of the programme in the creative stages, the appointment of the programme manager can occur after stage one or even stage two. In this case, the manager's skills must be oriented strongly towards implementation. Care must also be taken in transferring the programme responsibility and creative content from the business or product planners to the programme manager to achieve consistency and continuity of programme character and decision making.

In either case, once appointed, a programme manager should stay with the programme through to successful implementation in production which should mean staying on through the launch to the ramp-up to full volume achievement and to the achievement of cost and quality targets. At this point, the line responsibilities of manufacturing and sales and marketing take over the realisation of the programme's profit potential and the programme manager goes on to his next assignment.

There is no golden rule for timing the appointment of a programme manager. Much depends on the particular needs of the programme and the company organisation. Both forms of timing occur and both can succeed. On the one hand a programme where the product range is new, complex and risky requires maximum input from creative people at the front end who may not be best qualified as good implementers. A simpler programme, however, in a safer product area, for example a major update of an existing product, could benefit more from a good implementer appointed from the beginning.

DIFFERENT TYPES OF PROGRAMME MANAGEMENT

Apart from the timing of his appointment, four different kinds of programme management structure can be distinguished, as illustrated in Figures 7.1 to 7.4:

1. A Complete Programme Team.
2. The Strong Programme Manager.
3. The Weak Programme Manager.
4. The Very Weak Programme Manager.

1. *A Complete Programme Team.* The most extreme form is a programme manager who has all necessary resources reporting to him. This makes him a sort of general manager for product development, but the resources he controls should be company-wide and allocated for the duration of the programme. They must include product planning, purchasing, marketing, process engineering, logistics and not just product development (which means design engineering, test and development). There have been several new product projects run with programme teams composed only of technical functions. As a result, cross-functional working was less than optimal. The departments left out of the team, or that remained in the line organisation, did not feel a commitment to, or the benefit of, the team-working. A focus on concurrent or simultaneous engineering as the primary means of successful new product development – involving only engineering functions – can produce

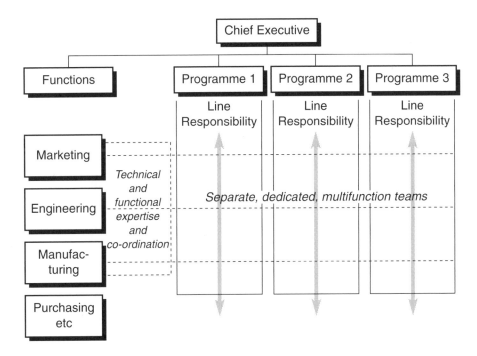

Figure 7.1 Forms of Programme Management: Programme Teams.

the same result. Under these circumstances programmes can be less successful because of the diminished involvement of the non-engineering functions. The simple creation of a multi-functional team and the appointment of a manager will not guarantee success. Therefore, before deciding on a particular structure for running a programme, careful thought needs to be given to the type of product involved and the objectives and needs within a team.

The type of programme requiring the complete team approach is often a venture into a new market or product area: for example, IBM's original development of the PC, which was handled by a specially established team. Compare also 3M's reputation for deriving a high proportion of its income from new products. 3M develops new businesses by appointing "product champions" and giving them the resources to create the complete new product line with their own teams. Companies that want a specifically strong focus on a programme, perhaps because of very tight targets, may also create a separate team for a single programme.

This approach, if used for one programme in a multi-product company, requires very careful handling when the programme finishes. The break up of the team, especially if there is no follow-on team project, can produce a great deal of dissatisfaction. Things they learnt in the team are often not accepted by the main line organisation that "stayed behind". Quite apart from resistance due to the not-invented-here syndrome a successful programme team will have developed some new, faster ways of doing things or adapted system approaches which conflict with the established order. These cultural issues must be worked out in anticipation of the end of the team's work and the benefits from the successful team performance must be transferred over to the next programme.

Volvo Holland introduced the 440 and 460 models, developed in the 1980s, through dedicated engineering and manufacturing teams. Several company functions were not represented on the teams, however, and the full benefits of cross-functional working and fast execution were never realised. The 1988 reorganisation with its matrix approach, as described in Chapter Six, was designed to obtain better performance in this area.

Rover, as already mentioned, creates complete multi-functional programme teams for all their major model programmes. Notably, the manager is appointed from the beginning of the programme.

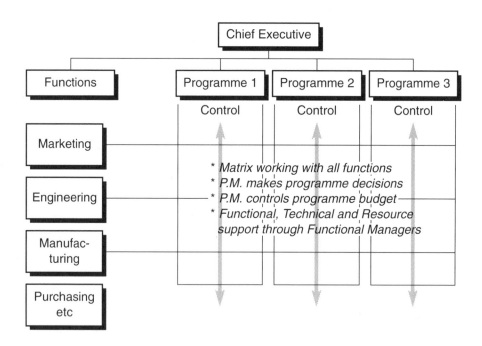

Figure 7.2 Forms of Programme Management: Strong Programme Manager.

2. *The Strong Programme Manager.* The "strong" programme manager usually has a small team of planners and specialists and real responsibility for bringing a programme through. The company works in a full matrix form and the functional line departments defer to his decisions and guidance on all programme matters. Apart from his own specialists, he buys all necessary resources from the line or outside agencies and consultants. This can be likened to the Toyota *shusa* concept or Honda's Large Programme Manager system. In this concept the high-level abilities of the manager himself play an important role in making the matrix work.

As with the integrated team, dedicated resources may be allocated to the manager on a short or long term basis but they remain in a matrix reporting relationship, owing allegiance to two bosses. One provides management and guidance of their work for the programme. The other provides functional and technical guidance.

With a large number of programmes, large and small, going through an organisation and with the changing resource requirements which that entails, the matrix is a good solution. It also has the benefit of keeping a functional specialist or technical view consistent across all the product programmes. This is important for controlling component proliferation, for preserving company technical and product image standards and for the economical acquisition of new techniques and technology. The downside is that Europeans typically find it difficult to report to two bosses and prefer a clear view of their own position and reponsibility.

Ford of Europe's re-organisation in 1985 offers one example of the "strong" programme management set-up. The fact that Ford made further substantial changes in 1990 shows that once again an organisational approach to successful product development must be supplemented by other measures to ensure that the performance of the organisation, the people and the processes are in balance.

3. *The Weak Programme Manager.* As with his "strong" counterpart, the "weak" programme manager may have his own staff but is of equal or lesser weight than the managers of the line functions. This may be due to his own capabilities and experience but is more often attributable to his position and reporting level. In this case, communication, negotiation, co-ordination and reporting are his main activities, rather than truly the hands-on management of the programme, once the programme targets have been set. This system can work where there is an acceptance by line functions of working together and of the board's authority vested in the programme manager.

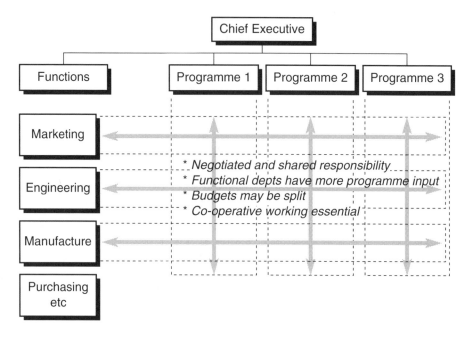

Figure 7.3 Forms of Programme Management: Weak Programme Manager.

There may also be a programme steering or product committee, on which all functions are represented, which helps the manager to obtain the necessary progress and decisions. This is not the most effective form but one that companies will choose if they have not faced up to the changing relative roles between the strong line functions and the new programme structure or if they are lucky enough to have a top management group who can really work as a team.

Both the Electrolux Floorcare and Philips Consumer Electronics organisations exhibit features of this kind of programme management. Perhaps the Philips example is more structured and heavyweight than Electrolux but both organisations rely on a committee structure for policy and progress and retain the strength and authority of the functional departments. The specific combination into one organisation of product planning and programme management is also a feature at Philips.

4. *The "Very Weak" Programme Manager.* This manager has very tenuous dotted lines between himself and the line functions. This kind of manager gets work done through consent and persuasion, through stealth or not at all. Sometimes his weakness comes from reporting into the wrong part, or at the wrong level, in the organisation. Sometimes it originates in lack of board

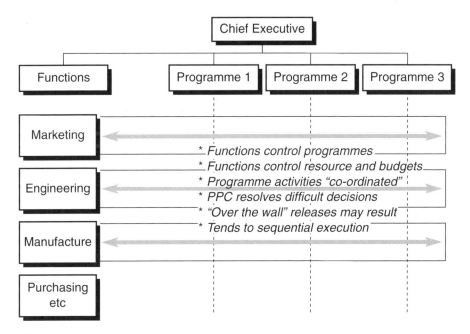

Figure 7.4 Forms of Programme Management: Very Weak Programme Manager.

support or understanding of the importance of the task. Sometimes, despite the best intentions in setting up a programme management structure, the functional line departments will not accept anything more than weak co-ordination of "their" activities.

Few companies should set out to run product programmes in this way. There will be no leap forward in programme execution quality. For this system to work at all in complex engineering product companies, there has to be a steering committee with a strong chairman to which the programme manager provides a secretariat and a problem reporting service. There certainly will be problems. Alternatively, one of the line functions such as marketing or engineering can have product or project managers under a powerful boss who drives their work through the board. Such structures are found in consumer goods companies where either the marketing or the research aspects of new product development and planning are of overriding importance and where product managers provide the nearest parallel to this form of programme manager. However, in consumer goods companies some product managers are empowered to perform more like the "strong" programme manager.

Apart from these comments it is hard to make a case for one particular type of manger. So much depends on the style of a company, the number of programmes being handled, the company's level of organisational development and the nature of the programme itself. The "strong manager" will work best over a long period because he gives the initiative to the programme and the company while keeping the functional and technical integrity of the line functions. This is essential where a company is handling a large number of different product programmes at any one time and where resources have to be switched from team to team as old programmes finish and new ones develop. This approach can also be used where the programme manager is appointed only at programme approval stage and performs mainly an implementing role. The front end of the programme can then be created and managed by product planning. For a large one-off type of programme however, the dedicated team is probably the best solution.

It has already been noted that the establishment of programme management on its own, even when effectively carried out, will not provide the necessary improvements in the output of the new product development process. The competence of practitioners in all functions is just as important as the quality of programme management. Their vocational skills must be constantly improved and they must be able to release their technical creativity as a necessary contribution to the performance improvement. This may come partly from the motivation of working together on a programme team, but it depends also on the support that comes directly from the company which must organise itself to make integrated product development work.

ORGANISATION AND MOTIVATION

The key to any form of successful matrix working resides in the motivation and training of people. This leads us to the next key necessity in the establishment and control of a programme management type organisation. The choice of any kind of programme management structure implies a changed set of responsibilities and operating methods for the rest of the organisation, including the board. These involve the following five aspects:

1. The Programme has Priority.
2. Shared Responsibilities.
3. Personnel Resourcing.
4. Reward Systems.
5. The Balance of Power.

1. *The Programme has Priority*. The project and company interests have to come before the interests of any single function. This is difficult for some

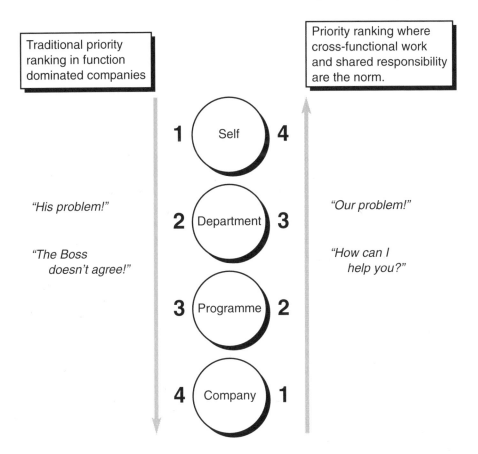

Figure 7.5 Functional versus Company Priority in Programme Decisions.

functional heads to swallow. For example, the large line departments in a company usually have the largest budgets, representing the bulk of spending on new projects. In a matrix organisation the demands of the budget holder can often override the requirements of the programme unless the budget situation is clarified in advance. With a separate programme team controlling all the necessary resources, budget responsibility usually resides with the programme manager. This has been found to be a desirable solution in making matrix organisations work where responsibilities are in fact shared and should not be overriden by one-sided budget procedures.

Figure 7.5 shows the priority order needed for effective programme co-operation as compared to the traditional approach. This is a motivation and training problem, one in which top management style and examples can work for or against the necessary atmosphere of co-operation.

2. *Shared Responsibilities.* People throughout the organisation have to accept the idea of working with others to achieve a common task. This can be a somewhat difficult concept when one of the central management tenets we have been taught to believe in is the clear definition of accountability and responsibility for each individual in an organisation. The point can be illustrated with two examples, one from Nissan and one from Rover.

Rover have, for many years, been running internal training programmes aimed at changing and modernising the performance and attitudes of their employees. One of the programmes concentrated on problem solving – not "his/her" problem, or "their" problem, but on "our" problem. Each employee must consider what could be done to solve the specific problem under discussion rather than thinking it should be solved by someone else. This training was given to multi-disciplinary and multi-level groups of employees to reinforce the idea of cross-functional working. The successful effects of this programme on the quality of their new product development is shown by the speed of introduction and improved product quality of Rover's most recent new product programmes, the 200/400 range, the new Metro and the new 800 range.

The Nissan example, from a conference on simultaneous engineering, has more to do with individual management motivation and style and stands as an example of the delegation of responsibility, combined with effective management control, practised by Japanese companies. While in Japan, a Nissan UK manager asked one of his contacts how he managed his people on a project. The answer was that each subordinate was given a clear task and a clear understanding of the area of flexibility and space he had to fulfill that task. The manager said that each employee knew that if he needed to go outside his remit he could come back to the manager and discuss the situation. The likelihood was that the extra room would be granted.

Both examples illustrate that it is possible for people to learn to share responsibility in a tightly controlled programme while having a clear view of their own room for action. This is a very necessary company-wide change of culture that must take place as part of any move to matrix type working practices.

3. *Personnel Resourcing.* It is clear that the establishment of a strong and effective programme management organisation at the top of a company, supported by the board, has to be combined with, and must not override, the need to push responsibility downward within the organisation and to advise each person of his room for action and, equally, when he must consult before acting. This requires the full involvement of a competent personnel

resourcing organisation as well as clear agreement on management style and delegation. Simultaneous engineering, parallel working, integrated product development all imply that the departments of a company are able to make their input as early in the programme as necessary. Personnel and organisation departments must be included at an early stage in each programme to ensure that the motivation and training programmes are in place and also to consider the organisational, personnel skills and remuneration effects of the move to programme-based working structures.

4. *Reward Systems*. Programme managers are usually chosen on the basis of their broad experience in the line as senior engineering managers, small division general managers, product planning or marketing managers. Since most career development systems are based on progression up a line organisation, how should a company reward success in programme management? The promotion expectations of most ambitious and high-performing executives involve a move every two to three years. However we have already seen that a programme manager, once appointed, should stay with his programme until successful implementation. What happens, then, if a programme lasts for four years? What happens if, when a manager has sucessfully completed a programme, there are no follow-on programmes of sufficient scope or if there is no space in the line organisation? In several cases a successful programme manager has been forced to leave his company to fulfill his future, perhaps expanded, aspirations.

Personnel working within a programme team environment have, potentially, two bosses: their line manager and the programme manager. Which performs their regular performance appraisal is a question of crucial importance.

The personnel, reward and organisation issues should be addressed early by any top management that wishes to implement a structure using the programme management concept.

5. *The Balance of Power*. A programme management organisation almost turns a typical organisation chart through ninety degrees. The programme heads fulfill the line, executive role and the functional managers become resource and skill managers in a support role. This change of relative roles between programme managers and the large line organisations must not be seen as a victory for one and a loss for others. Under "strong" programme management, the engineering department will become more of a resource management organisation, but will still be responsible for the technical competence, excellence and integrity of the engineers' output and for the technical performance of the complete product. The ingenuity and cost-effectiveness of the product solutions have to be improved each step of the

way. Without having to bother with overall programme progress, the engineering function is free to concentrate on its core expertise. However, many engineering managers will not see this as a step forward. To be blunt: working on projects or programmes and contributing to the progress or problem solving is more fun than just managing, say, an electrical engineering test programme or resource team. In other departments such as marketing or purchasing, external control over action programmes may also be unwelcome because these departments have traditionally fought for total responsibility in dealing with customers and suppliers respectively. However they must derive strength from being brought earlier into new programmes and from having a better level of basic certainty and information to enable them to negotiate with their internal and external business partners as part of the progress of the programme.

THE WAY FORWARD

It is not surprising, in the light of all the problems to be overcome in implementing programme management that many companies who have started some form of integrated product development are dissatisfied with the results. The idea of spending so much time and effort on cultural as well as organisational changes with a medium to long term payback does not appeal to companies with their noses to the short term grindstone and who face pressure for financial results next week – not next year. For the same reason many companies favour the separate complete programme team approach with all necessary resources allocated, because this is easier and more visible initially and just requires one big heave to gain acceptance and to get started. The problem is that programme teams for their own sake are not the goal. What should be striven for is continuous improvement in all aspects of the product development process in order to produce a continuous stream of profitable and customer-oriented new products. Success in this will enhance the competitiveness of all European and American companies, especially those that have not already started to strive for world-class product development performance standards. Even those that have made progress once, on one programme, must keep going in order to improve continuously. In the end, it does require substantial reorientation and remotivation to derive the full benefits of integrated product development. Using programme management techniques is but one tool, just as starting with effective business and product planning is indispensible in ensuring that programmes are started in the right way.

From the organisation descriptions in Chapter Six, it is clear that in real life there are similarities and overlaps between certain tasks and processes called product planning in some companies and programme management in others. The two roles can sit very happily side by side if a company picks those building blocks and processes that suit the needs of both the programme and its operating style. It is this factor that leads companies, after several years' experience, to develop organisations in which product planning and programme management responsibilities are combined. A study of the management aspects of the new product development process in Chapter Five shows that it is difficult to separate out the product planning aspects from the planning of other parts of the programme simply because everything stems from the product requirements of the customer.

8 THE BUSINESS PLANNING PROCESS

The business plan of a company and the actions that go into creating it are not necessarily a direct part of the product planner's function but it is impossible to create a business plan without a very large element of input from product planning. Equally, it is impossible for product planning to kick-off new product programmes until their implications and alternatives have been properly explored as part of the company's business planning process. The business plan process is described here sufficiently to illustrate this mutual interdependence. This chapter includes a definition of the business plan, and expands on its importance to companies and to product planning.

Business planning is presented as both a carefully timed and integrated process and a means by which a company can achieve a flexibility in its operations to guard against future uncertainty.

One of the most significant activities in the life of a product planner is the business planning process. This has already been touched on in Chapter Five as the starting point for the new product development process. Business planning is one of the organisational forms into which product planning can develop. The business plan and the actions that create it are one of the main environments in which the product planner participates. It is worthwhile taking some time to examine certain key aspects of business planning. As with programme management, dealt with in Chapter Seven, there are overlaps between activities defined as business planning and the tasks of both advanced product planning and product cycle planning.

Business plans mean different things in different companies and it is necessary to be clear as to the definition that is important in this context.

At the simplest level, a company's business plan is a description of future actions and progress, expressed in financial terms. New or growing companies seeking external venture funds or support from their bankers produce a business plan as part of the necessary demonstration of solid future prospects. Balance sheets are expected to be part of this plan. Produced for this purpose, the business plan is identical to a corporate or long range plan. The emphasis is on the validity of the financial figures used to judge the future viability of the company. Normally, such plans will be produced by small or medium sized companies. Larger companies seeking external finance will have to produce a greater variety of information.

As businesses become larger and more complex, however, it is necessary to distinguish between corporate plans that cover a complete company's activities in all its divisions and subsidiaries at a relatively high level, and business plans which focus both on the individual businesses within a company and on the business aspects of its future. A business plan would be created for each homogeneous business unit or division in a group of companies. Usually, the focus of a business unit will be the products or services that it sells and provides in its defined business sectors.

EMPHASIS ON THE PLAN CONTENT

There is an important distinction to be made between business planning that focuses mainly on future financial forecasts as a way of expressing viability and the assumptions behind that business plan, which represent a company's intentions and the predicted results of its actions. Financial forecasts are always used as part of such a decision making process but they are not the only yardstick for deciding what to do. It is this concentration on the content of a business plan that is most important in the context of a product planner's work and involvement.

A business plan will concentrate also on that content that is strongly related to the business such as strategy, products, competitors, markets, volumes, customers, resources and capacity, costs, operating targets and efficiency. A corporate or long range plan, with its heavier emphasis on the end financial result, must also concern itself with systems, organisation, facilities, financing, location, personnel and acquisitions. These aspects are also, of course, very important in planning a company's future but they are more supportive of the main business considerations than an integral part of them. In a sense they are a result of the individual elements of business plans rather than a determining factor.

In this business plan process, the product planning department plays a central role. As a minimum, it is the creator of the product cycle plan and project plans that lie at the core of the business plan. However, in some organisation structures, such as those described in Chapter Six, product planning and business planning go hand in hand. In one, the Ford pre-1985 organisation, business planning was part of product planning. In another, Volvo's 1988 structure, the exact opposite was the case. In a third example, the Ford post-1985 structure, business planning was separated from the programme teams but still remained as part of the vice president of product development's responsibility. The product planners themselves were absorbed into the programme teams.

These different organisational titles and reporting levels and their relationship to product planning are much more differences of emphasis or culture within a company rather than differences of substance in the new product process.

LINKS TO ACTION

The importance of the business plan is its link with the real action plans that are, or will be, taking place to allow a company to achieve its future goals. This is why business plans are made for operating divisions or business units and not at corporate level in large company groupings. Most business plans are expressed in financial terms and are often the creation of a financially-oriented department, but the real meat of a plan lies in its assumptions and decisions, especially in areas of high uncertainty. It is with these that the product planner must concern himself.

The business plan is the umbrella document or body of knowledge that is used as a bible by the product planner, as well as the rest of the company organisation, as a basis for forward planning activities. A business plan has to start by defining clearly the strategy that the company wishes to follow in the plan period. A business plan has to contain actions needed to ensure profitable survival. It will be a product plan driven document that sets out, for a period of up to ten years, depending on the type of company or industry concerned, the product actions to be fulfilled. This is elsewhere referred to as the product cycle plan. Starting from this, it should then describe what the company needs to fulfill the plan, the acquisition of technology, the resources of all kinds, the improvements in basic operating performance needed to achieve the plan's objectives and the main forecasts and financial calculations that are the results of the planned actions.

CONTENTS OF A PLAN

A large element of a business plan is represented by standard information similar to that needed to evaluate a product programme. This is natural: a plan is a collection of product and other action programmes.

However, the production of a business plan is not just a mechanistic gathering of figures and data. The best quality business planning companies attempt to forecast alternative futures. They attempt to devise strategies and action plans to deal with those possible futures. The link between the planning activity and operational actions is a key point. Another key is that the process must be organised in such a way that the commitment of all the functional areas of the company to the plan contents is secured at the end of the process. The process of the plan's creation usually occurs within an annual or bi-annual timetable which delivers its results at the same time each year. However, flexibility – which every company operating in today's business environment needs – should also be safeguarded by the process itself and the decisions made within it.

The value added by the renewal in each cycle of the business plan consists of the following.

1. Redefining the strategic positioning of the company in technology, core business, environmental performance, global positioning against competition, product systems and market presence.

In the last few years many companies have taken up environmental awareness as a basis platform for short term publicity. Several companies have decided to make the environment one of their long term focus points. Volkswagen has paid great attention to the recycling of cars, not just studying and arranging for the recycling of old models, but actually designing new models to be more recycling-friendly. Volvo, BMW and Daimler Benz are following similar strategies.

Volvo have placed great emphasis on exhaust emission aspects. They were the first to develop and adopt an exhaust catalyser for cars, and have recently publicised an advanced car project that involves a gas turbine and electric hybrid power unit.

Many companies are looking carefully at what they define as "core business" and are narrowing down the areas in which they will retain full technology, design and manufacturing capability. This is part of a cost reduction drive. Also, by relying on competent outside sources for the non-core components, they achieve flexibility in application of their own resources and lower break-even points.

2. Re-evaluating and, if necessary, adjusting business objectives and goals in areas such as product quality, manufacturing performance and sourcing.

Manufacturing efficiency and total quality have been areas of concentration for companies in the 1980s. Now new product development itself is the area where really aggressive companies are targetting quantum leaps in performance which require a complete re-appraisal of the way they do business. This affects the entire corporate infrastructure that supports the creation and production of products. Such a transformation can only be achieved on the back of an effective business planning process.

3. Reviewing alternative future scenarios or elements of the plan where uncertainty exists; devising counter strategies or back-up plans.

In the 1970s industries dependent on the use of fossil fuels faced considerable uncertainty because of volatile oil prices. This led companies such as Perkins Engines, the diesel engine manufacturer, to create within its business plans alternative scenarios for market development and economic growth based on different oil price levels and different reactions of vehicle buyers and users.

The 1980s and early 1990s have seen great uncertainty over aspects of European Community policy and legislation. Two examples involve the cross border movement of cars by distributors (which has been forbidden under the terms of manufacturers' distribution agreements) and the possibility of vehicle prices and specifications being harmonised in all the countries of the EC, from 1992. Both these factors have led all those connected with the automotive business to devise alternative plans to protect their own positions.

4. Deciding what to add to, or delete from, the plan, as previously established, in terms of new programmes and actions and where to modify and fine-tune existing plans.

This is the heart of the annual planning cycle where product cycle plans are tuned to resources. Much more is said about this aspect in Chapter Three (selecting new product ideas) and in Chapter Nine (product cycle planning).

5. Checking on the multi-project aspects of the proposed plan or scenarios – especially regarding resources and returns.

It is surprising how many companies formulate long term plans without subjecting the totality of requirements to an overall evaluation. The multi-project evaluation of plans is the third layer in the process after strategy formulation and the selection of desired action plans. It is, however, the most important layer because it allows plans to be seen in the light of resource reality and not just as something that should be done but never will be.

6. Ensuring that links are firmly made between future plans and programmes and current action and results.

1. External Environment.

2. Competitive Developments and Strategies.

3. Strategic Issues for Attention.

4. Global Actions, Plans and Objectives.

5. Product Market Strategy.

   - Current Products.
   - New Programmes.
   - Target Customer Groups.
   - Quality and Reliability objectives.
   - Option Strategy.
   - Marketing Programme Costs.

6. Product and Manufacturing Technology.

   - Property and System Developments.
   - Technology Research or Acquisition.
   - New Legislation.
   - Environmental Strategy and Plan.

7. Product Cycle Plan and New Product Programmes.

   - Alternative Scenarios.
   - Product Introductions.
   - Volume Plan per Market.
   - Major System Volumes.

8. Manufacturing Plan.

   - Strategy
   - Make-Buy.
   - Performance Improvements.
   - Capacities and Utilisation.
   - Operating Targets and Parameters.
   - Operating Cost Development.
   - Investment Plan.

9. Programme Plan details.

   - Objectives.
   - Product and Work Content.
   - Timing.
   - Development Resource Targets.

10. Financial/Profit information.

    - Variable Cost tracking.
    - Price tracking.
    - Running Product Change and Cost Reduction.
    - Margin Development.
    - Fixed Cost tracking.
    - Project Expenditure.
    - Alternative Scenario Evaluations.

Table 8.1 Typical Contents of a Business Plan

This is the reason why such a tight linking has to take place between the high level strategic aspects of the business planning process and the detailed operational targets and plans that assure implementation. In this chapter much is made of the mechanistic linking between the different actions that go into the creation of a business plan. This is deliberate. Business planning is not simply a process that involves taking the board away for a weekend's brainstorming. It should be a continuously evolving programme of activities interlinked throughout the year. It is this that gives the plan its robustness and in this sense, a detailed framework for achieving a successful business plan, with all functional input signed off and committed, is exactly the same idea as the detailed process steps which each new product programme should follow, as defined in Chapter Five.

In addition to programme-related information in the product section and financial summary, a business plan should contain a chapter for each major functional area of the company, setting out how it will fulfill its part of the plan and what targets or specific functional requirements it has to meet. Preferably, this information should spring from already agreed functional plans rather than being specially created for each planning cycle. If the company has organised itself into a matrix form with major product prog-rammes working cross-functionally, the business plan will also have to recognise this in its content and format. This is very important: a business planning document must form the link between the plan and day-to-day operational progress and actions of the company. Without these hard links there can be no continuity and the plan will be seen as an "ivory tower" document. A typical contents list for a business plan in a company making high volume engineered products is as shown in Table 8.1.

THE ANNUAL PLANNING CYCLE

Reference has been made to the plan as a document but really that is only the end point. The creation of the plan is itself part of a process that cycles throughout a company – usually each year. Figure 8.1 shows how the main actions in a typical yearly cycle could look for a company with its financial year tied to the calender year. The business planning activities start in Sep-tember, initiated and guided from the approval by the board of the company's strategy. This should be reviewed and reconfirmed or refreshed each year – an activity usually co-ordinated by business planning. Among the inputs to this strategic review are the results of the preceding business plan, which will show any need to improve performance or change direction.

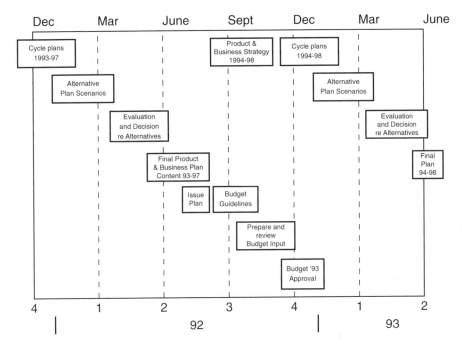

Figure 8.1 The Annual Business Planning Cycle.

The product cycle plan alternatives for the new planning period are then studied at the end of January in the following year. They are grouped into alternative scenarios and evaluated up to mid-May, so that by June the final business plan, together with the company-wide implications, can be discussed, approved and issued in time for July. Immediately following this, the budget guidelines for the next year are issued, based on the first year of the approved business plan. At the same time the preparation begins for the next plan cycle strategic review. So, while the detailed commitments of the next budget year are being hammered out, the business and product planners switch their attention to the next complete plan cycle.

Starting in September, the first year of the new planning period is current year plus two since the budget guidelines for the following year, current plus one, have been fixed in the previous round. The new business plan should be decided and issued in July not only to communicate the plan itself but also to enable each functional area to develop and refine in more detail its own internal and external plans – both those connected with the business plan and those concerned with their own organisational and operational development. In this way, all areas of the company are linked together both for short term operational and budget matters and longer term strategic planning.

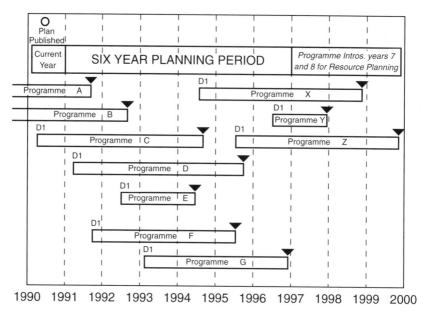

Figure 8.2 Programme Content of a Business Plan.

SCOPE OF THE BUSINESS PLAN

The kick-off point for preparation of financial and other quantified elements of a business plan is the publication by product planning of a detailed new product and project plan – the product cycle plan – for the period covered by the business plan. It is also necessary to add one or two extra years to the product plan so that departments working on long term projects can plan their own project resource needs in the final two years.

The approval of a business plan, in whatever form, should be seen as the reference point for serious and detailed project, product or programme planning activities. In this way, the plan's objectives are turned into a product programme with a set starting point.

This point is clarified in Figure 8.2 where the programme content, current and future, of a six-year plan is shown.

The current year in which the plan is published is 1990. The first year of the plan and the next full budget year is 1991. Programmes A,B,C had already started before the beginning of the plan period so the business plan content will be a reprise of the current programme status. Programmes D,E,F,G are all due to start and finish within the plan period. Programmes X,Y,Z are only described in the plan because resources will be spent on them

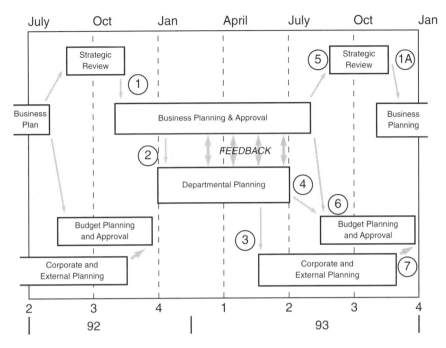

Figure 8.3 Linking of Strategic, Business and Operational Planning.

within the plan period, even though their introduction time and therefore their revenue earning potential lies beyond the period.

Five to six years constitutes a typical business plan period in the automotive industry. Industries or companies with a shorter product development life cycle will use shorter total planning horizons and may need to refresh their plans more often than once per year. Some companies for whom technology or product systems (rather than the products themselves) are important may produce a business plan that focuses on the life cycle and renewal of their technologies rather than finished products.

In Figure 8.3 the same planning cycle as in Figure 8.1 emphasies how the different elements can link together within a company to provide a common basis of assumption, information and commitment for strategy, corporate level planning, business planning at company or divisional level and for budget planning. Completion of each part of the cycle triggers and acts as a reference for the next stage.

In each company this linked cycle is an important part of forward operating activity. "Operating" is really a more appropriate term than planning here if only because many people see planning as a one shot exercise which is done with reluctance once a year, documented and then forgotten. A proper process that begins with an effective strategic review followed by a business plan can really help the chief executive of a company to drive forward operations with confidence. In creating the business plan, he will have looked at alternative scenarios and should therefore possess a degree of operational flexibility to deal with any adverse external conditions that may arise. He should also have the commitment from his divisional or departmental chiefs as regards their part of the plan and the related or supporting actions within their divisions. He should also have tuned his company resources to the needs of the plan. Planning in such a context becomes an integral part of the company's operations.

THE BUSINESS PLAN INFORMATION AND DECISION FLOW

Figure 8.4 shows in more detail the links between previously decided activities, the inputs into the new planning cycle and the feeding back of the newly decided plan into the operational areas. In a product-driven company, the plan and the streams of action within the company are firmly and continuously linked before the new plan cycle is started, during the preparation of the updated plan and as part of the feedback of decisions and action emanating from the new plan.

At the start of the cycle, the business and product planner does not have the luxury of starting with a clean sheet of paper. He must take on board the major lessons from the last cycle review plus all relevant inputs from within and beyond the company. His creativity in providing new and revised product actions for the new plan round forms the major input and influence.

Two other important elements of this initial input are: the status of current projects and functional departmental action plans. These are particularly important when an overview is needed of the total company implications of proposed new programmes. This review should cover manpower, financial resources, capacity, raw material needs, consistency of product or market position and especially performance objective setting for each major function.

The other important focus centres on the timing of input for new proposals that will take the plan forward another full year, or more if specific conditions require it, and which define the project start actions that must be taken in the next operational year.

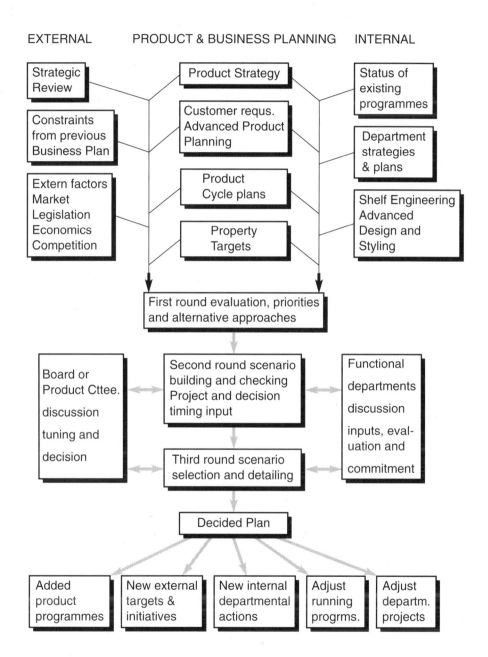

Figure 8.4 The Annual Business Planning Cycle; The Business Information and Decision Flow.

There is nothing holy about the timing of any planning process. Operational considerations of an urgent nature can often cause late changes within the planning lead time. In fact, one of the most important elements of good industrial management today is preparation for the unexpected. That is why the business and product planning process must accomodate alternatives and be prepared for flexible action or contingencies to take account of changing external or internal circumstances.

The bottom line of Figure 8.4 shows the plan's necessary outputs. The end of the successful planning process has an influence not just through the new programmes and targets which it adds but also on already existing operating actions and performance. In this way the links between planning and action are maintained.

PRODUCT PLANNING INPUTS AND ACTIONS

The input of the different product planning tasks can be seen in Table 8.2. A great deal of preparatory work must be completed before these can be finalised which has been explained in depth already. This means, however, that the starting point for product planning work and the critical timing of the readiness of programme information and studies for inclusion in each business plan round is a major product planning discipline.

The business plan as a reference starting point for any new product programme is explained in Chapter Five and this represents its importance also

---

1. The product strategy.

2. The product cycle plan; the rationale for replacing or renewing products.

3. The product plan: the content of all new programmes.

4. The advanced product plan: proposed new markets, new products, product features.

5. The technical development plan: shelf engineering and legislation to be met.

6. The property plan: capability targets for future products.

7. Competitors' product plans.

8. The project milestone and decision plans.

Table 8.2 Product Planning Input to Business Plan

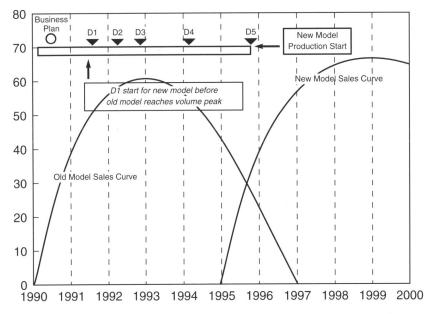

Figure 8.5 Decision Timing for New Programme Start.

as guidance for product planning. Product programmes that start without the backing of a thorough cross-functional analysis as part of a business planning process are either going to take more time to implement (because of this initial uncertainty over starting points) or else they have a smaller chance of success (because they will need to be adjusted more in the downstream phases).

The timing of a new product programme's starting point and preparation for that start are also important elements of the product planner's product cycle planning activities. In Figure 8.5 the role of the product development and business planning decision making cycle can be clearly seen in determining when a new programme must be fitted into a planning timetable. Assuming a four year decision-to-production cycle, as shown, the business plan in 1990 must offer a clear picture of likely volume and market developments between 1991 and 1994 to allow planning of the introduction of the new model in 1995. The D1 decision starting the programme must be planned in 1991. This means that the business plan for 1990 should have brought the project to a decision point D1 state of readiness. In 1990, the current product, destined to be replaced, is ramping up towards its peak sales rate. It is one of the characteristics of the world inhabited by product planners that no sooner is a "new" product in production than they consider it out of date and are busy working on its replacement.

Of all the major timing milestones in a new programme, the start point, D1, is the one often underestimated. An inadequately planned start can be just as harmful to the programme success as a technical problem downstream. The timing aspects of the business planning process and of the cycle plan content, therefore, are a primary responsibility of the product planner.

EXTERNAL LINKS OF THE BUSINESS PLAN

In addition to links within a company or group of companies, a planning cycle, and more importantly, planning activities must be linked effectively with major external entities such as the banks, suppliers and the marketing network. The banks will have to see a version of the business plan or the corporate plan each year. Purchasing depends on details in the plan for negotiating medium and long term agreements with suppliers. Marketing must be able to present the main product content of the plan to their distribution or customer groups to obtain commitment to volume and price objectives and to check out the visibility of likely future forecasts for new product actions.

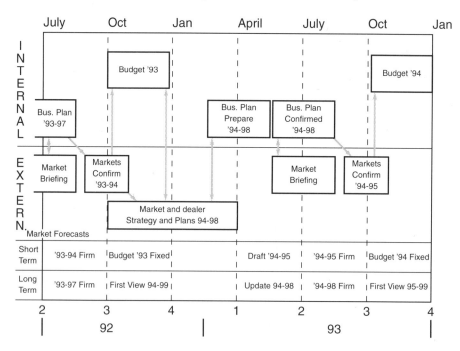

Figure 8.6 Relation of External and Internal Planning.

This linking activity requires parallel or simultaneous activities just as important to the company as the integrated product development activities. As an illustration of this, Figure 8.6 shows how an internal business planning process could link through the marketing function to the customer or distribution network. The future product plan should be discussed with the network as soon as it is finalised. The feedback from, and commitment of, the network must be timed to meet the needs of short term budget forecasting They must also feed into the next planning cycle.

Whether the business sells direct to customers or through a distribution chain there has to be a link between the business plan and the manner in which first, information is collected to support the creation of the plan and, second, the way a decided plan is used as a basis for action to plan the achievment of elements of the plan – in this case the short term sales forecast. Because a short term sales forecast often depends on actions taken before the forecast itself is frozen, the links between the business and product content of the plan and sales and marketing external actions are vital. The same could be said for the external links to suppliers, who also need firm figures and information for their own forward planning.

THE MULTI-PROJECT ASPECTS

By far the most important links emanating from the business plan connect to projects or programmes. As shown in Figure 8.2, the plan itself is mainly composed of programmes at various stages of implementation or study that therefore contain different degrees of firmness or commitment. Figure 8.7 is the same format as Figure 8.2, but has been amended to show the decision points for each programme in the plan. Despite the different levels of certainty represented by the different programme stages of each programme, the multi-project situation must be carefully reviewed. Concentrating only on individual programmes within a plan will not give a clue as to how the total resource, volume, capacity or financial burden will affect the company in a given time period.

The year 1994 sees four programmes at different development stages. In a new planning round it is proposed to add two new programmes to that year. Before a decision can be made to approve this new plan scenario it is necessary to calculate the total effect on, for example, product development resource or tooling costs. This involves taking a cross-section through the company to see the effects in that year. A multi-project analysis is therefore required for each year and each major resource element, in addition to the viability analysis of each of the individual product programmes.

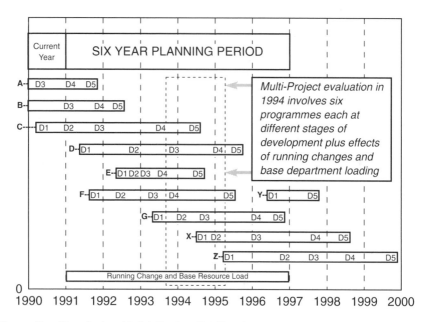

Figure 8.7 Evaulating Multi-Project Implications.

This is one of the most difficult things to resolve in planning. In creating a product cycle plan for his product range, the product planner will have to take into account not only what the market and strategy demand, but also what he is able to do under the influence of limitations outside his control. Limits on tooling spend, manufacturing capacity, product development resource, technical capability and finance exist in all companies. The sum total of all the product cycle plans is the total product plan. This also must be tuned against resource and capability throughout the company.

The strategy is formulated in October in the example above, the product cycle plans are ready in January, the business plan is issued in July and the corporate financial plan finished in August ready for the start of the next year's budget round in September. The multi-project implications have to be evaluated by an iterative planning and review process that is almost constant. If everyone waits until all plans are finalised before committing themselves then insufficient information will be available to do the planning. Working in a totally unstructured way, without prepared and discussed plans, will not achieve anything either. It is only by an integrated and continuous planning and refining process, as in a new product programme, that the connections between live planning and effective action can be maintained.

THE NEED FOR REGULAR REVIEW

It has been stated that there should be one and perhaps two business plan cycles per year. With an integrated planning process such as that described, there is no time for more. Yet each element of the planning mix must be under the responsibility of a specific department so that the individual elements can be regularly updated through the year in the light of changes in external circumstances, changes in company conditions and decisions in one project or function affecting another.

Product planning has received a fairly wide brief throughout this book. This is because product planners are best placed to take a cross-functional, multi-project view of a company's operations and plans. Product programmes themselves must now be planned and implemented in an integrated parallel working manner to ensure consistency and quality. By the same token, business planning is not a once-per-year activity but a continuous integrated process across all company functions. Someone must perform this task of integration. The content and assumptions within the business plan are more important than the financial summary that shows the total impact of a given scenario. Functions such as product planning should be responsible for the creation and consistency of this content and for the necessary assumptions and decisions lying behind it.

If the business plan process itself is to be almost a continuous process then what is the value of issuing a business plan document? The business plan document itself is only a moment in time, a snapshot of a moving process. It has the following purposes:

PURPOSES OF THE PLAN DOCUMENT

- To present or confirm a product-related strategic vision of the future of the company.
- To present a total update and overview of the content of business decisions for all operating divisions. To show their interelation across the company.
- To act as a basis for the continuing planning activities of operational departments who need central company reference points from which to plot their own action plans.
- To act as the input document for the annual process that leads to the firming-up of the next year's budget.

- To provide base information for the use of departments responsible for external company relations in negotiations, contracts and commitments with third party companies.
- To provide a basis for communication throughout the company, according to the style and needs of each division, of the opportunities and tasks facing the company.
- To describe and provide guidance for action on major alternative scenarios facing a company operating with major external uncertainties.
- To authorise certain long lead operational actions which need taking to protect a future company position.

WHAT THE BUSINESS PLAN IS NOT

- A decision and information base that will never change.
- A decision to proceed on any new proposed project appearing in the plan for the first time. Programmes and projects should only be started through the D1 programme decision process. The plan is, however, an instruction to prepare for the D1 start moment.

In summary, the business plan process has four levels of activity, each of which provides guidance for the next in the chain. These are: strategy formulation, preparation for alternatives, the definition and decision on future actions and targets and the link to current operations.

For these reasons a case can be made for business and product planning, in large complex engineering product-led companies, to be a separate department reporting into the chief executive. This is particularly true at the product divisional level where both product planning and business planning disciplines are required. In larger groups of companies, corporate planning or business development directors are appearing on boards more and more. There is no reason why the "product" responsibility and visibility should not also exist at board level. For most customer-oriented companies well designed and produced products can be a source of sound growth just as much as a concentration on diversification, general corporate development or acquisition.

In the next chapter, the emphasis moves away from higher level divisional or corporate strategic issues to look at some of the tools and techniques used by product planners to do their job.

9 THE TOOLS AND TECHNIQUES OF PRODUCT PLANNING

> **Some of the tools and techniques used in the product planning process are recognised and taught as part of marketing degree courses, MBAs and, to a lesser extent, they are found in engineering syllabuses. Many, however, are unique to the process. A critical overview is given of the principal tools of product planning in the areas of product strategy, market evaluation, voice of the customer, product definition, study of competitors, communication of product requirements and decisions. The focus is not placed on detail (the techniques themselves are described in outline with some illustrative examples) but on the value of the tool or technique to the product planning process and the principles for its successful application.**

So far the strategic aspects, objectives and activities of product planning have been defined, together with the way they fit within the new product development process and the different kinds of organisation structures and industries in which product planning may be found. The ways in which product planners work, the tools they have at their disposal and some of their typical techniques are also important for a complete understanding of the task.

The tools and techniques of the engineer are more familiar, even to non-engineers and, indeed are formally taught as part of engineering education or training: computer aided engineering in all its forms (CAE, CAD, CAM, CIM); stress analysis and finite element analysis; value analysis; predictive engineering such as failure mode and effect analysis (FMEA) and mathematical modelling of all kinds; thermodynamics; design for manufacture (DFM); the various material sciences.

How does a product planner define his field of expertise? What would a product planning degree course contain, if there were such a thing?

The tools and techniques described in this chapter are the main ones used by product planners. It is not my intention to provide an exhaustive description of these techniques, but to concentrate instead on how each one fits into the new product development process and to describe the principles for its successful application. Some of these techniques are recognised and taught in technical degree courses or marketing programmes and need no detailed explanation. Some are more specific to the product planning function; these will be illustrated with examples.

PRODUCT LETTERS: PROPOSALS AND DECISIONS

Most of a product planner's life is spent working with other departments and asking them to do work, perform studies or action a decision. Since inevitably this absorbs resources there needs to be a check that the request from product planning has been properly thought out, defined and authorised. A product letter is nothing more than a formalising of the many communications that need to go out during the life of a programme. The product letter originated in the automotive industry and was invented long before the days of computer networks. Electronic mail is a perfect medium for distributing programme communications but my insistence on using this other, formal expression serves to establish that at a certain level an official programme instruction method is necessary.

A product proposal letter can be used for communicating the start of a study leading to a possible new project or programme. It can be a request for some particular new idea or potential problem to be studied as part of a running programme. By contrast, the product decision letter is used to communicate individual programme content decisions or to confirm the formal start or transition of a programme from one "D" phase to another.

Consistency of communication requires some formalised communication method such as product letters. On complicated programmes or studies it is essential to have detailed terms of reference, visible to all involved in the study or phase of the programme covered by the letter. If not, then feedback may not be consistent and the effective implementation of decisions with all departments working together and in parallel will be threatened. Perhaps this statement clashes with some current thinking on team working, co-location of project participants and informality of working practices, but a structured form of programme communication seems still to be necessary, even though electronic mail may supersede the actual letter form. Complicated cross-functional programmes still require structured cross-functional information.

Content of a Product Letter

A product letter must always contain the following information.

1. A clear description of the decision or proposal in terms that link external customer needs to the internal requirements of the different departments, each of which is likely to need and want a different mix or presentation of the letter content.
2. A clear statement of the reason for the proposal or decision.
3. The source or authority for the decision or proposal.
4. The action requested and the name of the departmental head or team members responsible for taking action.
5. The relation to budget cover, cost allowances or investment targets, if relevant. This is especially necessary if other departments are being asked to use resources in their own budget.
6. The timing of the action and a definition of all necessary feedback to product planning and any relationship to other programme activities. If a decision is to be made on the basis of feedback, the date and venue planned for such exchanges should be included.
7. As much information as possible about the product or project details to assist understanding of the study or action requirements. This avoids confusion where letter recipients make their own incorrect assumptions due to being inadequately briefed.

The positive aspects of such letters are communication and consistency: everyone singing from the same sheet of music, all noses pointing in the same direction. Another positive factor is that decisions should be actioned quickly, and by all involved. Direct communication by letter is one way of trying to ensure this.

The negative side is that in the modern company where flexibility, a certain level of informality and working in harmony should be by-words, a bureaucratic instruction-giving and mailing process seems out of place. In fact the perfect non-political organisation has yet to be invented and an effective form of cross-functional communication will be required even if a company has already switched over to project team working, or runs its programmes through strong programme managers.

In a traditional atmosphere, officials can often hide behind procedure and refuse to do any work without a letter. Even sillier, they will question every detail of a given letter as an excuse not to implement it. Care must therefore be taken to produce letters that enhance the quality of inter-department communication and decision making in a programme. The only way to cope with problems that do arise is to work hard on an improved co-operative company culture and then the consistent communication aspects of product letters will be appreciated.

DECISIONS AND ASSUMPTIONS

Because a product letter must provide an information base against which action can be taken or information provided, it is desirable to say something about the decisions and assumptions themselves, which are a very important software tool of the product planner.

From the earliest stages of a study or programme it is necessary to describe, as fully as possible, the product item in question. This means that the product planner, in advance of any definitive information or guidance from the company management, must make many assumptions in writing the product description that describes the programme being started. The purpose of the new product process is to move the project along through the various decision stages with an ever greater degree of certainty until everything is firmly decided and implementation is fully underway. Thus it is, in part, a process for translating these early assumptions of the product planner into decisions. At the same time, many of these early assumptions made will have a big influence on the early stages of engineering, styling, supplier and manufacturing process studies. Indeed, some early assumptions have the character of decisions and this is why it is a subject for the product planner to pay attention to from the earliest beginnings of a study.

Examples of Early Programme Assumptions

1. *Volumes*: One of the first assumptions needed by both design engineers and process engineers concerns the various combinations of volume required for the new programme. These have an influence on such factors as plant capacity, the degree of automation in the process, the type of material to be used in a component design, the exact design configuration, the component variety needed, the trade-off between tooling and piece cost and so on. At the same time, the product planner may have some alternative ideas for product markets. He may have some inkling about different versions that could generate extra volumes. He must therefore structure his volume assumptions very carefully, in consultation with his design and manufacturing colleagues, to ensure that early investigation and planning work is not carried out on the wrong volume basis. Purchasing also have a strong need for early volume information – especially now that suppliers are brought into discussions about new products at a much earlier stage. Wrong volume assumptions and guidance at the start can result in wasted initial work. The early studies must produce the information and results that allow firmer volume decisions. At the same time, the product planner must know when final decisions on different aspects of volumes have to be taken in

order to preserve the flow of the programme, for example to support official component information release to suppliers and manufacturing.

2. *Legislative Provisions*: Different countries have different legislation for the manufacture, sale or operation of products. This is certainly true of motor vehicles. Computer and telecommunication products are also increasingly subject to regulatory frameworks.

Current and future legislative conditions should be a major consideration at the start of a programme. If not already addressed by the product planner in his first document, this should be one of the first questions asked by the engineers. Designing in provision for a difficult piece of legislation can severely compromise a design, delay a programme or involve new technology not already developed by the company. Under such circumstances it is likely that the product planner will want to know the implications of the piece of legislation before he can make a firm decision. Decisions on such matters should be bound up with the iterative procedure of the planning process. This emphasises the need for parallel working so that the implications of alternative assumptions or potential decisions can be studied across the company before making a final commitment.

3. *Product Configuration:* A new range of computers is planned which will have several models of different performance and capacity. A major consideration at the design concept stage will be the amount of commonality between the top and bottom models. Too much, and the performance of the higher models will be compromised and the costs of the lower models pitched too high. Too little and the component proliferation for design and manufacturing could strangle the project at inception. I cover this subject of trade-offs within a range of products later in this chapter but before trade-off decisions can be made it is necessary to define them in outline terms at the programme start. For many companies, rationalisation of product proliferation is undertaken after a product is launched to improve an unsatisfactory situation. The task of first the product planner and, second, the design engineer, is to maximise market coverage while minimising component and product proliferation before the new product is released into production. This involves some high quality assumptions on product configuration and rationalisation at the outset.

PROGRAMME PLANNING DOCUMENTS

As a programme develops and the quantity of product information increases together with the degree of certainty, the quality of the communicated product information should be increased. Taken to the ultimate, this means the implementation of sophisticated programme control information systems with screens of information available to those with a need to take action or a need to know. Major automotive OEMs have gone further than most in developing integrated programme control information and product specification systems that improve the accuracy and speed of cross-functional communications. For many companies, however, off the shelf systems are scarce, especially those that can cater for more than pure engineering-related data. Lacking are systems that can also integrate such information as volumes, cost targets, customer requirements, make-buy assumptions and product configurations in a form accessible to a variety of people in a variety of departments. This issue lies at the heart of integrated programme development: without a common information base, people working in parallel can still be on different tracks.

In the words of John Gault, corporate director of engineering services for US company John Deere: "parallel tracks that hardly ever meet because of the lack of real integration and communication."[1]

Whether or not the product information can be described and linked into other parts of an engineering data system, the following section describes the data to be provided by the product planner, at the different stages of the programme, to guide the study, design, development and release of the product. The need for cross-functional availability of all such documentation, regularly updated, is stressed, in order to avoid John Gault's problem. Successful companies pay great attention to this aspect of programme control. It doesn't need to be bureaucratic but it does need to ensure that an appropriate level of information is available to everyone with a need to know.

The business plan has already been covered in earlier chapters, where it was presented as a necessary precursor to the start of a new programme. Other crucial information sources for formally starting or guiding a new programme are as follows. The terminology may differ from company to company, but the needs are common.

The Product Description

The product description is the overview of what the new product should contain and what it should be, in terms that are as precise as possible. It should not be a generalised description or an essay on what somebody in product planning thinks the product should be. That may sound strange, but there have been many documents issued to kick-off new programmes in which the description of requirements left so much open to interpretation that it was quite impossible to use the document as a control tool, which is its main purpose.

			Product Programme: 1994 21/22 model upgrade				
Product Structure			Model	Usage			
Code	Sub	Description	X21	X22	V21	V22	Remarks/Cross-refs.
12300		Engines					
	12345	New X25 Diesel	*	*	*	*	All new installtion: see code 14567
	12346	Carry-over current 2.0 litre engine.	*	*	*	N/A	
		New manifolds to suit installation	*	*	*	N/A	Other installation items; see code 14568
	12348	New ZB40 V6 premium engine.	N/A	N/A	N/A	*	All new installation see code 14573
	12380	Emissions All engines to meet US '94 legislation	*	*	*	*	See property requs. PPL/25/92
12600		Body and Trim					
	12660	New exterior details	C/O	New 1	New 1	New 2	Styling guidelines PPL/49/92
	12601	C/O Body in White from X/Y 20 models	C/O	C/O	C/O	C/O	
	12621	Modify rear panel for new Tail lamps.	Mod 1	Mod 1	Mod 2	Mod 2	New Lights in code 16435

Table 9.1 Product Planning Programme Description (Sample data only)

As a control tool, a product description must be exact in its requirements. It may contain alternatives – but with a clear view on when and how the alternatives are to be decided. It will certainly contain decisions emanating from the strategy review and business plan that have gone before. It will also, especially in its initial form, contain many assumptions or preliminary decisions and wishes that will require further study and input to clarify. The distinction therefore between "musts" and "wants" in a programme is also important. A "must" feature is required; a "want" feature is desirable – but not "at any price" and so it requires feedback before a firm decision can be made.

A product description should be arranged structurally with the same precision as any other technical document: it is, after all, a document that guides technical people. An example of a half page is shown in Table 9.1 from which some other important elements can be seen.

Product Structure Coding: All information is grouped into coded categories. Many companies employ product coding at a much higher level than part or sub-assembly numbers. This is useful in a variety of engineering and non-engineering tasks, such as costing, supplier or material planning. The coding provides the link between product documentation, which is written in customer-oriented language, and the eventual specification release of the product. Often this higher level code is referred to as the product structure. Its particular importance is seen not only in the logical, structured presentation of documents but also in any automation of the programme planning and data communication process in which a common product structure language is essential.

New and Carry-Over Systems and Components: Against each sub-code there should be entered a description of the relevant part that may require the creation of a new set of parts or involves the carry-over of existing parts. The concept of carry-over is one of the most important focal points for a product planner working with his engineering colleagues. The whole resource and time pattern of a programme can be influenced by its degree of engineering carry-over. This is a field in which Japanese companies score heavily, maximising carry-over but minimising the visual effect as perceived by the customer, so that the product appears all new.

Carry-over involves those parts of existing products that must be used in the manner defined in the new product. The decision on the carry-over content of a new programme is one of the earliest and most important dialogues between product planning and their engineering and process colleagues. The term engineering carry-over is appropriate because there are three main kinds:

1. The carry-over of a part or assembly literally unchanged from its use in a current model: thus the costs of new tooling and engineering expense, design and testing, are saved.
2. The carry-over of an operating mechanism, sub-assembly or perhaps proprietary component where the main design, quality, reliability and operating features are carried over wholly unchanged but the precise size or shape of the housing, attachment bracket or frame may be changed. Here the main carry over element resides in the engineering and the essence of the device or mechanism. Installation engineering and some tooling will be new.
3. The third category of carry-over is where a major component, such as a vehicle floor, compressor housing or diesel engine cylinder block is carried over in design terms with perhaps only a few external or major features changed, but where the specific tooling has to be wholly new because of the part which is changed. The manufacturing processes, however, may also carry over. Here the skill is in limiting the engineering changes to those parts that must change and carrying over the rest of the design.

The natural inclination of design engineers is often to redesign a part that must be re-tooled anyway – an action guaranteed to result in higher costs for re-testing and modification of other carry-over parts downstream in the programme. Thus what carry-over really means is the preservation of engineering, design or process work that is satisfactory enough in operation to be used in the new product. The customer should not perceive it as an old part or feature. The negotiation of what is carry-over and what new is a major part of the cross-functional relationship between product planning and engineering at the start of a new programme.

Option use: Another feature of the sample page is the beginnings of an options usage chart. This is a necessary early definition from product planning so that, at the engineering level, the degree of complexity and interaction between different parts of the product can be decided. Options in this context can mean pure customer choice variants, legislative requirements not common to all models or countries of sale, variants for differentiation between low and high line models. Some option features may only be required in a few countries due to consumer choice. Technical additions may be required to meet different market, climate or operating conditions.

Product Requirements

Product requirements may be part of the product description described above or a separate document. The requirement part of the title refers to performance standards; conformity with specific legislation, technical test standards, if defined, and specific characteristics that must be built into the product. In short, a product requirements document covers what the product should do; the product description covers what the product is or must contain.

Many companies will have a standard set of product performance standards that all products must meet, and many will do a new study for each new product programme. Best of all are those manufacturers who try to tune their product standards to what the customer in the target group expects and wants from their brand name for this particular new product. The best product requirement documents focus on this and result in the most customer-oriented and cost effective products. The dangerous product requirement statements come from those companies where internally generated product standards dominate new product development programmes to such an extent that the product usually breaches cost and weight targets, comes in late and, in any case, is not designed principally to meet customer requirements.

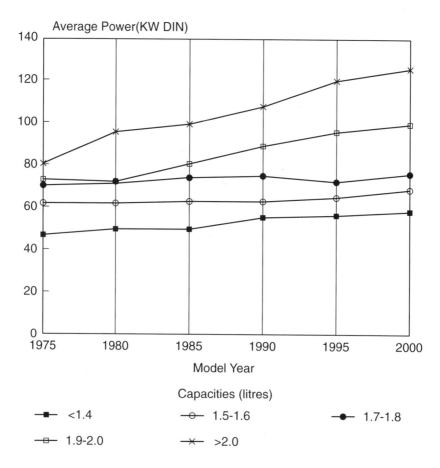

Figure 9.1 Engine Power Trend: Compact Segment.

There is nothing wrong with high technical standards provided they can be related either to what the customer wants or to specific product characteristics that the company wants to offer as part of its product platform or image. Volvo and Mercedes are good examples of the latter: the best safety standards and the best engineering standards are pursued by the companies as a cornerstone of their product profiling. IBM, too, have traditionally matched this kind of high product standard both in their mainframes and personal computer products. Recently, however they have introduced a range of PC products under a different brand name designed to compete with lower priced competitors in segments where the traditional IBM technical standards are inappropriate.

For each new product programme, discussion between the product planners, the engineers and, if necessary, the product committee, should tune product requirements to the specific positioning and market requirement of the new product and not just project the past into the future. Thus a product in a smaller, cheaper, less demanding segment should not have to meet all the same technical standards as its bigger brothers.

This approach can result in tougher standards for some product areas. As an example of this, Figure 9.1 shows a projection of power output requirements for engines used in the compact car segment: the Ford Mondeo, Honda Accord and VW Passat are compact cars. A company which operates in an average engine power output position in the market today must make significant improvements in its next new product to keep pace with the average, because the market is improving all the time with each new product entry from competition.

This is a key feature of targetting the product requirements for a new product, especially in programmes with a long implementation lead time, where competitive performance is moving up all the time. Translating these requirements economically into product specifications is also a key product planning concern. A technique called QFD (quality function deployment) is used for this. This is described with an example later in this chapter. It is a structured way of ensuring that what starts out as a customer requirement gets into production as economically as possible but with technical and process performance safeguards to protect the customer features.

Model, Option and Country of Use

Model and option usage charts have already been mentioned; they are a motor industry method of breaking down very complex, interdependent product ranges into manageable forms. They form part of the product structure definition which has to remain valid from the first glimmer in the product planner's eye through the design and process engineering phases to production and to the input of orders through the sales organisation.

Each part of the company will want its own view of the product at a detailed technical breakdown level, for its own information processing and action purposes. However, it is essential that what was originally requested by the customer, what is designed, procured and built by the company and what is finally ordered by the customer is wholly consistent throughout the new product creation process. The product structure provided by product planning ensures this consistency. A product structure as in the model and option usage charts should be part of every engineering company's armoury. In fact, because of the complexity of different inputs required to define a new product, information is needed in three-, not two-dimensional form, with one

Model Family: 8000 Series   Model Year: 1991

Model Variant	Engine 1	2	3	Transmission 1	2	3	Body Style 1	2	3	Trim Levels XE	GL	GXE	Turb
Options													
Customer specified													
Wheels & Tyres													
5J 145 HR.	S	S	NA	S	S	S	S	S	S	S	S	NA	NA
5.5J Alloy Sports	O	O	NA	O	O	O	NA	O	O	NA	O	O	NA
5.5J Alloy prestige	NA	NA	S	NA	O	O	O	O	O	NA	NA	NA	S
Interior													
Plush trim	S	S	NA	S	S	S	NA	S	S	S	S	NA	NA
Leather trim	O	O	O	O	O	O	O	O	O	NA	O	O	S
Sport Seat	NA	O	O	O	O	O	S	O	O	O	O	O	NA
Electric Options													
Windows front	O	O	O	O	O	O	S	O	O	NA	S	S	NA
Windows Front/Rear	O	O	O	O	O	O	O	O	O	NA	O	O	S
Sunroof	O	O	O	O	O	O	O	O	O	O	O	O	S
Legislation/ territory specific													
French Lighting	NA	O	O	O	O	O	O	O	O	O	O	O	O
German Lighting	NA	O	O	O	O	O	NA	NA	O	O	O	O	O
Swiss Cat. Shield	O	O	O	NA	NA	O	NA	NA	O	NA	O	O	O
Australia Windshield	O	O	O	O	O	O	O	O	NA	NA	NA	O	O
Emissions 1505	S	S	NA	S	S	S	S	S	S	S	S	S	NA
Emissions US '83	O	O	S	O	O	O	O	O	O	O	O	O	S

Note: The indicator 'S' standard, 'O' optional, or 'NA' not available, is a key definition for each group of components which must be provided by product planning well before the engineering release stage. When combined with a definition of the complete product requirement for each market and model, this chart is a powerful tool for the engineering group to specify and control component proliferation and to structure prototype and test specifications for each system of the product. Eventually the product release and bill of material will be based on this information also.

Table 9.2 Model and Option Chart: Example for Car Model Range

axis for different models, one for different option offerings on each model and one for the different combinations of models and options required in each country of sale. Perhaps the automotive industry has highly complex needs for product structure and variety definition, but every pre-designed, pre-configured range of products, offered to a wide range of customers in a variety of markets has a need for some form of structured definition.

A sample model and option chart for a car model range is shown in Table 9.2. The data are fictional but the chart is similar in outline to the approaches used by Volvo, Mitsubishi and Chrysler.

I said earlier that one definition of an option could reside in legislative requirements not common to all models or countries of sale, or features only required in a few countries due to consumer choice or climate and operating conditions. These country definitions, together with model and option, are important to have at an early stage of a new programme. This ensures that the total engineering workload can be tuned to the required product variety. It is impossible for engineering to start on detailed component engineering without this structure definition.

They are also very important at the point when the manufacturing specification is created. Combinations of options that must be specified to meet legislative or climatic conditions must be "hard-wired" into the manufacturing specifications. Failure to do so could result in severe product liability for the company or simply bad product performance for the customer. Options available, but not mandatory, in a given country must also be defined together with options not available, or not suitable for a specific country.

A specific subset of models and options must therefore be defined for each market territory. This could be called a territory option schedule (TOS). This kind of model and option chart acts as authorisation for manufacturing to release certain option combinations, for logistics to procure specific volumes of each option and for sales to order the right specifications for each country. It also offers a check for the invoicing and audit systems that the correct model specifications are being built and delivered against the agreed prices. Indeed, if adapting products more to meet consumer choice in different markets becomes necessary because of increased international competitive pressure, the TOS may become ever more widely adopted.

Timing Schedules and Plans

Timing schedules as such are not unknown in the engineering industry and require no separate description. As already described, they are not always defined by product planners. However, a valid set of timing objectives laid out in management chart form is a necessary part of any programme documentation issued for the guidance of implementing departments.

The important part for the product planners consists of what is often called "coarse timing" – management meetings and decision points, financial release points, and styling or design approvals for products with a strong consumer or user orientation. Also included are corporate approval timing for some heavily structured international companies and the cross-functional points – the major points at which several departments interface. These are the elements of a programme that must be planned just as efficiently as any part of the engineering or manufacturing process. They have as much to do with resulting product quality and the introduction timing as do the technical processes. They also play a very important role in departmental and company resource planning. A programme may be feasible from a purely timing point of view but when the multi-project situation is reviewed, overlaps in critical areas may throw up resource bottlenecks or unfeasible timing lead times. Timing programmes are therefore coupled here with the more specialised product planning related documents because they should have the same status as company-wide guidance and decision documents to ensure an effective programme planning and implementation. A high level coarse timing chart should follow closely the product development process overview described in Chapter Five but should focus more on the major action and decision points within the programme and their inter-relationship.

A timing plan should be created to back up the timing charts which provides the following key elements:

1. A map of the whole process that the company must follow to achieve its targets, including especially the key interface points between functional departments.
2. A basis for monitoring and controlling the project, focusing on the programme objectives and deliverables as well as key activities and events.
3. Management decision dates.
4. Timing of resource needs throughout the company.
5. Expenditure commitment milestones.
6. Individual department budgets and action plans.
7. A check on the feasibility of the whole project including an identification of critical timing events or issues.
8. A means to link the project in with other, internal activities, including other product programmes.

This is the timing plan that covers the complete company and not just the critical path analysis of the technical and procurement activities. Unfortunately, the two are often confused. The technical departments must be capable of planning and monitoring their design, development, test and release activities and must also be able to link into the process planning activities of manufacturing and the procurement activities of purchasing with the suppliers down to a fine level of detail. Manufacturing and purchasing also should have their own timing activity plan. The product planning timing plan should not need to interfere in those relationships.

The overall management time plan, created and controlled by product planning in this instance, must be tied in some way to the detailed departmental timing plans but this connection does not need to be monitored in the same way. The one covers a company-wide activity reported to senior management and concentrates on the major objectives and milestones in the programme, allowing each participating department to see the complete structure of the programme and to fit their own departmental plans into it. The other is the information system which allows each resource manager to manage the inputs and outputs of his department and that must be linked centrally to the detailed plans of other resource areas so that interactions of changes or status reporting can be seen in their effect on the overall timing.

Volume and Capacity Schedules

As with timing above, volume and capacity plans are nothing new. They have already been mentioned several times in the context of essential information or assumptions for all departments in the planning and implementation of programmes. They are so important that a company should have an agreed system of producing, approving and communicating volume forecasts that contains the following elements.

● *Short term forecasts linked to the budgeting process.* These cover a period of one or two years, are strongly linked to current order intakes or rates of sales and also have to be connected to the longer term demand forecasts for new products that are shortly to be introduced. They are normally produced by sales and apart from their uses in financial budgeting, they can be used to double-check tooling volumes for the release of components in the last two years of a product programme.

● *Longer term life cycle forecasts for individual product ranges or families linked to the timing and product content of each new product programme.* These may also need to be in the form of "do" and "do nothing" forecasts that show the "before" and "after" effects of adding a new product programme to a company's product range. They are particularly useful in enabling an effective financial evaluation of potential new programmes. The "do

Year	1992	1993	1994	1995	1996	1997
Sales Trend	100.00	123.00	134.00	120.00	155.00	150.00
Capacity Planning (1) = Salestrend plus 10%	110.00	135.30	147.40	132.00	170.50	165.00
Financial Planning (2) = Salestrend minus 15%	85.00	104.55	113.90	102.00	131.75	127.50

Note:
1. The linking of sales trends and capacity by adding ten per cent, or a variable figure for each main capacity area, is a simple approach to allow a capacity reserve for production flexibility or capacity for spare parts production.

2. The linking of sales trend to financial planning volumes allows a cautious evaluation to be the baseline for decisions, not the full optimism of the sales forecasters.

Linking these different uses of volumes to a common base avoids the proliferation and mis-use of multiple forecast versions.

Table 9.3 Volume Forecast Sensitivities for Programme Planning

nothing" forecast shows the timing of the fall in revenue and profitability against which the timing of the new programme start can be set.

● *A long term company sales forecast covering all products in the range.* This should contain all the approved projects in the business plan. It should be linked both to external forecasts of market developments and to the short term forecasts that show the direction in which the company is currently proceeding. As part of the business planning process, there may be alternative volume scenarios of this kind to reflect different external conditions. However, there should always be a "most favoured" version that illustrates the company's preferred course.

It is possible to use the same volume forecast for different planning or operational purposes within the same product programme by adding factors as shown in Table 9.3.

As with timing documents, volumes for a new product programme may be produced by departments other than product planning, but they form an essential part of any new product programme documentation from the very earliest definitions and are required by everyone working on the new product. Product planning must therefore initiate the production of volumes at the appropriate time for both the business plan and each product programme and should define the terms of reference and product assumptions.

Product Information Releases

The product description, the product requirements, the model, option and territory requirements and the master timing and volume plans will have to be updated and issued several times during the life of a product programme. They are the product planning releases that act as the basis for and, in their final versions, the authority for engineering and purchase commitments and releases. They are the link back to what is wanted by the customer and what should be developed and produced by the company. They are also the links that tell marketing what to prepare to sell, that tell logistics and sales programming what should be provisioned and what will eventually be ordered. They must therefore be treated with the same consistency and professionalism as any other formal releases made by a company to introduce new products, such as engineering and manufacturing specifications.

The Programme Book

The programme book, programme bible or red book, as it is variously called, is a much used, misused and misunderstood document. Even the understanding of the concept varies from company to company. The following approach, then, is a distillation of much experience.

First of all, it is a good thing for a company that believes in programme planning as a necessary prelude to excellent programme implementation to have a programme book system. The book itself will usually contain sections covering all the elements describing the product that are covered in this chapter. It will also contain quantified information pertaining to the programme as described in the chapter on the overall new product development process.

Some companies insist on having the book at the start of a programme (D1) as a sort of bible. Others only issue it at programme approval (D3) in which case it should contain only firmly committed programme specification and decision information. For some companies it is only a briefing document for top management, designed to support one of the major decision points, either D1 or D3. In this case, it should be only a management summary. However, some top managements insist on seeing as much information as possible within its pages.

The Preferred Approach

● *Use for programme start*: At the start of a programme it is dangerous to issue large books containing detailed information pertaining to the new product programme. At this stage in a programme, information will be changing very quickly and it is quite impossible to use a thick document as a parallel working communication tool because of the massive editing, updating and distribution task entailed. Furthermore, the programme may still have major alternatives to be evaluated: in this respect too, a comprehensive programme book is not appropriate.

The preferred approach for kicking off a programme is a concise, structured document such as the product description, a summary of the main strategy and objectives contained in the business plan and a product requirements list, together with an intelligent covering product letter that details the main issues and alternatives to be addressed in the first stage of a programme.

- *Use for management decision points*: For the management decision process at D1, D2 and D3 only an executive summary is needed. Management have limited time for reading large tomes. Correspondingly, bosses should be prepared to delegate responsibility for the detailed programme content provided the financial, policy and strategic issues in the programme are properly covered in the executive summary.

Too often, corporate bureaucrats insist that the programme book presented to management for each decision has to contain every detail of a programme. Some functional heads will not sign-off to a programme unless they or their people can read everything in a book beforehand. However, a printed book is not a suitable place to record the dynamic content of a technical product programme in such detail that it can be used as a sign-off document. This sort of approach is not helpful in achieving world-class product development standards which are based, among other things, on speed, co-operative working practices and efficient methods of handling and sharing the large amount of data and decisions that a new product programme generates.

- *Red Book After Programme Approval*: The executive summary is the right approach for product planning committee decisions. The only time to issue a comprehensive programme book comes with the programme approval point – or preferably after a successful programme approval decision (D3). What the company needs then is a clear, unequivocal and comprehensive statement of the approved programme and its objectives, main contents, targets and key attention areas suitable for guiding the heads of all the functions charged with the implementation and control of the programme. After D3, the content of such a book should have a high degree of stability and so a major subsequent editing and updating task should not be needed. Major programme decisions and adjustments after D3 can be handled by the manual or electronic product letter.

The Advanced Parts List

This has been kept until last in this survey of product planning documentation because it is a controversial but important part of the product planning process. An advanced parts list (APL) or bill of material must be created as early as possible in a new programme. All the above product planning documents, if well produced, should act as input to the engineers who must create and structure an APL. The APL in turn acts as one of the major guideline documents, ensuring that all departments, planners, cost estimators, layout engineers, implementers and buyers can lay their hands on the same information base. We are now back to singing from the same sheet of music. It is worth putting a lot of resource into this area because its value as a control and communication tool is of a very high order. If it can be automated, so much the better.

The larger automotive and electronic product companies, accustomed to parallel or team working, will already be using APLs at an early programme stage. There are still many companies, however, where the APL does not get the attention it deserves. In some cases it gets no attention at all. The problem goes hand in hand with the over the wall engineering mentality. Often you hear from engineers the complaint: "How can I write an APL when the product is not yet designed?" Of course it has not yet been designed, but it should have been defined. That is the purpose of all the product planning discussions, decisions and documentation produced at the programme front end. Most reasonably sized engineering companies have specification databases or bills of material containing product specifications and giving immediate access to current data, including changes and additions. These can usually be used as a basis for creation of the advanced list for the new product which will contain carry-over parts, or at least parts comparable to some in current production, as well as new parts.

Many departments other than engineering need a list of parts during the preparatory phases of a programme to do their work satisfactorily. The costing department needs a list to make a cost estimate; the investment planning department to run a proper investment estimate; the purchaser, first to do his make-buy analysis and then to start early supplier planning. The engineering controller needs one to do his workload and engineering cost estimates; the process and capacity planner needs to check his first process and layout concepts; the engineering release department must have one to estimate its future workload.

In the absence of an official APL, each department will try to produce some list for its own purposes based, more or less, on the product planning documents. However, each such list is guaranteed to have a different content, to be created within a different time frame and to place different emphasis and importance on the same things. Under such circumstances, the achievement of parallel engineering benefits is already made impossible. How much simpler, then, to recognise the value of the APL from the outset and to organise its creation and regular updating on a centralised, consistent and controlled basis.

This book is about product planning – but also about the process of planning products in the most effective manner. It is not suggested that product planning should produce APLs. That should be done somewhere in engineering planning or specification control. The absence of a proper APL system will certainly be a major handicap to the smooth operation of the total product planning and programme implementation process. To those engineers who say that this cannot be done, my answer is that this task is better performed by engineering from the best available assumptions. It is certainly a number one requirement in Japanese companies planning new programmes because it is the only way to guarantee consistency throughout the parallel working planning process. It is also a potential information basis for the development of computer-based programme planning and control activities in companies interested in getting information technology to help control their new product introduction processes.

What has been described in this chapter so far goes under the general heading of product programme documentation. In fact, it represents the substance and result of the product planning work for new programmes. It is official information, released by product planning to drive or support the different stages of the programme.

The following section concentrates more on the expertise or work methods used by product planning to arrive at the decisions leading to the creation of product requirements and specifications.

THE TECHNIQUES OF PRODUCT PLANNING

Much of a product planner's work is informal in the sense that he works outside his own department, researching, advising, persuading, negotiating, synthesising ideas, attending meetings, resolving conflicts or trade-offs. In this activity he uses both inter-personal skills and analytical capability, both of which are demanded by many management functions. However, there are some specific techniques that he may use on the way from the first germ of an idea to a fully defined programme. For some of these he will hire in specialist help. In other areas, he will exercises his own skills. There are eight important techniques used by product planners.

1. Demographic and Segmentation Analysis.
2. Market Clinics.
3. Focus Group Discussions.
4. Competitive Product Evaluation.
5. Product Cycle Planning.
6. Product Positioning.
7. Trade-off Analysis.
8. Quality Function Deployment.

It is not the intention to give a user manual-type definition of each of the above. Definitions of some can be found in marketing or business literature, some are taught at business schools, others have been mentioned already in some detail as part of the product planning building blocks or in the description of the new product development process. The following illustrations cover only the essence of each technique and why it is important to the product planner's task.

Demographic and Segmentation Analysis

The first requirement must be to know where the customers are and who they are. Hence the requirement for demographic and other customer profiling information. The product planner also needs to know how the markets are structured. Usually there will exist an accepted industry or market segmentation, perhaps developed for common sales reporting and statistical gathering. In any case the product planner must adapt it for his own use so that he can ask the following questions.

1. Where are his current and future products in the overall market?
2. What is happening to the different segments or groupings of product in the market?
3. What kind of people or companies buy his products now or could buy them in the future?
4. In what way will the characteristics and requirements of these customers change in the future?
5. How can he use this knowledge to maximise his product's success: by niche marketing, by adding appropriate product characteristics, or by moving across to other segments?

In the absence of an industry standard segmentation for his markets, he will have to develop one in conjuction with his market research colleagues or an outside research bureau.

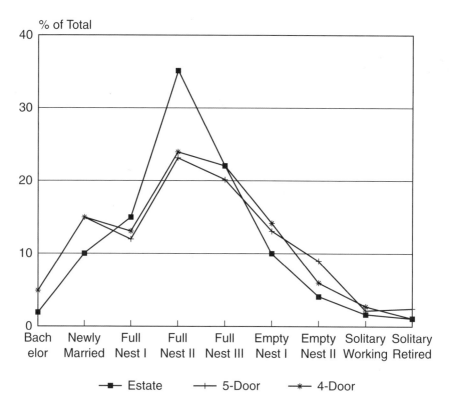

Figure 9.2 Family Life Cycle Stages: Preference for Vehicle Body Styles.

Often such segmentations operate at too high a level for effective analysis. Markets for industrial machinery may be split by power or performance classes. But within each class, buyer types or needs may differ widely. The standard European motor industry segmentation, for instance, divides the market into six main segments: mini-cars, small cars, sub-compact cars, compact, large, and luxury cars. These are based mainly on size/price/ quality classifications. However, each segment contains different product types such as saloons, estate cars, sports, off-road or hatchback models, and different models in the same segment may be bought by quite different customers. There are also high-volume and premium quality sub-segments that further divide up markets and customers. Hence demographic analysis creates a far finer analysis of customer and product demand patterns.

Figure 9.2 shows the preferences in one market for three car body styles (4-door, 5-door and estate models) in the compact segment. The demographic information shows the "family" profile of the buyer – from the bachelor on through six marital stages to the solitary retired person. It is probable that each competitor sells his products to a different mix of these segmented customers and so the research profile for future product positioning must focus on the correct mix of customers for each company.

The structure and buying patterns in the market and the profile, both current and future, of those customers is an essential area of knowledge for the product planner. He can begin a new product programme without this information, relying on experience, subjective judgement or the hope that what is known and valid today can be projected into the future. The likelihood is that his new product will be outclassed by the products of those competitors who have taken more seriously the task of gathering basic market data.

Market Clinics

Clinics are a specific way of testing product concepts with groups of target customers. These can range from members of the buying public to mass users of products, such as fleet or plant hire operators, and can also include distributors or a company's own internal sales organisations and internal management groups.

The evidence from successful companies is that they use clinics extensively throughout a new product development cycle and cover one or more of the above groups several times as the product is refined. These clinics may involve many hundreds of customers in all the main target markets. The manner of presenting the proposed product can be in viewing model form, as a working model if feedback on specific operation is important, on video and even with good quality photographs or projected slides. It is not always necessary to have fully representative models. Especially for concept or alternative checking, visual representations can give good results. Photographs and projected slides have been found to be an excellent way of checking product concepts at the start of a programme where ideas are fast-moving and it is difficult to stop progress long enough to use or make actual representative models.

The timing of clinic investigations should always be attuned to a specific progress or decision point in the programme. It is no use doing a clinic when the product is going to be further changed or refined immediately afterwards, before the clinic results are even known. The timing of clinics and the creation of the models and prototypes for the clinic must be carefully negotiated with engineering and styling colleagues so that the results of the clinic can be both meaningful and timely.

Clinic audiences are not often accustomed to handling products in the development phase that may not be perfectly finished or made from production tooling. They can therefore sometimes be put off by features that stem from prototype or mock-up condition. Hence clinic investigations must be carefully tuned to the condition of the product samples presented. However well finished a model is, you will only get an appraisal of the modellers' skills and not of the finished engineered product. On the other hand, clinic audiences can be remarkably perceptive and enthusiastic if they are properly acquainted with the condition and status of the models or prototypes.

Some stylists, engineers and industrial designers see clinics as a slight on their professional competence. This issue has to be handled carefully. There are three points which should help in getting acceptance.

1. Involve the stylists and designers in the preparation of clinic questionnaires and of the approach to the whole evaluation.

2. Make it clear what sort of feedback is being sought and how the information will be used. A clinic should never be seen as the only decision maker on a specific product issue. It should be much more a check on the status of the product execution against the guidelines for the product laid down by product planning. It should also be a support for future decision making. This is particularly true at the early stages of a programme where concepts, images, trends and a product's relationships to current competition and existing products are being tested. Later on, clinics can be used for more decisive tasks such as selecting specific product features, determining relative price positioning or choosing the right features or colour schemes.

3. Be sure that the clinic results are fully fed back at the working level with an opportunity for comment and questions before they are used formally in any project review or decision making meetings.

Focus Group Discussions

These are related to clinics and usually take place at the same time but have a specific character of their own. Typically, a small number of the target customer group is gathered together and invited to express judgemental or interpretative views on the clinic subjects.

In a clinic, questionnaires are filled in and comparisons are made by a large number of respondents from which average, trend or rating conclusions can be drawn. In focus groups the leader is able to pick out and prompt discussion on specific issues where shades of meaning might be important, where the information would not naturally come from a mass questionnaire or where the discussion itself can stimulate the thinking process of participants – as is the case especially when future concepts are being tested. Two examples from automotive experience illustrate this application.

1. During a focus group discussion in North America centered on some advanced styling concepts, the general reaction was unfavourable because of the very advanced nature of the concepts presented. Then one of the group members said that three years ago he had exactly the same reaction to a then new model in the market, the Mercedes 190 E. He had said to himself that he could never buy such advanced styling. However, he now admitted that he had recently bought a Mercedes 190 and could therefore imagine that the very advanced styles being presented at the focus group could in three or four years time be the norm – instead of looking way-out and unacceptable, as they seemed at that time.

2. The second example comes from a European focus group discussion of the proposed facelift of a uniquely styled existing model. In the facelift proposal, some of the very individual features of the old model had been refined and even somewhat watered down in an effort to give the facelifted model its own separate identity.

Initially, reaction in the questionnaire clinics had shown no specific preference for either the old or the new model. However, in one of the focus groups it became clear that the image of the company and its brand name was so strong in this particular market that the customers would accept almost whatever the manufacturer put out into the market as a new model. Thus the manufacturer concluded that he could not simply ask the customers to decide. Instead, he would have to make his own decision – based on his own view of the product's required image and positioning.

This kind of information is impossible to get from a sample questionnaire: carefully structured and managed discussions can reduce future uncertainty by uncovering real customer motivation or concerns.

Competitive Product Evaluation

Evaluation of what competitors are doing in markets and with their products is a vital input to any company. Product planning must have a principal role in a company's competitive product evaluation and should also ensure that the product lessons are properly drawn out and followed up. Using information and good ideas from competitors should not be seen as just "me too" product planning. There is no point in re-inventing the wheel if a competitor has an idea worth copying. This is sometimes a difficult point to get over to industrial designers and engineers for whom their own latest creation is always the preferred solution. There are several different sides to competitive analysis.

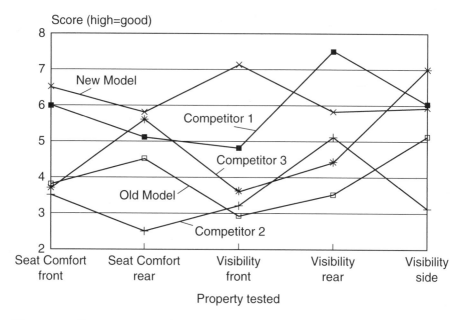

Figure 9.3 Competitive Product Evaulation: Sample Extract Interior.

- Performing a functional test of the competitor against other competitors or against an in-house product. This is used for initial benchmarking in a new programme, for establishing state of the art product performance standards to be met by new products, or for checking the progress of a new programme. Part of a typical benchmarking comparison is shown in Figure 9.3 for a number of competing car models. The cars are driven and evaluated by a panel and scored for a large number of product features. The technique is also valuable for any consumer or industrial product that can be operated in a customer use environment.

- Carrying out a teardown, whether destructive or non-destructive, is aimed at finding good component or system ideas for design or manufacturing purposes. This is the most common form of competitive analysis, but unless it is done at a time when the findings can be utilised in a new product programme, the costs in terms of staff time and the purchase or hire of competitive products are not always justified.

- Teardown for costing purposes can often yield much more than the above since good ideas hidden in the depths of a competitive product are easily adopted into a new product programme – once again, provided the timing is right. Teardown of competitors as an aid to effective cost targetting for new product programmes has already been covered in the building blocks chapter.

● Simultaneous engineeering-based competitive evaluation is quite a new concept that aims to combine all three of the above teardown aspects. The idea is to look at the cross-functional aspects in the competitive product that have contributed to a highly competitive feature, system or even the whole product. Then comes an assessment of how the different actions of the competitor have combined to provide this good result. This is perhaps a difficult concept to grasp, but if a competitor, through good integrated product development processes has produced an advanced product idea, then the competitive evaluator has to work out how to initiate, in his own organisation, cross-functional actions to gain similar benefits for himself.

Product Cycle Planning

In Chapter Three this was mentioned as one of the building block responsibilities of product planning. The concept of product cycle planning is based on the premise, widely described in marketing text books, that all products have a natural cycle in their market places that looks something like Figure 9.4. As a separate evaluation, the profitability curve does not proportionally follow the sales curve because successful new products are most profitable in early life.

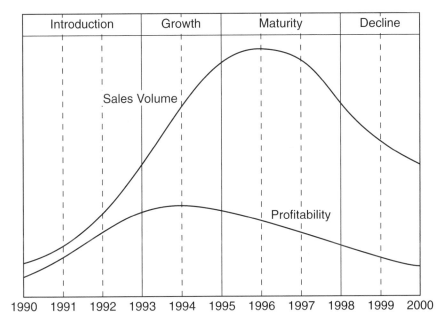

Figure 9.4 The Product Life Cycle.

The curve is not of the same shape or duration for each product and market but it represents an analytical approach on which a company can base its forward product planning. The fall-off in volume at the end and the very rapid fall-off in profitability make the timing and nature of the replacement product a key issue for the product planner.

System Cycles

It is also possible to see system cycles where technology or sub-system elements of products need renewing, usually on a different cycle from the complete product. Examples of this can be seen at work in the process plant industry where systems within the total process will be refined and improved even though the basic plant design does not change. The development of new engines and emission control approaches in the car and truck industry is another example. Here, a basic engine development will be utilised over several model cycles but must eventually be replaced or updated. As already noted, the decision making and preparation cycle for this system and major component cycle planning is longer than it is for the whole product. This means that the creation of a cycle plan for a system element of a product – or for a major system supplied by a company to an OEM customer – is most complex. It involves looking beyond the whole product using the system to the future markets and environment in which the whole product will be used.

Influencing the Product Life Cycle

The shape and duration of these cycles are affected by many factors peculiar to an industry or company, and each company should try to develop its insights into these factors. A mechanistic method of calculating life cycles expresses each year of the life cycle as a percentage of the maximum annual sales potential. Thus, the early years will build up to a maximum based on the factors combined with the planning of the launch and market introduction. The run down in the later years will follow the percentages based on experience from other similar products or competitors.

A company can influence the shape of the product life cycle with actions such as product improvements and facelifts. Examination of Figure 9.5, the Volvo 300 series life cycle, reveals the effects of successive incremental efforts at new product development aimed at extending the life cycle and increasing the height of the total volume curve. The individual product actions and additions introduced by Volvo are seen as a series of overlapping life cycles. The total increase over the period was achieved by introducing

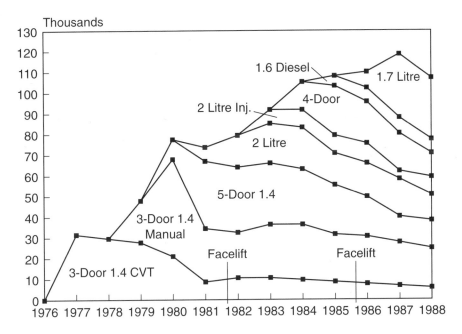

Figure 9.5 Life Cycle Volvo 300 series.

several major new derivatives of the original 300 model. It is interesting to note that each new version reached its own lifetime volume peak somewhere between one and two-and-a-half years after introduction, whereas the whole range had an eight year cycle.

External actions by competitors can also cause the product life cycle in a segment to shorten. This has happened in the camera and consumer electronics industries in the past ten years. This has been partly due to the sheer thrust of the players in the market to beat the competition, but also to the growing efficiency of product development processes that dramatically shorten time to market. There is evidence that the dash to ever shorter product life cycles and more new products is slowing down under the influence of the economic climate and of the product producers' desire not to confuse the customer with too much product proliferation. Under such circumstances, the focus will change to starting later with a new product programme so as to have the most up to date market feedback and customer knowledge built into the new product. Naturally, improvements in time to market will still be a competitive issue. The OEM that continues to shorten his product development cycle times will be able to do more new products, or react more quickly to market changes.

The Steps to Product Cycle Planning

For a company trying to manage the life cycles of all its products and product systems, there are four key steps:

1. To make a decision when a product will need change or refreshment because of its natural life cycle and to restore profit or volume levels. This is what has been previously called a "do nothing" forecast, which charts change in the market based on the current decided product status.
2. To tune this replacement plan to the company's strategic objectives and evaluate other external inputs, competition, legislation, market conditions and their possible effects on the product in question.
3. To consider what alternative forms of product renewal are possible; a minor or major facelift, a new product in the same category, a completely new type of product, or the phase-out of the product line. The examples of Volvo (above) and BMW (Chapter Three) demonstrated a policy of incremental improvements to sustain the life cycle. The Ford Sierra-Vauxhall Cavalier example illustrated the effects of bigger steps taken at shorter intervals.
4. To look at internal pressures impacting on the proposed product renewal action including finance, human resources and its relationship to other decided product programmes and other non-product strategic needs.

The result of the above four-step evaluation should be a product cycle plan for each product family, one which can be achieved by the company because of the fourth stage in the process. In the real world, plans that are not tuned to resource capability are not worth having: inevitably, they will have to be modified later.

Product Positioning

There are so many facets to product positioning that it is only possible to relate a few here. Attention to correct positioning of the company and its products in main markets is one of the most important actions for top management and one in which product planning must play a significant role. Product positioning also has a significant influence on pricing – a shared task that involves product planning, marketing and finance. Positioning can be viewed from different aspects.

The Company Position

This is directly connected to the mission or strategy statement whereby the company positions itself in its markets and in relation to its customers and competitors. Positioning a company is a necessary precursor to being able to position products correctly.

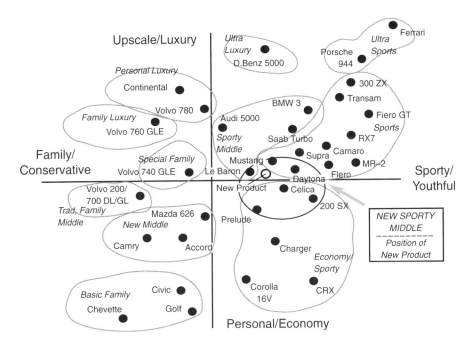

Figure 9.6 Perception Map of Car Market: USA 1986.

Positioning Products in a Market

The positioning of a specific new product in a market must be thought out in preparation for the whole development phase and must be kept in view throughout the programme development. If this is not done thoroughly, the presentation of the product at market launch can go wrong because of inconsistency between appearance, real and perceived quality levels, cost of the product, price at launch and statements made at launch about the company's intentions for the product. Hence positioning is a complex mixture of quantitative and qualitative elements. To clarify these, it is often useful, during the development of a new product, for product planning to produce positioning charts. The basic data in these charts are obtained from market and demographic research.

The first example, shown in Figure 9.6, is a so-called perception map showing the US car market in the mid-1980s. Two different axes are used to locate each product: family/conservative and upscale/luxury. The new product being planned fits in the sporty middle area of the market.

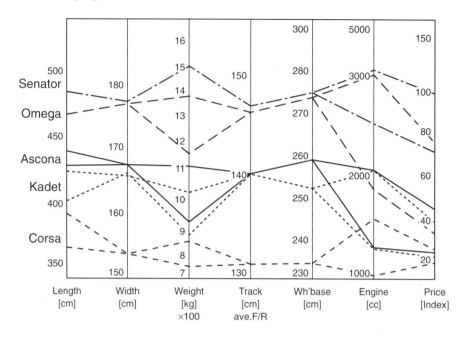

Figure 9.7 Product Positioning Comparison: Opel Range 1988.

Positioning in a Product Portfolio

Another way of looking at positioning is to consider the product against the others in the same family. It is essential that a new product is positioned in a good and logical relationship to the others in the same corporate stable. Otherwise, it will send confusing signals to customers and may, for example, end up substituting too much for one of the company's existing products. Usually, it is helpful to present positioning visually. Figure 9.7, from the vehicle market, shows an example from Opel in which the physical characteristics and specifications of cars are used to compare one car with another.

Figure 9.8 shows the same situation for the BMW model range and both sets of data come from a 1988 analysis. Two important things can be seen from these charts. The first is that in each company's product range the models stand in a very logical relationship to one other. This would produce a good impression in the showroom and mean that the relative visual and value impression given by each model should help the customer understand how much product he gets for his money. The higher-placed product in each range scores better on all main characteristics than its smaller brother. Opel and BMW have both been successful in broadening their product ranges over the last few years and in creating a consistent model image from product to product.

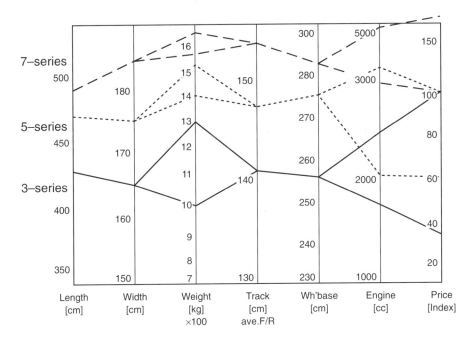

Figure 9.8 Product Positioning Comparison: BMW Range 1988.

In product planning studies for new products, this chart format enables the size of the gaps between products to be assessed easily, allowing space for a new entry or a positioning adjustment for the next replacement. In both charts, the spaces between models show where a possible increase in size for a new model can be introduced without encroaching too far on the next one. The Opel Vectra in 1989 and the new BMW 3 series in 1991 moved closer to their bigger brothers. Both were able to offer a better customer package in their segment without substituting by being positioned too close.

A perception map can also be used to show relative positioning *within* one company's product range. Figure 9.9 shows the relationships between different products in the 1991 Volvo range. Volvo clearly has decided on the role of each of its product ranges and how each should be perceived in relation to the other. This is reflected in the initial development brief for each model and in the promotion of the models in the market place.

Competitive Product Positioning

Another way of using the same chart technique as in Figure 9.8 for competitive analysis is to show competitors from the same market segment. Figure 9.10 ideally needs colour to show the relative positioning clearly. Neverthe-

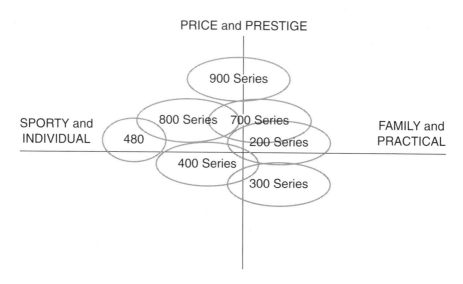

Figure 9.9 Product Positoning Map: Volvo Car.

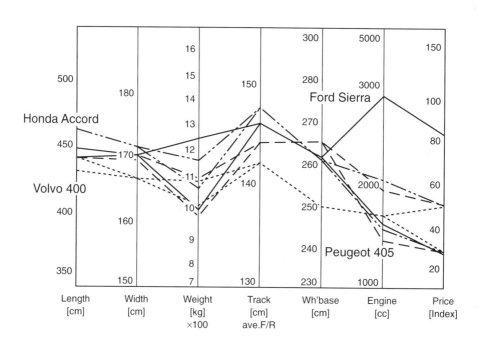

Figure 9.10 Product Positioning Comparison: Compact Segment Competitors 1988.

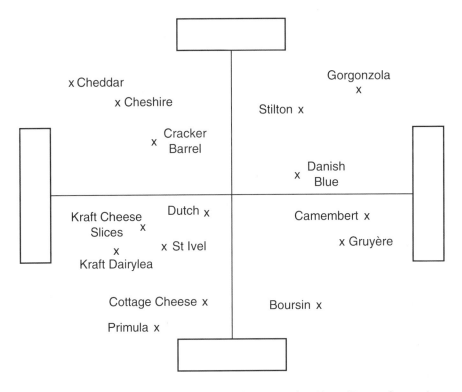

Figure 9.11 A non-metric map of the UK cheese market (from Trevor Sowrey).

less, the purpose of the chart is to see how closely the four competitors match up on major product positioning features. Any vehicle in the same segment that deviates significantly from the main competitive parameters must have a specific reason for doing so. It is a disadvantage to produce a new product priced in a segment head-on with other products and aimed at the same customer group if that product is deficient in a significant product feature of size or specification. In this comparison, the price ranges of all models lie very close to one another, except for the Sierra's price positioning advantage at the top end, based on a larger V6 engine. In 1992 many more competitors in this segment have V6s. The Accord is clearly the biggest car, the Volvo the smallest. Volvo also suffers from having only one engine size at the low end of the segment range.

For products such as personal computers, where performance-oriented features as well as size are important differentiators, a tabular form of comparison would be necessary though visually less informative. However, the product planner must always plan very carefully the steps from one product family to another, relationships with competitors and the spread of different models within one family. He must use whatever assessment tools are appropriate. If the products are positioned in a logical relationship to one another and to competition, they have a better chance of success. If the customer is confused by overlapping product ranges without separate feature or price justification, then he will not buy. However, smart positioning and specification planning can lower the product cost for the OEM and maximise visual value to the customer.

Positioning charts and perception maps come in many forms and are used in many industries. Figure 9.11 comes from the FMCG sector[2] and shows relationships between different brands of European cheese. Charting is a good way of showing the multi-dimensional relationships between products and, when combined with customer research, it is a good way of checking that a company's products are perceived by the customers in the planned positioning.

Trade-Off Analysis

The ability to decide between competing and often conflicting requirements within a new product programme is an important factor for success. With their multi-functional overview, product planners should be skilled in making trade-off decisions and having that skill accepted by the rest of the company. This is part of their professional stock-in-trade.

Trade-offs are more than just a financial evaluation since often situations cannot be totally evaluated in financial terms. Nevertheless, the criterion for good trade-off decisions is the benefit that accrues to the product throughout its life cycle and so the financial side is also important. It is a skill that comes only from being competent in analysis and from experience in as many aspects of the new product process as possible. Hence the really important trade-off decisions will be made by product managers or the programme director himself. What must be avoided are decisions that have a multi-functional effect but that are made within individual functional departments and often based on purely single function criteria. This has been a problem of functionally-based organisations that lack the benefits of team working, product planning or programme management help.

Two typical examples of trade-off decisions are described below.

1. *Car Wheel Trims*: This scenario concerns a car family with a range of different models that product planners and stylists want to differentiate as much as possible by external styling features. Thus a range of four wheel covers or trims is designed to cover the different models from family to

luxury to sporty to super premium. Since one of the difficult design features of wheel trims is a cost-effective and reliable method of attachment to the wheel rim, the engineer suggests a common outer rim for all designs with a clip-in centre section for the differently styled versions. He then only has to develop and test one rim.

This proposed rationalisation does not please the stylists who want form and depth in some versions, but not in others. Neither does it please the purchasing man, who has to fund an extra set of tooling for the common rim as well as separate inner sections for each version. The supplier is pleased because he can have one line for assembling the standard rim assembly and the added centre piece just in time to the customer's factory. The logistics man in the factory is also pleased: he can run with shorter inventory cycles. The cost target man, however, is unhappy because the extra tooling and the two-piece nature of the proposed wheel trims appears to break his cost targets.

This is a typical trade-off situation. The product planner must decide. In this case, the logistics, development and supplier benefits and savings won the day. But if the only criterion had been lower piece-cost then the one piece rims would have been preferred.

2. *A Range of Small Excavators*: A manufacturer of small hydraulic excavators planned a new range of models from 1.2 to 3.5 tonnes capacity. He wanted a combination of low cost and manufacturing commonality together with minimum engineering spend because his resources were limited. The key question was how many versions of each major system or component were required to span the total model range. Table 9.4 shows the main decisions made. These are typical configuration decisions which must be made right at the beginning of any new product programme where a range of sizes or performance levels is required from one product range. Other examples

| System | Model | | | | |
	1.2 tonne	1.5 tonne	2.2 tonne	3.0 tonne	3.5 tonne
Cab	1	1	2	2	2
Chassis	1	2	2	3	3
Arm	1	1	2	2	3
Tracks	1	1	2	2	2
Undercarriage	1	1	2	2	3
Engine/ Hydraulics	1	1	2	3	3

Table 9.4 System Variations in a Hydraulic Excavator Range

might include air compressors, industrial gearboxes, refrigeration units, personal computers.

The actual data shown in Table 9.4 are realistic but fictitious. The total product range contained far more system decisions where trade-offs were necessary.

Commentary: 1. The 1.2 tonne model was derived downwards from the 1.5 tonne model. Ideally, a large amount of re-engineering was required to achieve a lower cost price to preserve margins at the lower selling price. Since the 1.5 tonne model was itself a unique design because of the size and price restrictions in that market place, the extra volume of the 1.2 version plus some cost reduction of high cost items and some performance restriction provided an acceptable balance between lower costs, minimised engineering development costs, extra sales revenue and the risks of substitution with the 1.5 tonne model.

2. The cab for the two bottom models was common but too small and narrow for the higher ranges for which one new, wider, rationalised cab was designed.

3. The chassis needed three versions to cover the range, partly because of the wider 2.5 to 3.5 tonne models and partly because the extra loading demanded a fundamentally stronger design for three tonnes and above.

4. The digger boom, the undercarriage and the engine/hydraulics combination also each required three variants to span the five model range though some component and development commonality was achieved.

5. The track systems used only two variants of track link width and handled the greater weight of the larger models by spacing the front and rear drive axles in the undercarriage more widely.

Each of these final trade-off decisions would require a great deal of cross-functional engineering, costing, process discussion and product analysis work. There is, however, little commonality of experience between different manufacturers in this kind of decision making because of differing internal and external factors. What is common is the need to have available a qualified group of people to make the appropriate trade-offs for each new product programme.

Trade-off problems in an integrated product range such as this occur because, at one extreme, factory and logistic rationalisation and scarce development resources tend to push for maximum commonality between top and bottom models. This forces pressure on margins and makes the lower models loss-makers because they carry the unnecessary cost penalties of design standards aimed at the higher placed models.

Pressures from the market, customer and cost/margin ratios work in the opposite direction. These impulses demand that each model should be unique and have a design cost standard that reflects its own market segment requirements without penalties. In such a way, each model can be competitively priced and earn maximum profit.

Our examples are large, high profile instances of trade-offs that would be handled by a formal study process and perhaps even in a product policy committee. During the course of a typical product programme, however, there are many simpler, but no less important problems constantly presented to product planning for resolution.

Quality Function Deployment

QFD means translating the voice of the customer into the product. The essence of the product planning process also is to define customer-oriented products and programmes that engineers can turn into technical, process and product hardware to be produced profitably. Quality Function Deployment assists this process. This is a formalisation of what takes place in every company to decide on how to translate customer requirements into hard products. It originated in Japan but is now widely adopted both there and North America and is increasingly used in Europe, especially among electronic, computer and consumer products companies.

The QFD process is also about trade-offs because at each stage of QFD, conflicting requirements between what is wanted and what is possible are analysed against internal and external company criteria, preferably quantified, in order to arrive at a set of decisions that move the QFD process on to the next stage.

QFD 1: Product Planning: The first step is to match agreed customer "musts" and "wants" for a new product or part of a product against potential design, specification and quality requirements to arrive at a balanced result in which all conflicts have been resolved by prioritising programme needs and trading-off unachievable elements for achievable ones. A complete cross-functional team should participate in each of the four QFD phases – preferably the same people. The output of this stage is an agreed set of technical objectives containing specifications and design standards, together with some measurable test criteria for judging the relative importance of each feature including part and tooling costs.

QFD 2: Part Deployment: The next step is to turn these specification requirements into actual designs that meet other technical criteria such as reliability, tolerances, system needs. Shape, material and expected performance should also be specified.

QFD 3: Process Planning: The third step is to match these proposed design solutions against manufacturing process requirements. Of particular importance is identifying those process activities that could have a beneficial or harmful effect on the product standards laid down in QFD 2. As in all stages of the process, quantified criteria for measurement and comparison with existing or competitors' practice and with internal process requirements and standards should be used. The result of QFD 3 is an agreed set of product and process solutions designed to meet the original customer requirements.

QFD 4: Production Planning: The fourth step involves matching agreed process requirements against logistics, production, quality control and sales order processes and thus closing the loop back to the customer and ensuring that the plant has the tools to deliver the original customer requirement.

In fact, each company can choose the number of QFD phases. Some only use formally the first two, which are considered to be the most important. Others can use up to five. In addition, the phases can be carried out in part simultaneously to achieve more rapid time to market. They can also be merged with other multi-functional product development processes.

The QFD process uses a visual chart planning technique called the House of Quality. An extract from an actual QFD exercise to plan a new car seat makes up Figure 9.12, which is shown in the QFD 1 form.

The vertical axis of the so-called House of Quality contains the customer input requirements – the What – at the start of the exercise. They are expressed in plain language and the four illustrated are only a part of the complete analysis. The horizontal axis shows a number of possible specification or design requirements – the How – which could be built into the seat design. The boxes in the "house" itself show the degree of correlation between the specification features and the customer requirements. Thus, foam quality in the seat cushion will have a big influence on "feel" and seating comfort, but comfort will also be strongly influenced by the ergonomics of the seat. The "house" roof shows the correlation between the different technical solutions being studied. Here, for example, the seat suspension medium is shown to have a strong effect on three of the other parameters and is therefore one of the key specification items for an early decision. The correlation boxes help to identify the trade-off areas where compromise, or

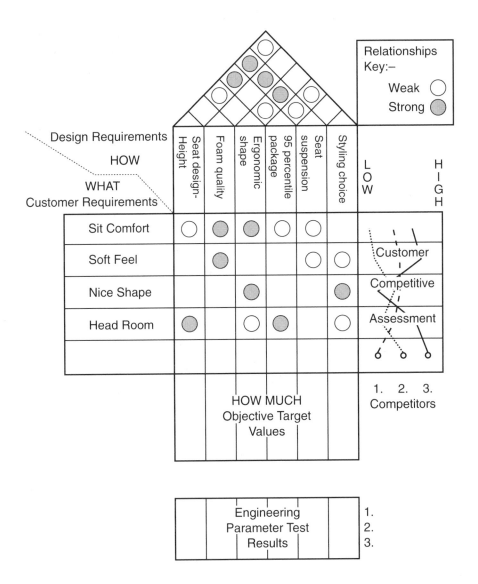

Figure 9.12 The House of Quality - Example of car seat exercise.

rather, optimisation decisions will have to be faced. The boxes to the right and below the main "house" contain quantified information on competitor rankings for each requirement, viewed from both the customer's and engineer's point of view, and cost or other target parameters, all of which will assist in formulating the most appropriate design specification for the seat.

The completed House of Quality becomes a structured information base to assist in the incorporation of customer requirements into a new product programme in a way that meets the company's combined objectives of cost, performance and quality. Thus in QFD 1, the real customer is represented; in QFD 2, the customer becomes the product planner looking to have his specifications met by the designer; and in QFD 3 the designer is the customer of the process engineers. The technique requires, at each stage, cross-functional working and that people from different disciplines sit together to understand each other's problems and requirements. Mutual decisions should be reached.

There is no room here to give a complete manual of QFD, but the technique nicely illustrates the creative conversion process that product planners must bring about. In Japan, QFD stands as a good example of the way they adapt and polish a common sense process into a fine management tool. There are many recognised courses for companies wishing to start using QFD and to train their people, or just to learn more about its benefits. ASI, the American Supply Institute, based in UK in Milton Keynes, is one of the largest companies offering them.

A summary of the key considerations for QFD use follows.

1. The customer requirements must be just that – not the voice of the engineer or product planner saying what he thinks the customer needs. Deciding on the real customer requirements is crucial and will be very difficult for a company using QFD for the first time. The initial customer in a QFD exercise can be any part of the organisation: the QFD technique is not just for use in designing consumer products.

2. Confusion between an internal product standard and a customer requirement should be avoided. For example, a requirement that a car seat should fit a 95 percentile male ergonomic profile is an engineering interpretation of the fact that customers come in different shapes and sizes. Even though it is dictated by customer requirements, this is not, in itself, a customer requirement. What the customer wants is comfort and space – as shown in Figure 9.12.

3. QFD analysis charts can get very large and unwieldy if a complete product or major multi-technology system is being studied. QFD is, therefore, more suited to self-contained components or systems rather than complete products.

4. Once a QFD analysis has been completed it represents a piece of company knowledge that is usable for the same type of component or system specified in other products. "Wheel inventing" can then be minimised in future product programmes and knowledge transfer from one programme to another can be

safeguarded. This principle can be seen at work often in Japanese cars where the same type of design solution or idea crops up time and again in different products both within the same manufacturer's range and even between competitors.

5. In the case of "sky blue" creative new product ideas, the technique is not so easy to apply since customer requirements are difficult to define for something of which the market has no knowledge. For this reason, QFD is more suitable for the improvement or replacement of existing products.

6. QFD means multi-functional team working and the sharing of responsibilities; it is not something that one department can pick up and do on its own. It is also a technique that requires training and discipline because its methodology is very formalised and precise. However, extensive use of QFD can assist in bringing about culture change in the new product development process.

7. The objective of a company in starting with QFD should be to make it part of the normal work process and not something added in from outside or imposed by management. If it remains a separate technique rather than being built into the thinking and working processes, it will not deliver its full potential.

The QFD technique is strongly recommended but companies trying it for the first time should choose carefully a product area in which it will show quick results. Accompanying culture and work process changes should also be taken on board at an early stage as part of the initial decision and training process.

Notes

1. Article by Chris Lorenz on John Deere's use of teamwork in improving product development performance, *Financial Times*, September 1991.
2. Trevor Sowrey, *The Generation of Ideas for New Products*, Figure 6.2 page 65, Kogan Page Ltd, 1987.

10 CASE STUDIES PRODUCT PLANNING AT WORK

> These case studies and examples use well known companies and products. Most describe successful product programmes and show the contribution made by different aspects of product planning excellence. Reference is also made to less successful products because good product planning lessons can be learned from failure as well as success. One case attempts to describe, using a much simplified version of the full product, the whole product planning process for a new diesel engine programme in order to bring out the inter-relationship of the cross-functional issues which arise. Other cases deal with cars, industrial and construction equipment, consumer electronic products, copiers and vacuum cleaners.

There are two main methods of demonstrating the worth of a particular management technique. The first is to describe what it is, how it works, where and when it is useful and why it is the right thing to do. This has been the primary approach used in this book so far and a large number of different perspectives on the product planning function have been presented. In each chapter describing the different viewpoints or cross-sections of product planning, a number of examples have illustrated the points raised. However, none of these constitutes a comprehensive specific case study. What follow now are some expanded examples of product planning at work.

This is the second way of proving a point: by showing how the various principles and skills of product planning work in practice. Yet it is not always the most successful products that offer the best examples of industrial practices so though I mention some household names widely regarded as successful, I also point to some products that could have been made better by the application of product planning expertise. In some ways, one can learn more from failed product cases than from brilliant successes.

Some failures have been executed brilliantly, by very capable people, except for one major input missing, one aspect badly planned, or one piece of bad luck or timing. Bad luck or timing cannot always be guarded against but the omission of good product planning principles, especially in the preparations for, and early stages of, a new product programme will undoubtedly jeopardise chances of success. In the cases that follow, it is possible to see where the application of a wide range of product planning skills and principles has been effective and where the major product planning success or failure criteria lie.

It would have been ideal to present a complete product planning history, showing the process in its entirety. However that would have occupied a book in itself, even supposing that the originator of that product would allow a full description of the programme, warts and all. As a compromise, Case Five describes the complete product planning process from first strategic conception to implementation for just two components in a product programme for a new family of diesel engines.

CASE ONE

Philips Consumer Electronics Division and the Product and Market Positioning of the Digital Compact Cassette

I am indebted to Philips Consumer Electronics Division, Eindhoven, for provision of material for this case study.

The Home Audio Market

In the market for pre-recorded music, three distinct product types have been in use since 1945. The vinyl record in various forms enjoyed its heyday up to 1983 when it was overtaken, in unit sales, by the analogue compact cassette. This product in turn was overtaken in 1991 by the compact disc.

The main characteristic of the cassette which the compact disc cannot reproduce is recordability by the consumer. The other difference is that the cassette is more widely used in portable players than the CD; in the car, in the open air and around the house. Hence there are really two distinct markets. First, the active, foreground, household music system, as now fulfilled mainly by the CD and previously by the vinyl record. Second, the portable system, fulfilled almost entirely by the cassette. For these reasons, cassette sales are not falling as fast as the vinyl sales did after the analogue cassette became established. Instead, the cassette market and the sale of cassette players has stabilised. Table 10.1 charts the sales of all three products from 1983 to 1991.

Million units	Vinyl	Cassettes	Compact Discs
1983	536	480	4.9
1986	390	608	131
1989	210	780	599
1991*	86	638	899
*Estimates		source: IFPI/BIS	

Table 10.1 World Shipments of Recorded Music Albums

Source: *Financial Times* July 10th 1992

In addition to pre-recorded cassettes, some 1.2 billion blank cassettes are purchased annually, together with some 180 million new cassette players of all types. This compares with a total population of CD players of some 120 million units after the product has been on sale for ten years. Therefore the cassette and player market is still extremely valuable. Consumer electronics companies' efforts to revitalise it are therefore sound.

The analogue cassette cannot achieve the highest recording quality by using digital techniques as the compact disc does. Nor are such features as direct track access, error correction and both digital recording and playback features available.

Two New Competitors

Two new contenders are now entering the market. The Sony Mini-Disc and the Philips Digital Compact Cassette (DCC) both offer high quality pre-recording and digital recording capability to the customer. Each, however, is a unique technical concept. Each will also try to carve a big niche for itself in the home audio market and, perhaps, create a new standard.

This situation has some similarities to the development of the video market in the Eighties when different players – Sony Betamax, Philips V2000 and JVC/Matsushita with the VHS system – offered slightly different product mixes to fulfil the same group of customer needs. The battle resulted in the eventual victory of the VHS system which is now the standard adopted by all producers.

The question is: what product characteristics of these two competitors, Philips and Sony, give them the best chance of success in the high quality pre-recorded and recording market?

Undoubtedly the market is at another change point because of the availability of a combination of digital technology and recordability. New technology usually gives companies an opportunity to change the rules in a market and both Philips and Sony must see this as such a moment.

The Mini-Disc

The compact disc market is the fastest growing of the two formats and the introduction of a recordable mini-disc by Sony might enhance that growth, as often happens when a second generation product enters the market. The fact that Sony are also the creators and market leaders in sales of the Walkman, for which the mini-disc is ideally suited, is another point in the product's favour.

On the other hand, the new mini-disc, being closely based around existing CD technology, will inevitably substitute for the compact disc if consumers are willing to commit their investment in the recording/playing equipment to the new format. Substitution may therefore be a negative factor in the development of the overall market. It could particularly affect the recording companies, for whom the current CD market growth must be very satisfying. In addition, the mini-disc players are unique and take no other disc. Nor can the mini-discs be played on current CD players.

The Cassette Market

The analogue cassette is running at a sales rate some 25 per cent lower than the compact disc but currently there are far more cassette players in use world-wide than compact disc players. This is due to the recording capabilities of the cassette, the fact that nearly all cars have cassette players and because most households have several multi-purpose radio/cassette players. Allied to this is the fact that compact discs are not as portable as cassettes for use in cars and around the house, so the cassette should still remain a valid long term product. CDs have a slight reputation for fragility and need careful handling but the cassette and its box, while being more portable than the CD, definitely has some durability problems of its own.

The Digital Audio Tape System (DAT)

Before looking at Philips creation of the DCC, I should add that in 1987 Sony and other manufacturers including Philips, introduced a consumer product, based around a digital audio tape system (DAT), which combined the qualities of high quality digital reproduction and recordability. The technology was complex, involving multiple recording heads to achieve high digital quality. However, the players involved brought yet another unique product form on to the market. Both Philips and Matsushita introduced DAT models and there were deep negotiations on common technical standards and music copyright protection leading up to the launch.

Despite competitive pricing for such a new product and strong efforts to make pre-recorded tapes available at launch, the product has not been successful. Sony is the main manufacturer with about one-third of the world market which may be as high as 200,000 player units in 1992. The company's product and market approaches were based around DAT's technical performance rather than real market and customer needs and DAT has been bought mainly by professional recording organisations and hi-fi enthusiasts and has not reached the mass market. In fact, there are some product characteristics of DAT that limit its application to the mass, lower cost market such as the complexity and cost of the player/recorders themselves and the difficulties in high speed recording for the pre-recorded tape market.

The Philips Product Planning Approach

In the meantime the product planners and marketeers at Philips have returned to basics and have evaluated what they and the consumer would really like in the cassette field.

The market for cassettes has already been shown to be both separate from CDs and in a mature stage. Philips' first objective, therefore, was to create a new development to revitalise the market in the 1990s.

From market research, it was clear that three characteristics of the cassette rated badly; image and attractiveness, sound quality and durability.

In addressing these product issues, Philips also established a number of other product strategy points that were to guide its product planning.

1. Any new hardware had to be capable of developing sales much faster than the CD player. This was necessary to create a customer demand base for the new digital cassettes themselves and to compensate for a drop in sales of the old analogue cassette which would inevitably occur with the launch of the DCC.

2. The potential low cost and price target for any new product meant that the design and technological drive should be for simplicity and ease of manufacture as well as for quality recording and playing performance.

3. The new product had to be backwards-compatible and attract not just the "novelty" customer, who always goes for the latest new product, but also the regular cassette customers, still buying 180 million new cassette player recorders each year.

4. The system had to include, from the start, the four main product elements of the current analogue systems: pre-recorded and blank cassettes, table-top, home cassette decks as well as portables and car systems. Unlike the CD player, the recording facility in the cassette units was found to be important to the customer since a very high proportion of players are bought incorporating a recording facility even though these are seldom used on many machines.

Product Planning and Realisation

These market and product strategy objectives were converted into objectives for the product itself.

1. The portable, outdoor aspect meant the choice of a standard low-coercive tape quality, with error correction built into the system and a protective sleeve for the tape.

2. The need for a large amount of pre-recorded music led to a linear track format, allowing high speed duplication.

3. The low cost design solutions required to reach a mass market quickly meant specifying relaxed tolerances in the player construction and the specification of no more than eight tracks for the DCC recording and playback system. This in turn allowed the use of carry-over technology, for example in tape mechanisms, where high reliability low cost components were already established.

4. Nevertheless, the need to hold high recording and playback standards and therefore to remain of interest to professional and serious users meant remaining competitive in performance with the CD, which, in turn, required a re-think both of the method of recording, to get more data into a smaller space and to devise a special head design using thin-film technology. This also enabled one head with eleven tracks to be made: eight for digital recording, two for reading analogue tapes and one for providing customer-related information in an LCD display on the player. Because the digital play back occurs through a buffer, controlled to an accurate clock speed, the well known "wow and flutter" of tapes is also eliminated.

With all the extra features and constraints, consumer tests still showed that the sound quality was perceived as equivalent to that of the CD.

5. The cassette itself was redesigned to be more robust, more temperature resistant, attractive to look at, more handleable and to conform to the same basic dimensions as the old-style cassette, only slightly slimmer. Access holes for the drive are on one side only and the graphic artwork for the pre-

recorded versions is sealed under a transparent window fused to the cassette. The new players can take both new and old cassettes, a very important consumer feature.

The Benefits for the Customer

With this technology and product planning approach, the DCC is a product that can ride on the back of, and enhance, the existing cassette market rather than make it obsolete. Old cassettes can be retained, new cassettes to the old analogue standard can still be bought and used on old or new players, and the gradual replacement of old cassette players and recorders by DCC versions can proceed at a speed the consumer will accept because he controls it; his old system and tapes remain usable whatever he decides. However, this growth in the population of DCC players is likely to be quite rapid. Currently, the cassette player market is in the replacement phase of the product cycle and a large number of replacement players are bought each year. This seems to be a very fundamental difference between the product and market positioning of Sony's Mini-Disc and Philips' DCC. The latter also can ride on the back of the DAT market, such as it is, by offering itself as a second generation, more user-friendly and mass market development.

Philips' own consumer research showed the need for a product to replace the cassette tape and they have developed their DCC ideas from a customer-driven approach. They have also learnt the lessons of DAT which was far too technology-driven. They have laid great emphasis on having a wide variety of pre-recorded music available at launch. As many as 500 titles were ready. It was hoped that this would avoid completely one of the problems – lack of pre-recorded tapes – which influenced the final choice of VHS as the consumer video standard as well as causing the slow start in DAT equipment sales.

Pricing and Positioning

The initial launch prices for both DCC and mini-discs have shown a slight advantage to the mini-disc. Sony is offering a player in Japan at a price eqivalent to $465 and a player recorder at $650. The launch price for the Philips DCC 950, the table-top model, is set at £540 in the UK and at a dollar equivalent in Japan of $799. In Japan and Europe the Matsushita price is $999 for a table-top model and somewhat lower for a portable.

It is not possible to conclude anything from this but if the Philips market research and product planning has been well-founded, and it seems to be, then the mini-disc will perhaps need a lower price to compete.

This is a classic illustration of the connection between developing the right kind of technology, acquiring the right understanding of customer needs on as broad a front as possible and the right product planning approach to create a potential winner.

CASE TWO

The Hydrovane Compressor Company, Redditch: Planning the Successful Introduction of a New Air-Compressor Range

I am indebted to Hydrovane for permission to use this case study first presented at a London conference on new product development in 1989.

Hydrovane, which specialises in the manufacture of sliding vane compressors, forms part of the CompAir Division of Siebe plc. This study describes improvements in product planning and product development processes developed over several new model programmes. The following description relates mostly to the new 9 Series compressor range, comprising four models that deliver from 296 to 410 cfm (cubic feet per minute).

The drive to introduce new products in a different, more effective way came from a realisation in 1987/88 that the company had to perform a complete overhaul of their product planning and product introduction processes.

Studies of competition, customer requirements and the needs of their distribution showed that success in their markets was based on staying competitive technically, converting new technology into product features and controlling costs. In such a way, distribution would be motivated to sell more product and the company would be more profitable. In fact, Harry Craig, the company's engineering director, decided that change was inevitable because their historic approach had not yielded the right product, at the right time, at the right cost: the classical product planning challenge.

When he looked at their internal processes to find out why this might be, Harry Craig concluded that there were several different problem areas:

- The initial product and project objectives at the start of each new project were not clear enough.
- The process involved too much sequential or "over the wall" project activity.
- The company spent too little at the front end of projects and therefore encountered too many problems downstream.

- The company was not clear on the use it could or should make of supplier capabilities.
- The company carried out insufficient testing and thus the production launch was always disturbed by last minute changes and releases.
- They company had an inadequate management visibility of the progress of new projects – both from a control and a communication point of view.

These are all well known problems of the new product process which Hydrovane decided to eliminate so far as possible in the development of their new 9 Series range.

The Hydrovane Approach

The problems were attacked in four different ways.

1. They used the already existing product policy committee to approve planning and specification details and to monitor the introduction of the new project.
2. They spent time researching the market so as to start the project with a clearly-defined set of product objectives.
3. They created the position of product planning manager to ensure effective project planning, monitoring and programme communication.
4. They organised a team for the project and supporting systems to allow the team to work efficiently. The team included creative and marketing people at the outset but they varied the team personnel to suit each stage of the project.

Product Planning

Improved product planning quality at the front end of the project was achieved by specifying the essential information that was to be available before the project could officially start.

- A detailed product specification.
- Volume projections including specific export territory needs.
- Cost targets and selling price projections.
- Styling and product image objectives.
- Crucial product performance targets and features.
- Project time targets.
- Capital and budget cost requirements.
- A full feasibility and return on capital analysis.

Project Planning and Control

Project planning and monitoring were greatly helped by the use of a Hoskyns Project Manager Workbench package to control time, cost and manpower. In addition to this, Hydrovane created a separate project data base that included an advanced parts list, supplier data, key project dates, functional responsibilities, project and product costs and cost tracking. This was for the exclusive use of the team until the time came to release the product into the company's main line systems. This gave them all the essential information for effective project management and led to more comprehensive data for management than previously had been available.

Successful Results

There is no doubt that this structured approach greatly helped in avoiding misunderstandings and time wasting because of lack of clarity about responsibilities and objectives.

This study is interesting because of the way that Hydrovane tackled the complete process from the first concept to successful introduction – driven by the knowledge that they *had* to improve. The company put big emphasis on the need to "do more early", on customer analysis, product positioning and product definition. These are essential ingredients of good product planning practice. The company also intends to continue improving its product planning and development processes in each succeeding programme.

CASE THREE

The Land Rover Discovery. Introducing a New-to-the-Market Product with Maximum Use of Carry-over Engineering.

I am indebted to Land Rover for contributing information to this case study.

The Land Rover Discovery, launched in November 1989, has been rightly praised for its attractive and customer-oriented design and for its success in the UK and Europe at a time when other models were having difficulties because of adverse market conditions. It is also widely reported as being a product programme that was executed quickly and efficiently using the latest techniques of team working, simultaneous engineering, early involvement of suppliers and modern computer-aided design and manufacturing systems.

The following stages in the initial product strategy and planning work describe the main elements of the programme and the excellent up-front planning that was a major contributor to high quality programme execution.

Effective Programme Planning

Market studies in the period up to 1986 showed the potential in Europe for a vehicle in the middle segment of the specialised four wheel drive market, at that time dominated by Japanese models.

A concept study group was set up in spring 1986 to study what kind of product could attack the market opportunity. Vehicles in this class were more used in substitution for upper class family saloons and less as true agricultural or off-road vehicles, so the studies had to embrace both off-road vehicle and saloon car characteristics.

The design brief followed two months later. It showed that an all-new interior geared to the tastes of target customers was required. For speed in market introduction, the new exterior styling had to be based on the existing Range Rover package, but it had to look as individual as possible.

The first clay model was ready in autumn 1986 and the programme was approved for implementation by the board at the end of 1987. In that intervening fourteen months a full scale multi-disciplinary team under a programme manager had been working out all details of the product and its implementation programme. They strove for the maximum certainty of success and the minimum of risk prior to the final board approval. This involved in-house design and test work but the team also made the best use of external resources by bringing suppliers' capabilities in early. Also present were the skills of an independent design house, Conran Design, which advised on the interior.

Rapid Launch Timing

Since the market launch took place in November 1989, that meant just under three years from concept clay to production start – a very competitive lead time for a programme that effectively created a new vehicle in a new market sector.

The Discovery is admirable as a vehicle. The professionalism and speed of the whole of its product creation programme was of the highest order. However, the most significant product planning aspect of the Discovery programme is the team's clever use of carry-over engineering from existing models. Starting from a clean sheet of paper, it would have been impossible to achieve that speed of introduction for a complete new vehicle. Yet the Discovery presents itself to the customer as all-new.

I mentioned in Chapter Nine the value of clever carry-over product planning between old and new models. The part number itself can carry over and the manufacturing process itself can be carried over with a modified component. Alternatively, just the essential elements of the design can be utilised for the new model with all part numbers and manufacture being new. The design carry-over is the key time and development cost saver. That is what happened in the case of the Discovery. I have said that many apparently new Japanese cars have a very high degree of carry-over from previous or sister models. Likewise, the Discovery was based largely on the Range Rover package and body/chassis layout. Even so, it was developed as a separate model and presented and fully accepted in the market as a unique model – albeit with a strong Land-Rover family resemblance.

It is normally good product planning practice to stretch new products up from smaller cheaper ones and so get a low cost base for a new product that can then be sold at a higher price. Deriving a vehicle downwards from the base of a more expensive brother runs the risk of carrying unnecessary cost and weight penalties. But it can be done. The BMW 7 Series and the 5 Series have many parts and systems in common including major parts of the underbody. The larger 7 Series entered production first, so the 5 Series was "stretched" downwards from the 7 Series.

In stretching a new product up from a smaller one, if too much carry-over from a cheaper to a dearer vehicle is apparent to the customer, this can have an adverse effect on the image and perceived price value of the new product. The Discovery was derived from the package of the Range Rover, a much more expensive and up-market product. I cannot imagine, however, that Land Rover would have worried if any of the Range Rover image rubbed of on the price perception of the Discovery. That would only enhance its value for money qualities.

The derivation of one model from the other was very successful, as the following two tables show. Table 10.2 compares the main package dimensions of the two vehicles; Table 10.3 compares the respective prices and model line up in the UK market as at September 1992.

Dimensions and Price Comparison

The width, wheelbase and track are very close between the two vehicles. The Discovery is slightly longer but that can be accounted for by the modern bumper design and the spare wheel mounting on the tailgate. The Discovery is also higher because of the kick-up in the rear roof profile, which is raised to give more window area and light for rear passengers. On the road, the Range Rover and the Discovey retain their individual character.

	Discovery	Range Rover
Length (mm)	4521	4450
Width (mm)	1793	2080
Track (mm)	1487	1487
Wheelbase (mm)	2540	2540
Max. Height (mm)	1928	1835
Kerb Weight-4Door. (kg)	1986	1967
Fuel Capacity (galls)	18	18

Table 10.2 Product Comparison: Range Rover and Discovery

Model	Discovery	Range Rover	Model
3-Door Tdi	£17760	£25326	4-Door Turbo D
3-Door V8i	£18454	£27365	4-Door Vogue Turbo D
5-Door Tdi 'S'	£20721	£28999	4-Door Vogue 'S'
5-Door V8i 'S'	£21417	£34528	4-Door Vogue 'SE'

Table 10.3 Retail Price Comparison: Range Rover and Discovery (Prices valid at September 1992)

To achieve a price difference for the base diesel model of 43 per cent from Range Rover to Discovery, or of 46 per cent between the lowest priced models with the V8 petrol engine, is a very considerable product planning achievement. It was no doubt based partly on design specification and manufacturing changes built into the more modern vehicle design. The Range Rover, after all, had been in production for nearly 20 years. The level of specification required in the Discovery market segment would also be lower than that of the Range Rover. However, the targeting of more efficient processes of manufacture, the use of supplier skills to optimise purchased component costs and the design cost targeting of all the new components against the market requirements were obviously carried out very well to retain profitability in the much lower priced Discovery market segment.

It is also clear that by basing the new vehicle on the package and chassis layout of the tried and tested Range Rover, there had been a considerable saving in new design and development costs and perhaps some tooling. There was also the benefit of accelerated introduction timing. Thus the appropriate carry-over elements of the Range Rover were married with the all new elements targetted at the customer needs in the Discovery market sector.

The Product Planning Achievement

I do not say that the Discovery is in any way a cut down Range Rover: it is a vehicle in its own right, with its own character, and it probably shares few part numbers with its big brother. However, it shares those appropriate elements of the Range Rover engineering history that have helped to shape both the new vehicle and the efficiency of the development programme which created it. Speed of implementation and cost saving are part of the benefits gained but the use of carry-over components in a new vehicle will also enhance its quality, reliability and profitability.

That is really creative planning of a product. It represents a degree of partnership between the product planning, design engineering and process engineering functions that is often hard to achieve but which gives outstanding results when it works.

CASE FOUR

Electrolux UK: The Development of a Successful New Vacuum Cleaner

I am indebted to Electrolux UK for their help in compiling the details of this case study.

The European white goods market has over the last ten to fifteen years seen a great deal of rationalisation and consolidation of the competing companies.

AEG is now part of the Daimler Benz group. A second large German grouping contains Bosch, Siemens and Neff. GE of America and the British General Electric Company have merged their white goods interests into GDA, General Domestic Appliances. Whirlpool, the largest American company, has recently acquired the interests of Philips. Meanwhile, Europe's largest white goods company, the Swedish Electrolux group, has been steadily acquiring other major European brands including Thorn and the Italian Zanussi. Based on 1991 revenues the league table in Europe is shown in Table 10.4.

Electrolux has four main product divisions: in the UK, floorcare, refrigeration, cooking and washing. In 1986, the floorcare division launched a new product that had a dramatic effect on their fortunes in the market. This was the 600 series upright vacuum cleaner which included built-in tools, and was the first to do so.

1. Electrolux	$3,930
2. Bosch-Siemens	$3,525
3. Whirlpool	$2,250
4. Miele	$1,538
5. AEG	$1,474
6. Thompson EM	$1,138
7. Gen. Electric	$1,032

Table 10.4 The European White-Goods Manufacturers (Sales, $millions)

Source: *Financial Times*, June 24th 1992

The effect of this new development was to increase the market for models with built in tools; 17 per cent in 1987, 55 per cent in 1990 and up to 70 per cent today. It also caused competitors, notably Hoover and National Panasonic, to react with similar but lower priced products.

A Product-Led Strategy

For its next major initiative, designed to counter this competitive action, Electrolux decided on another product-led strategy. Regular investigation of market trends and consumer preferences indicated a requirement for different styling, more performance and features and an opportunity to go for a younger group of customers in addition to satisfying their existing customer base in the 32-45 age bracket.

The strategic product and marketing objectives of the new programme were laid out as follows.

- To create a range of products which, through design and image, would give the products a unique profile in retailer's showrooms.
- To position Electrolux as brand leader in the upright market by the end of 1991.
- To incorporate productivity improvements in the new product to reduce costs in all areas of manufacturing.
- To broaden the Electrolux appeal to younger customers.
- To further enhance product quality to meet global quality control standards.

This was followed by a design brief that further refined the product and marketing objectives for the industrial design and engineering people and included such elements as differentiation from competitors, styling trends, customer requirement and feature content, ergonomics, cost targets and image positioning.

The resulting product broke new ground in styling terms with its integrated body and handle and neat rear compartment storage for tools. It also provided all user features in an economical design form, combining a high quality image and improvements in cost effectiveness both in design and production. Two basic models, the Contour 1410 and the Contour Pulse 1450 (now the 1460) were created, together with a range of options.

Rapid Results in the Market

What is impressive is the way this new product allowed Electrolux quickly to realise its objectives in the market.

- Market share of the upright sector rose by seven percentage points at the expense of its main competitor.
- In April and May 1991, Electrolux became brand leaders in the upright market.
- The new product had a tractor effect on the rest of Electrolux business. Total share in the floorcare market increased to market leadership in six out of seven months in 1991. There are signs that this success is continuing in 1992.
- The positioning strategy has also been successful with the new product in that the top two price/product sectors – £120-140 and above £140 retail price – have increased their proportion of the total market by sixteen and three per cent respectively.
- Lastly, the new styling of the product is evidently more attractive to a higher proportion of younger buyers than are traditional Electrolux products.

Further premium products are being launched higher in price, performance and features than the 1460 model. Electrolux continues to pick up awards from design and consumer organisations. So it is clear that the product, design and marketing strategy of Electrolux with their Contour range has been fully succcessful and has created a base they can continue to build on.

New Products as the Drivers of Success

Floorcare Product Manager, Elisabeth Farmer sums it up as follows: "Electrolux has never been brand leader in uprights before and we believe our success is due to Contour's distinctive showroom presence. Basically, it's the right product for the market. If the product is not right, it does not matter how much you spend trying to promote it."

The Contour project is testimony to Electrolux's long term commitment to investment in the development of new competitive products. By fostering an atmosphere in which success is perceived to emerge from new product generation, Electrolux encourages bold strategic steps within its product development organisation.

CASE FIVE

Component Product Planning for a Multi-Purpose Family of Diesel Engines

Introduction

This product planning case history charts the development of a new family of diesel engines by one of the world's leading manufacturers of diesel engines. This company manufactures several different engine families at their home factory in a horsepower range from 30 to 200. These same engines are made in several overseas licensee operations and are sold to a wide variety of industrial product makers for whom the expense of designing and producing their own diesel engines for every one of their needs is too great. The company did not wish to have its name specifically mentioned in the case study, but the events and actions described are based on a real new product programme.

The company's customers include multi-national and major European companies making motor vehicles, construction equipment, agricultural machinery, stationary and mobile industrial equipment and work and pleasure boats. The company also has an extensive world-wide network of distributors who sell engines direct to medium and small sized customers.

The case study deals with the product planning of two groups of components in a new engine engine family: the exhaust and inlet manifold assemblies. By limiting the components described, the cross-functional planning and decision issues can be illustrated clearly. Trying to focus on the whole product would only make the explanation too complex.

Product Complexity in Manufacture

An issue which that had caused the company problems during the 1970s and 1980s was the high degree of product complexity in its plants, due not only to the number of engine families but also to the component variety within each engine type. This arose because many customers needed a special version of the engines to satisfy their own product installation requirements. It was in the optional installation components attached to the basic engine that much of the component complexity lay.

In order to maximise their competitiveness and penetrate markets all over the world, the company had a policy of tailoring the engines to customer requirements. The application engineers, who advised customers on how to install the engines into vehicles or machinery, often had to design new components to satisfy certain specific customer configurations. This enabled them to propose an optimum technical solution for the customer. It also meant that component variety expanded. The company saw that this was beginning to have an adverse effect on inventories and product costs and on the company's ability to deliver specific batches of engines on time to meet specific customer needs. This last point was critical because a diesel engine is only a component, though a major one, in someone else's product. Unreliable delivery meant that the customers could not manufacture their own products. In the short term, it was not possible for them to go elsewhere because the diesel engines were tailored to fit their products.

The problems were particularly acute on the two most successful engines – let us call them the X9 and X10 – which were both built in high volume and sold into all the main application types. The company first tried many short term measures to reduce variety and improve delivery reliability. These efforts were always limited by the fact that these two engine families were already designed and running in production. Therefore major configuration changes were impossible to consider. A strict rationalisation and reduction of low volume components was also out of the question since the special components were tailored to customers' products which could not be re-designed overnight. However, when the time came, in the early 1980s, to plan a successor range to these two engines the company management decided that the new range should not repeat the component proliferation of the X9 and X10. Product planning therefore took a careful look at how best to proceed to overcome the complexity problems from the start.

The Approach for the New Engine Range

In the automotive industry, the product offered to the customer is usually pre-designed and configured from a menu of options aimed at satisfying the widest possible spread of requirements within a rationalised design, manufacturing and logistic approach. It seemed, therefore, that a similar approach could be the basis of the new product and option structure for the new family of engines.

In 1982 the terms of reference were laid down by management for a new family of engines to replace the X9 and X10. We will call this the X20 programme. The X20 was an integrated and common range of four and six cylinder diesel engines. The X20 project started in 1982 and went into production in 1986.

For the new engine it was not possible to make a completely clean start because the new engine family had to be manufactured on the same basic facilities as the X9 and X10. Although some plant upgrades were allowed, the old engines also had to be produced on these facilities. This meant that many of the principal dimensions and layout features of the old engines had to be retained. In addition the performance of the new engines had to be enhanced with power and torque up 13 per cent and 17 per cent respectively and fuel consumption improved by 8 per cent. Manufacturability and cost levels also had to be improved.

To start off the new programme, product planning set out to rationalise and optimise the way the base engine offering and options would be planned, designed, specified, procured and offered to the customer. This was to ensure that component proliferation could be controlled as a major programme objective from the start and that the early buy-in of all the company functions to the programme objectives would be achieved. The steps in the programme were as follows.

A Detailed Market and Competitive Analysis

The programme started with a very thorough analysis of all market sectors in which the new product was to be sold. The sector characteristics, the volumes and trends, the base engine characteristics and the future performance needs both from legislation and the users were all carefully collected and screened.

The new engine was targetted at the existing X9 and X10 customer base as well as at new customers due to its enhanced performance. The current and future properties, performance and design characteristics of the major engine options were examined so as to obtain a view of the degree of product complexity that would be needed to satisfy market needs. This was checked against the current X10 and X9 option offering and customer requirements as well as against the main competition. In particular, the product planners wanted to ascertain the reasons for the different option versions and to distinguish between options that were segment-specific and those which were customer-specific. In particular, they were on the look out for multi-customer versions of the options.

Item	Old X9/X10 Family	New X20 Family	Reduction %
Ratings (Fuel pumps)	160	80	50
Transmissions	2	2	0
Flywheel housings	87	8	91
Flywheels	85	17	80
Starter Motors	47	12	74
Oil-filter & coolers	30	20	33
Crank Pulleys	24	5	79
Water Connections	16	3	81
Fans	36	8	78
Alternators	28	3	89
Induction Manifolds	33	16	52
Exhaust Manifolds	23	11	52

Table 10.5 X20 Diesel Programme: Old and New Option Variety

Product planning targets for design engineering

This comprehensive specification and option analysis enabled the product planners to define an idealised but rationalised option range as the engineering team's target, complete with cost and investment objectives, performance requirements and a statement of key competitor features. There then followed an iterative design, costing, process, purchasing, product planning discussion in which various alternative technical approaches were schemed and evaluated. One of the key targets was a reduction in option variety. Table 10.5 shows how the old numbers of optional components and the new targets compared. The reductions sought were considerable. The aim was a significant reduction in logistics and manufacturing costs as well as a reduced design and tooling investment for the new product.

To simplify the issues involved, this case will concentrate on just two component groups: the exhaust and inlet manifolds. In real life the complete analysis and planning task had to be carried out on several different base engine configurations as well as on all the option groups shown in Table 10.5. This illustrates the complexity of the initial product planning task which is not, as some think, a simple one-off definition of the products the customer wants but, rather, a thorough analysis and decision making process to find the most effective way for a company to provide those wants.

Analysis of Customer Needs

Product rationalisation is of no value if it results in reduced choice for customers and the eventual loss of business. In parallel, therefore, to the internal design and manufacturing engineering discussions, the possible customer impact of a reduced option list was evaluated. Specifications and configurations in production were compared with the new option offering. Thanks to the quality of the initial option and market analysis, a high percentage of customer specifications could be switched to the new engines without creating cause for concern. The difficult specifications were then singled out for more detailed evaluation. A benefits package was worked out to enable sales engineers to sell the new rationalised configurations to their customers and the final design and test programme of the new options was started. The reduction in total components was originally earmarked by management as one of the key programme targets: tight product introduction timing depended on the maintenance of the planned variety levels.

The Product and Process Solutions

The product design and manufacturing solution chosen for inlet and exhaust manifolds was ingenious and economic and overcame many of the problems of excess component variety. Base components were designed with adaptor parts which could be quickly fitted in the factory with computer controlled fixtures and modern engineering adhesives, yielding a good variety of different layouts from a small number of base components. Thus the manufacturing variety for the suppliers of the base components was considerably reduced and the company plant was asked to produce the correct option part number only at the time the component was needed on the assembly track; in effect, an in-house just in time approach. Plant inventories and work in progress were also considerably reduced by this rational, planned product range and the cost structure of the different manifold options was similarly controlled. Supplier inventories could also be reduced. Likewise, the number of schedule changes and last minute requests they would receive for component deliveries, since the plant would make the final sub-assembly operation which determined the final part number.

Sales Aids for Technical Sales

At a certain point in the product programme, it was necessary for the salesforce to introduce the new engine concept to customers and to encourage them to include it in their new products or install it as an upgrade for existing machines. To assist in this, product planning prepared an advanced prod-uct launch briefing pack for the sales force. Besides describing the product range in full detail, the launch pack and the sales training sessions emphasised the market and product analysis that produced the specification and option levels and why the rationalised range was strategically necessary for the company. Maintenance of the targetted variety levels was clearly important during this phase of the programme. It would not have been acceptable for the customers to demand, or for the sales force to allow, a completely different set of options to the ones already designed and planned. This position was safeguarded by three key points.

1. The quality of the market and competitive analysis which ensured that a very high proportion of future customer demands were already covered by the pre-defined option offering.

2. The pre-check against existing customer specifications which showed that most of them fell within the new reduced complexity option range.

3. A system that allowed the company to evaluate the costs and benefits of new option requests so that the customer could decide whether to accept the disadvantages and extra price of a special version. Alternatively, of course, he could modify his own vehicle or machine installation to take a standard component. This last point was of paramount importance in keeping the proliferation of unplanned options down to a minimum whilst still satisfying the customer.

The Involvement of Suppliers

During the development of the product, discussions were held with key suppliers to obtain their input. On the manifolds in particular, bad supplier experience with product variety in the past stimulated a host of suggestions that contributed to a more rational and more cost effective range of options and a more efficient logistic and manufacturing process.

Two major supplier roadshows were mounted; the first focusing on the strategic objectives of the programme and getting suppliers to buy-in to the idea of cost reduction. The second was a more operational discussion on the benefits of low variety and a move towards single sourcing of components. These contacts helped to ensure that suppliers contributed their ideas and commited their efforts to the programme at an early stage.

Component group	Original X9 & X10 Models	New X20 Target	1986 Plan X20	Development status @ 4/86 X20
Inlet Manifolds and Turbochargers	33	16	4	5
Induction Manifolds and Air Filters			16	13
Exhaust Manifolds	23	11	11	10

Table 10.6 Progress Towards Manifold Variety Reduction; X20 Diesel Programme

Variety Reduction Progress

Table 10.6 shows the progress on the variety of manifolds at two stages in the programme compared to the old engines and the new targets. These variety numbers are shown at option code level. Since several options could be produced from one base component with in-factory adaptations, the actual component and tooling reductions due to the product rationalisation was even more impressive.

Conclusion

This case shows how the effects of good product planning can work to the benefit of all departments contributing to a new product programme as well as helping external suppliers. Almost all the excessive variety and the supply problems identified in the old product offering were eliminated by the quality of the up-front planning and analysis and the design briefs for component engineering that resulted. A repeat of the component proliferation, which had occurred after production start on the old products, was also avoided by putting in place an effective training and decision making process once the programme reached the stage of customer contact and buy-in.

To return to the company's original concern about product proliferation: the effectiveness of product planning in creating rational product ranges requires that their input comes right at the start of a programme and not after the programme has started or the product is in production. The cost of making good decisions early is very low compared to the costs and problems involved in re-designing and rationalising products later. This is especially true with industrial products where the users of the products are committed to the design configuration of that product fitting with their own products and equipment.

This case study shows a company making great strides in customer-oriented planning between old and new products. This enabled them to reap a variety of benefits in terms of component rationalisation, ease of scheduling and manufacture, reduced inventories and manufacturing costs and, above all, an improved product and service for the customers.

CASE SIX

Canon Copiers: The Development of the Small Personal Copier Market

I am indebted to Arthur D.Little, the international management consulting firm, for permission to use this case study which first appeared in their brochure *Managing Product Creation* in 1989.

'Canon was number one in medium and small copiers. Management was convinced that growth would come from smaller copiers rather than larger systems. Would there be a market for personal copiers, as there is for personal computers? The size of the market, if it developed, would be enormous, and well worth the development effort. Thanks also to its strong retail distribution, Canon would be uniquely positioned to sell personal copiers.

Preliminary research was undertaken to discover key market requirements. The results indicated that the market would develop under two conditions.

- First, personal copiers should be priced below $1000.

- Second, they should be literally service-free. A single service call on a personal copier would wipe out all the cost benefits of having such a machine at home.

Many companies – and Canon's competitors were no exception – would have given up if confronted with such a formidable challenge. Canon's management decided it was worth a try. They immediately focused their innovation efforts on two critical areas; low cost and service-free operation.

Existing copier concepts with their drum and toner system, required service. All competitors recognised this and focused on reducing service requirements, not on eliminating them. Canon therefore, decided to focus on real service-free copiers and a major corporate innnovation project was launched around this objective.

The research programme was extensive.

- Externally, management needed to find out what customers really meant by low cost service-free copiers. The answer came back loud and clear. Service-free did not really mean no service at all. It meant that all servicing should be done by the user himself without the intervention of external service staff.

- Internally, management focused its research on the origin of the high cost and service requirements of the original copier concept. The answer was encouraging. One element, the drum/toner assembly, was responsible for both a large part of the cost and most service calls on current copiers.

Canon management then set up innovation teams with the objective of finding a new concept to replace the current drum/toner assembly. They wanted a design that would be cheaper and user serviceable. Several innovation teams were set up in parallel because management wanted to explore all possible ways of meeting the target.

The breakthrough ultimately achieved by Canon with its personal copier was to re-design entirely the drum/toner assembly, and to come up with a user-replaceable low-cost cartridge. Canon was also aware that its product innovation would soon be copied unless it was protected by a proprietory, patentable manufacturing process.

Overall, more than 200 people worked over four years to allow Canon to achieve its personal copier breakthrough. Market results were worth it. The Canon copier was a superb example of focused innovation. In 1987 the company sold more than 400,000 personal and home copiers worldwide, capturing the bulk of the world's market.

Like other successful innovators Canon started work on successor products even before it had launched the new personal copier. Its objective was to develop a second generation of smaller, lighter and cheaper copiers for home applications. By this move, Canon was protecting itself from competitors undermining it from below.

Having made the first breakthrough with the first drum/toner cartridge, it was easy for the company's development department to improve its concept and come up with an even smaller, cheaper cartridge.

Canon was ready to introduce its second generation of home copiers just as competitors were launching their first generation. At the same time the company exploited the principle of product proliferation, adapting its drum/toner cartridge for use in smaller laser printers and, latterly microfilm printers.'

This is a fine case example of three aspects of the product planning process.

First, is the effective use of product/market analysis to understand exactly the customers' requirements before starting engineering.

Second, the advanced product planning approach to direct the technical innovation search for product features that could make feasible the new product concept. The parallel innovation teams idea also speeded up and sharpened the quality of the technical solutions.

Third, there was the product planning of a second generation product before the first generation reached the market to anticipate and fight off the first wave of the expected competitive response.

CASE SEVEN

Examples of Less Successful Product Planning

The Market for Home Video Player-Recorders

One of the most interesting examples of competition in the consumer durables market has been in the market for video recorders and players. At the beginning, three companies came out with their own systems – the Sony Betamax, the Philips V2000 and the VHS system originally by JVC, part of Matsushita, but later made by almost all competitors in the market.

The Philips product is said to have been the first available. Philips certainly believed it to be technically better than the competitors. A number of European manufacturers also signed up with Philips to produce video recorders using the V2000 format.

The Sony product was also thought, by the Sony engineers, to be better than competition. Indeed, Akio Morita acknowledges in *Made in Japan*[1] that it was, in fact, too good technically, with its two reading heads, and that it cost too much, while focusing on the wrong product elements to be sure of success.

The VHS system manufacturers however, while ensuring that the product was technically, and from a quality and consumer point of view, fully acceptable to the market, though not as technically advanced as the other two, concentrated on the in-use qualities of their product by ensuring that a high volume of recorded video material was available for their customers to rent or buy and that the VHS recorders were widely available in the retail network. The wide availability of recorded material alone must have had a big influence on the eventual victory for the VHS system which is now the only consumer video standard, since between the three original systems no major differences were visible in the recorder products themselves or in their physical user interfaces.

In this case, the planning of the less successful products concentrated too much on the technology or characteristics of the product itself rather than on the customers' needs or the total environment in which the product was to be used. The parallels between this case and the launch of the Sony Mini-Disc and the Philips Digital Compact Cassette are interesting.

The Sinclair C5 Electric Vehicle

Sir Clive Sinclair has been responsible for a stream of new products, many of them breaking new ground technologically or conceptually. In the case of the Sinclair C5 electric vehicle however, product planning input could have improved the end result.

Technologically and from a manufacturing point of view, the project was well-conceived. A one/two person vehicle suitable for electric power by virtue of its low weight. The small, city electric car runabout had been long awaited. Was this it?

The manufacturing was sub-contracted to a manufacturer whose plant already had handled the same components, materials and assembly processes that the C5 demanded. Thus the reliance on an existing technology and investment base for production speeded up the launch and kept the break-even as low as possible.

However, any sensible evaluation of the product concept and configuration carried out by experienced product planners would surely have modified or stopped the project either at the concept planning stage, at the styling and design approval stage, or at the customer research stage. Just imagining the effect of the small low-slung C5 product operating in its intended environment of suburban traffic should have sounded alarm signals. The imagination and experience to see critically the potential effects of a product in both its manufacturing, retail marketing and user environment should be one of the primary qualities of the product planner. In the case of the C5, the focus was too strongly directed on the technical derivation and manufacture.

The Advanced Passenger Train (APT)

Someone in British Rail did some excellent product planning on the APT – at least in the initial concept work. The objective was to design a train that would have superior performance compared to the interim design of the High Speed 125 trains, but which would still run on the standard British track layout.

The economic and infrastructural sense of this as an objective was shown by France's subsequent success with their high speed train, the TGV. This has required the building of a dedicated high speed track and, though successful, has had a serious environmental impact on the French countryside and has been very expensive in terms of infrastructure investment. The need to construct new permanent way everywhere has also been a hindrance to getting the full European network in place within a reasonable time frame.

The problem with the APT was the tilting mechanism deemed necessary to bring the vehicle around the curves of existing track at high speeds. Despite the large amount of time and money spent on the project and the fact that a version briefly reached passenger service, potential customer reactions to such a novel idea should have been evaluated much earlier. With a proper product planning, decision and risk evaluation process, this would have been the case. Perhaps a more customer-focused product design could have been developed, allowing the original objectives to be realised. Certainly the benefits of achieving the target were high enough but the project became impossible after the premature and unsuccessful trials of the early versions.

Passenger Air Transport Development in the 1960s and 1970s

The Comet was the first all-jet passenger airliner. The Boeing 707 was the first commercial American equivalent. Boeing certainly learnt something from pioneering work on the Comet. Enlarge the interior to make it more passenger-friendly and separate the engine pods from the body structure both for reduced noise inside the cabin and to assist servicing. No doubt there were structural and other reasons also.

In considering the possible product planning briefs for the two follow-on aircraft models to the Comet and the 707 (the Boeing 747 and Concorde) the following points come to mind.

The Boeing 747 Product Brief: Something along the lines of: "Create a new model, based on all the good features and lessons of the 707 but capable of carrying more passengers, at a higher speed, with greater roominess, over longer distances, with equal or greater safety and, most important of all, at a lower cost per passenger mile."

Concorde Product Objectives: Now the possible guidelines for Concorde: "Develop a supersonic passenger carrying aircraft, about the size and carrying capacity of the Comet but with Mach 2 speed, high safety and reliability and having the possibility to reduce the flying time from London to New York from eight to three hours. We can probably use a lot of the technology already used in large, high speed military aircraft to keep overall programme costs down."

Technology-Led versus Commercially-Driven: It is not that one was right and the other wrong; simply that one was appropriate and commercial in its orientation and the other was appropriate mainly to pushing the bounds of technology. Concorde therefore ran the risk of becoming an inappropriate commercial venture. Both are superb aircraft in their own right, but I am here applying a product planning judgement on something which is appropriate. Unfortunately, the technology-led product looking for a market still appears from all kinds of industries, when the application at the outset of some professional product planning discipline would have oriented it more to the market and customers and would have given it a better chance of success.

The single linking theme of all the above examples of less than successful product programmes is the dominance of the technological idea over more mundane issues of market and customer acceptance. To paraphrase Morita: technology creativity is no good without product planning creativity.

Notes

1. Akio Morita, *Made in Japan*, William Collins, 1987.

11 PRODUCT PLANNING AND ITS CROSS-FUNCTIONAL RELATIONSHIPS

Because product planning is one of the truly cross-functional departments, it is worth examining the advantages and problems inherent in its working interfaces. Co-operative working across a company, team work and less formalised and bureaucratic organisations are the characteristics recommended for success today, and so the traditional responsibilities of the big line departments are being challenged by matrix or team working practices. At the same time, many more departments have an important input into the new product process, especially in the early stages.

Product planning must act as a catalyst in encouraging these new ways of working. On the other hand, product planning as a "new" and unusual cross-functional department can encounter resistance from the vested interests of entrenched line functions. How to mitigate the effects of non-co-operative working is a key task for top management.

We have seen that the work of product planning is strongly intertwined with other functions that contribute to new product programmes. We have also seen cases where, in particular activities, working with a product planning structure has caused friction. We have said that in a perfect organisation, all traditional line departments work smoothly together and produce exactly what the company needs. We also know that there is no such thing as the perfect organisation. The result: some parts of the organisation must take on a more cross-functional role on behalf of the board, which cannot be expected to ensure that daily cross-functional issues are properly co-ordinated, nor even to arbitrate on every clash of requirements.

Because it evaluates the cross-company implications of every new product programme, change or idea, product planning must be seen in this role so far as the new product development process is concerned. This is a key starting point for the establishment or operation of a successful product planning activity. There have been many situations where the lack of acceptance of this point has caused major friction in getting new product programmes successfully implemented. In over-the-wall organisations product planning was seen as just another ivory tower whose occupants were expected to perform and then throw out their work to the next department without any cross-functional consultation.

This chapter aims to show the key aspects of the inter-functional working, offer advice for good working relationships and point out some common problem areas. Even with team working, the different ways of working and the conflicting requirements of each function need to be taken into account. Neither the formation of teams nor the creation of programme management matrix structures automatically guarantees that people from different functions will work together. The diesel engines case showed the cross-company benefits of good quality product planning at the front end of a programme that has an effect on engineering, purchasing, production control, logistics, manufacturing, suppliers and customers. The following sections try to explain other functions' view of product planning as well as the product planning side of the same relationship. By trying to put both viewpoints on the table, the possibility of better cross-functional co-operation is created.

SALES AND MARKETING

There is a difference in operations between sales and marketing. Sales should be in direct contact with the customer and should control the distribution system as well as being the people charged with selling today's products. In this respect, sales need not pay attention to what product is needed tomorrow. Marketing provides sales support to sales in the short term, in what is often called merchandising. Marketing must also pay some attention to the longer term's strategic aspects of the company's future: the marketing strategy and planning activities.

Sales

The first key relationship point between product planning and sales should allow product planners access to the customer and the distribution network. This is often jealously guarded by sales. But it is an essential input to new product thinking to know as much as possible about how customers and distribution view the current products and the manner in which they are presented to the market. This is no substitute for market research focused on the end customer, but a means of viewing the whole distribution network as part of the customer structure for the product offering.

Volvo Holland organised a very successful product market feedback sys-t-em precisely to get this view on current products. Rather than have piece-meal complaints and suggestions fed back to product planning from diff-erent points in the network, sales were encouraged to organise the feedback on a regular basis so that:

1. The feedback represented the views of sales as a whole and was not just a few isolated complaints.
2. The value of correcting the various problems identified was to be stated, if it could be quantified.
3. Product planning guaranteed a response on each item so that feedback in the opposite direction could reach the originator who would then know the resulting action.
4. A possible outcome was a decision to take no action and to handle the problem through the aftermarket system. This cleared up many points of minor dissatisfaction that were widely discussed in engineering and service but were never worked through to a conclusion because of low priority or lack of resources.

The regular feedback system was backed up by visits to the distribution network for point-by-point discussion on distributor or customer problems from a purely sales point of view. The feedback resulted in product improve-ments that generated an excellent sales response in the market areas visited. The "customer voice" comes not only from the end customer. It comes also from distribution, which must be listened to and motivated as well.

Matching the short and long-term

A second aspect of the relationship with sales is the gulf that often opens up between the strategic product issues decided at high level in the product policy committee and the messages that sales puts over to customers. The diesel case is again a good example. A component rationalisation had been decided by the PPC for the new product. However, product planning still had to provide arguments for sales to use with the customer to ensure that individual one-off customer demands were not allowed to proliferate the rationalised and integrated product offering without full justification against the criteria provided. It is essential that the strategies developed in the PPC should be good enough to put over to the market – and that sales should push the strategies right through to the customer rather than operate in an inconsistent or opportunistic way. Equally, if sales are proceeding short-term in a specific direction to meet their budget objectives, which implies a change in the longer term strategic positioning of the company, then these two positions must somehow be reconciled.

The changeover from the Ford Cortina to the new Sierra mentioned in Chapter Three is another example of this. The addition of high cost specification items to the Cortina to stimulate falling sales in the last year of its life meant that specifications for the new Sierra had to be raised, at launch, so reducing its profit margins below the programme objectives set by the product planners.

Marketing

The breadth of a marketing department's responsibilities can vary greatly. There are companies where marketing has full responsibility for all forward planning of market-related activities including volume planning, consumer and market research and the product requirement input to new product programmes. In others, the long term volume, research and requirement planning is handled by business planning or product planning. Marketing therefore concentrates on the short to medium term situation, with merchandising, sales and market statistics and support for the achievement of sales performance.

Whatever the exact splitting of activities in this area, the following points are important.

• There must be no inconsistency between what the sales and marketing group is achieving and planning in the short or medium term and what the forward product plans contain. This consistency must cover volumes, strategy, product positioning and pricing policy.

• There must be a capacity planning aspect to the marketing network development activities, just as the process engineers must plan the factory capacities for a new product. This requires early consultation and input to the product and business planning process, since lead times to develop distribution networks can be as long as those for manufacturing equipment.

• If the product strategy, positioning and description for a new programme have been done well by product planning, and implementation has met all the requirements, then it should be possible to create launch marketing material using as a basis the original product planning strategies and product description.

Sometimes a marketing department will develop, in conjunction with an advertising or public relations agency, a somewhat different story, trying to create a product afresh for themselves rather than adhering to the original product strategy and programme objectives. This is dangerous: it can lead to inconsistency between the actual product characteristics and the way in which the product is put over to the market.

A second aspect of the same thing is that the product data used in sales literature can often deviate from the product, engineering and legislative standards against which the new products have been developed. This is due to the natural desire of marketing people to present any product in as favourable a light as possible. The increasing strength of consumer legislation and the notice taken in courts of law of excessive claims made by salesmen for products makes this a dangerous practice, too.

● The best way to overcome both of the above problems is for product planning to work closely with marketing and any outside agencies in preparing the launch of the new product. This will ensure complete consistency with what has gone into the programme from the outset and avoid unnecessary wheel-inventing of image or strategic product aspects not actually present in the product.

● Market research and analysis about new product concepts and details, or market clinics with early models must be performed under the direction of product planning, which is better aware of the issues involved and decisions being evaluated. This is often a bone of contention. Market research and statistical departments are usually part of marketing, which is a primary user of market data to support the development of short term sales and marketing activities. Joint working through an outside research agency is often the answer because a shared view of both needs and results has to be the out-come. The brief for the clinic, the interpretation of results and the resulting decisions and actions for the programme should be handled by product planning.

● Quite often, marketing will have its own opinion about what a product should, or should not be. Indeed, this is not confined to marketing, since in products with a consumer orientation everyone in the company becomes an expert. Nowhere is this more evident than in the automotive industry. However, there must be a truly expert view on the product in every company. Product planning must be the custodian of that expert view. Other functional views, though they should be put forward, must take second place – even those of the board. This places a requirement on product planning to be professional in justifying their product proposals and decisions: their subjectively expressed view is no better than anyone else's.

• Just as sales and marketing might guard their right to be the main interface with the customer and the distribution network, so product planning must have the primary responsibility for instructing engineering to create or change products. This is another problem area, especially in industrial products, where a product manager in marketing or a salesman may want to short circuit the product approval procedures. This is a delicate point to handle. It is pointless working hard through the product development process to introduce carefully studied, rationalised products designed for manufacture if the short term product change system is busy changing or adding to the product via a separate influence network. At the same time, as illustrated by the Volvo product market feedback system, sales and marketing must have a means of getting reaction and action to major points of customer dissatisfaction.

Product planning and marketing have to work hard together in all the above areas. These are the first links in a parallel working chain that goes right through the new product process.

INDUSTRIAL DESIGN AND STYLING

Industrial design is not a necessary input for all new product programmes although everything under the heading of consumer durables should have it. More and more items of industrial equipment – diesel engines, compressors, electric motors – are benefitting from it. For all programmes the styling and product planning considerations and inputs go hand in hand.

In the big consultant design houses, the industrial design responsibility embraces some product planning, some design engineering and even some process planning activities, as well as styling. This may be a valid approach with simpler products where the dictum "form follows function" can be applied. However, in the complex product development processes where we have shown product planning to be necessary, the industrial design and the styling input should be broadly the same and for the purposes of this discussion they are considered to be the same.

Styling is a main partner of product planning at the front end of a product programme. It is essential that relations should be close, communications clear and that there should be mutual respect for one another's professional viewpoint.

A good styling department can often originate product ideas and so advanced styling work can precede any product planning and have considerable influence. A look at any international motor exhibition will show the wealth of new styling and product concepts created by independent styling houses and automotive stylists. Many of the concept cars, based mainly around styling input, are an attempt to test public reaction to an idea or to start a new design fashion. Sometimes, advanced styling work can influence a whole new product concept.

Styling guidelines for products

In all serious new product projects entering the D1 programme phase, styling guidelines should be laid down by product planning for package, image, specification content and sometimes aesthetic points. It is therefore essential that mutual respect should exist between the two departments where the senior product planning managers have a respected creative opinion and the senior stylists understand the relationship between their creativity and the total new product creation process being started. In this latter category come issues such as the importance of packaging, of product positioning in a market segment, of cost targetting and control and the importance of carry-over product items. These may be seen as a restriction on the creative freedom of the stylist.

Sir Terence Beckett's speech to the London Business School has already been referred to[1]. In it he emphasised that a strong input by product planning to the styling and design function should be a source of strength to the stylist rather than an unwelcome restriction. Styling creativity can then be aimed at a specific customer- and market-oriented target rather than operating in an open field with a risk of missing the target altogether. This is what Sir Terence Beckett recommends.

> Design should be practised, not as an art in itself, aesthetically and intellectually fascinating though that can be, but as part of a business activity as a whole and of product planning in particular, if it is to fulfil its proper role in creating our future prosperity.
>
> We have to design to satisfy the customer, not design primarily to satisfy design itself. Innovation is essential – but as Quiller Couch said on the art of writing, what distinguishes good craftsmanship from the rest is whether it is appropriate.

"Appropriate" is an important word here and it applies across the whole spectrum of product planning activity. Statements of product requirements that are *absolute*, with no concern for the implications across a company of meeting the requirements, are not professional in a product planning sense. Instead, the product planner must strive for what is *appropriate* to the objectives of the programme. Few product requirements are wanted at any price. Perfectly good or even brilliant styling may be inappropriate to the product being created or to the name on that product.

Styling and clinics

A potential conflict area between product planning and styling lies in the area of performing clinics on early design themes. The styling viewpoint is that the customer cannot appreciate future fashion or design themes, but that the stylists' main task is to create these on behalf of the company. The product planning view is that if tight terms of reference for image and positioning of a new product have been handed over, it is reasonable to check the styling interpretation and execution of those guidelines against customer opinion – notwithstanding the stylists' point on future fashion. The conflict of views, if it arises, can be overcome by involving stylists in the preparation of the clinic, the orientation of the questioning and the feedback of results. Participation in, and understanding of, what is being done in a product clinic should strengthen, not weaken, their hand.

The packaging or layout of the product is also an important consideration between product planning and styling. This is valid for all product types, not just cars and trucks. Quite apart from aesthetic considerations, the early terms of reference for a new product will include what components have to fit within the product envelope and be accommodated in the style and some carry-over items and features with a visual content may also be specified. In addition, the way the customer will use or interact with the product may create restrictions or opportunities that the stylist must take into account.

The product planner must always be interested in whether the presented style fits the package and carry-over criteria. Often the stylist prefers to tidy up a chosen style after approval has been given and before the final release.

As a final note on this styling-product planning relationship, it should be noticed that most styling departments report at the same level in the organisation as product planning or engineering. Some come under engineering itself but, for example in the Volvo Car Corporation organisation in Sweden, product planning and design are contained in one department, headed by a vice president who is also a member of the VCC board. This works well and emphasises the very close working relationship necessary for successful product planning and styling. This approach is the same now in the Ford of Europe organisation where design reports directly to the vice president programmes and is no longer part of product development, as it was previously.

DESIGN ENGINEERING

From what has already been written, the close relationship between product planning and engineering can be appreciated. The two functions provide the main drive to create the content of a new product programme. In the sharing of responsibility, the potential for friction arises. This is natural: in many companies engineering has felt responsible for the product as a whole and the product definition task of product planning, if it exists at all, is seen as no more than a kicking-off of the product creation process through engineering.

The potential for dissent still exists in situations where both product planning and engineering exist as independent line departments and work together on new projects through a matrix or project co-ordination structure, rather than as part of an integrated project or programme team. In the latter case, unnecessary friction should be submerged in the team identity.

The difference between the two roles should be clearly understood: product planning must be responsible for saying what the product should be. Engineering is responsible for the individual technical solutions and the technical integrity of the whole working product. One of the difficult aspects arises from the cross-functional role of product planning in defining the key elements of both the product and the project. Product planning is the art of the possible; the art of what is possible technically and the art of what the company can deliver profitably from available resources and skills. This iterative process of study and evaluation at the front end of a product programme that firms up these product possibilities can cause problems because there has to be a deep dialogue between engineering and product planning to reach the necessary conclusions and terms of reference. Many engineers, however are more comfortable with a higher level over the wall guideline from product planning that they can then turn into a product through their own processes.

I have watched Japanese engineering and product planning groups fight very hard over particular issues. There, however, the outcome is always a decision that benefits the programme. The conflict is regarded as natural due to the separate interests of the two groups. It is also seen as creative. Parallel and interactive working between product planning and engineering is accepted as a natural means of starting a programme. Successful companies devote a lot of time to the front end dialogue in which the whole product can be virtually configured and designed before any significant design or test engineering work is done. For many European engineers this is a new approach, but it is the same as the styling to product planning relationship just described; the combination of product planning and engineering creativity should produce a better product. Conflict occurs also during Japanese product programmes between, for example, engineering and manufacturing personnel; this is also creative and stems from their different viewpoints. In Europe, too many conflicts are political in nature and tend to end up as victories for one side or another, and not necessarily as victories for the company or the product programme.

Advanced engineering and research

The particular periods where product planning and engineering need to work together occur throughout the front end of a programme and up to the D3 point, but also in the pre-programme phase where advanced or shelf engineering is necessary. Product planning must provide guidelines for a proportion of the advanced engineering work to develop technological advances or product feature improvements for use in future product programmes. Product standards for each new product, or properties, as the Volvo Car Corporation calls them, are also the subject of an increasing dialogue. This can be a delicate area since the origination and management of technical standards and research is traditionally a preserve of scientific or technically-qualified and responsible people. However, the modern trend is to treat research and advanced engineering programmes in exactly the same way as programmes that produce an end product; that is to say, they must be focused on a strategy and a market need and be subject to a planning, timing and control process. The shelf engineering of technology and systems is becoming more and more a part of competitive, integrated new product processes. The companies who have traditionally developed all-new products and new product standards as part of a new product programme itself, incurring extra development costs and a long lead time to market, are having to learn the value of pre-engineering and planning of the key elements of new programmes. This is perhaps one of the most important areas for the development of closer relationships in the future between product planning and the advanced or research and development departments in engineering companies.

Cost Targeting and Carry-over

Returning now to co-operation in specific elements of new product programmes, cost targeting is one area that has been mentioned where only by treating it as a shared responsibility can a satisfactory solution be reached. Cost targets must be seen and accepted as objectives for the work of the engineers. The cost targets must also add up to a total that meets the pricing and business objectives of the product programme. Therefore, the creation of the design cost targets must be a joint effort between the product planners and the engineers.

The definition of the carry-over elements of a programme is important both in the target setting phase and the implementation. Carry-over of design, tooling or process aspects of previous products into a new product is difficult enough to negotiate at the front end of a new programme. During implementation the training and the inclination of engineers leads them to prefer designing something new, making something better, or using the latest material or technique rather than older, satisfactory, approaches. This goes back to choosing what is appropriate for a particular product programme rather than always trying to start from a clean sheet of paper. The product planning requirements should represent a challenge for engineering in the interests of both profitability and time to market. The art is to give the impression to the customer of an all new product while controlling the amount of new engineering content. I have also seen product planners, interested only in defining what a product should ideally be, take the same clean sheet approach. But the product planner who always keeps the cross-company implications and the total business objectives in mind will stick to the carry-over objectives.

Timing and programme control

A further aspect of a programme where engineering and product planning should work closely together is in the planning of all implementation details: the linking of the engineering timing to all the other key timing activities in the company; the collation of advanced parts lists to allow estimating and planning by other departments and the structuring of the engineering programme itself. Engineering often appoints its own internal project co-ordinators, if only because of the complexity of the engineering programme itself and the linking process with purchasing, process engineering and suppliers. Usually these groups will be one of the main links with product planning on programme timing and progress matters. However, it is also essential that product planners maintain a close, but often informal, working relationship with the component and system engineering groups themselves, just as they do with styling. It is never possible to perform truly integrated product development if each department is forced to talk to its colleagues only through arms-length project co-ordinators.

In the Ford of Europe example in Chapter Six, the departments of product planning and vehicle planning (formerly part of engineering) were combined to make the "strong" programme management teams and timing was separate. However, these groups, together with product engineering, reported to the VP for product development and were jointly responsible for setting new programmes on the right path. In the Volvo 1988 organisation, timing, product planning and programme management each reported to a different board member from the board member responsible for product engineering. Separate project managers also existed in engineering. Obviously, then, there can be no prescribed way of setting up the relationship on timing issues between product planning and engineering in organisational terms. The key is co-operative and integrated working at all stages of a programme and a clear, shared view of responsibilities. That there will always be some kind of conflict – this is not a problem. What is important is to channel the energies to a creative and not to a destructive outcome.

MANUFACTURING ENGINEERING AND LOGISTICS

Sometimes manufacturing engineering can be two separate departments; process engineering, which is close to design engineering, and manufacturing engineering, which is close to, or part of, the production plant. Logistics can also be attached to the production plant or it can be part of purchasing. They will all be treated as one entity for the purposes of this discussion.

Manufacturing engineering

Traditionally, product planning has not had such a close dialogue, at the front end of product programmes, with process as with design engineering. This is a pity, because, as already demonstrated, process input at the beginning of a programme is as important, and should be as timely, as any other form of input. The lack of contact occurs because product planners come mainly from a product engineering or marketing background and apart from general issues such as capacity, plant investment or specification rationalisation, they have insufficient knowledge of the process implications of new products. At the same time, process engineers are often hard at work implementing the latest product to hit the plant and have little time available to talk about new long term concepts. However, I do have experience of two companies, Perkins Engines and Volvo Car, that both placed some manufacturing engineering resource directly in product planning with the specific objective of improving the input early into new programmes. This made a big difference both in understanding and resolving joint manufacturing and design issues at an early stage.

At the beginning of a new programme concept, perhaps at the product and business plan formation stage, it is essential that the product planner takes as much notice of the process technical as of the product's technical issues. This is a time when new design or process engineering study work will not be available to the product planner. So initial input will have to be based on experience and a lot of discussion. The presence of people with manufacturing experience in product planning is invaluable during this phase. Later on, at the actual start of a new programme, manufacturing is usually pleased to be consulted so early in a product programme. For companies not yet used to having full-scale design and manufacturing participation early in the programme, the first contacts may be difficult. As with design engineering, manufacturing engineers may be less willing to be targeted on performance improvements for the new product and may not understand how to define their input at this stage. To get the programme to a competitive level, or to meet a difficult economic objective, the product planner may have to look for manufacturing improvements in labour efficiency, quality levels, scrap rates, manufacturing lead times and carry-over plant utilisation. The manufacturing engineer may only be ready to talk about more general issues such as overall capacity, new process technology and factory layouts.

Referring back to the European-Japanese joint venture cited earlier, it was most interesting to note how many process guidelines and parameters were put up from the Japanese side as terms of reference to influence the design and product aspects. It was quite clear that these guidelines were not just dreamed up for this project but instead represented past process decisions that had been beneficial. Once again, good wheels don't need to be reinvented.

There is in fact a tremendous part of the front end of a product programme dependent on manufacturing input. If this is not defined at the correct level of detail the results may deviate far from the programme objectives. In addition to capacities and process technologies, such items as overall lead times to production, process targets for design, the number of pre-production products, the product characteristics and options to be made available through specific manufacturing processes, the labour and overhead elements of the cost targets: all of these are key inputs. The results of decisions and assumptions about these manufacturing aspects will not be felt until much later in the programme. However, the cost of changing them then will be very high compared to the effort involved in getting the manufacturing input in early. It is not just simultaneous engineering activities that bring process issues into the front end of the product design process. The whole programme planning process has to have all the necessary inputs available simultaneously, and in an integrated fashion. Manufacturing engineering may have to learn how to make their input proactively, early in a programme, having been used to working mainly reactively in the implementation phase.

Logistics

At first sight it does not seem that product planning could have a fruitful relationship with logistics, but there are several areas where information input at an early stage can be beneficial.

The product structure and offering issued by product planning as a guideline for engineering to design and release is, or should be, exactly the same structure that sales will eventually use to order products and that logistics will use to provision material for build. The volume of each major component and option, the make-buy policy, the timing of product releases to suppliers and the whole manufacturing cost structure as applied to the logistic system for the new product: these matters can be heavily influenced by decisions taken at the front end.

Most logistics personnel are only too willing to discuss their necessary input in any new product programme because normally they are left picking up the pieces after releases have been made. Unfortunately, logistics, as with manufacturing engineering, is not normally geared up early enough to provide a full analysis for the new product – not least because of its greater pre-occupation with short term events. JIT and MRP systems have been widely developed with suppliers, to reduce manufacturing costs and inventories and to handle the growing complexity of product specifications. However, this is usually done not as part of a new product programme but using the existing product specification as a basis. New logistic and material release and procurement systems and warehouses have been such big projects in themselves that they have their own project teams and management decision and reporting circuits.

In their 1988 organisation, Volvo Car Holland made an attempt to get more focus on manufacturing and logistic issues early in new programmes by having an advanced manufacturing engineering department sitting alongside product planning and engineering. However, this produced a split of another kind because the upstream department had two tasks: first, it had to create the input for the new programme and then it had to tune its input with what was going on in the logistic and manufacturing departments working on implementing short term programmes. This involved settling differences of technical opinion about what should be done and negotiating the handover of the plan to the implementing departments after the D3 decision.

Experience of this way of working suggests that there should be only one major department for each functional specialisation, each of which should have the capability, the will, the budget and the responsibility to provide an upstream input for new programmes and subsequently handle downstream implementation. Reconciling two technical opinions within the same functional discipline, a frequent problem should be the job of the head of that function. In this respect, it is more difficult for a separate non-specialist manager, such as a product or programme manager, to mediate between two separated parts of the same basic function than it is to treat the function as an integral group.

A variation of this, in which team formation is more familiar as a way of implementing new programmes, is to allocate the members of that function to the various programme team units. This ensures that their work and technical input is united at the programme level and that no handovers are involved, even though manufacturing engineering as a working function is split between the different programmes. Here the product planners and the manufacturing engineers are working together from the first start of a programme. Rover's way of keeping the team together even though the reporting level of the team changes after programme approval acts an an illustration of this.

In the diesel engines' case, the beneficial effects of the rationalised product planning and design approach to the new diesel engine components was a major factor in improving the logistic costs and effectiveness. This in turn improved delivery reliability to customers. Without that early input the benefits would not have been realisable.

PURCHASING

The purchased-out content of a typical engineering product can be anything from 50 to 85 per cent of the total manufactured cost. It is therefore surprising that more weight has not been given in the past to purchasing input and indeed suppliers' input early in the product creation process. This is now changing rapidly as European and American companies try hard to reduce their manufacturing cost base. It has been further stimulated by Japanese OEMs moving into Europe and bringing in their own, more co-operative, ways of handling supplier relationships. However the habits and training of years in what is euphemistically called a "firm but fair" purchasing approach will take some companies a long time to change.

Like the sales department with customers, purchasing always seems jealously to guard relationships and contacts with suppliers. To a product planner looking for input and ideas for his next new programme this is often a barrier to bringing in new ideas. There are advanced purchasing operations at some OEMs that seek to know everything the suppliers have to offer which could be useful to the OEM. Daimler Benz has one such operation. It tests every new supplier product quite rigorously and examines the commercial conditions – regardless of whether it sees an immediate possibility of using the product. Thus it builds up knowledge for the future and a reference base for those involved in planning the next new products. By contrast, some OEM purchasing departments erect huge barriers against potential new suppliers or new ideas from existing suppliers being communicated to product planning and engineering. The *status quo* on suppliers and their technology is preferred for a variety of reasons. At one OEM, I worked with an advanced purchasing operation capable of no more than a literature and trade show search that provided little useful input to product planning. In another, there was a strategic working group, run by product planning, that operated between the OEM and some of its key suppliers to explore ways in which joint activities could provide the OEM's future needs and also fit what the suppliers could do.

It is essential that product planning has an effective access to, and dialogue with, the outside sources of new product ideas that suppliers represent. This may come from attending trade shows but the direct contact with certain key suppliers in both process and product development areas is also very important. This message is also for the salesmen of suppliers: don't just deal with purchasing but try find the people in your target OEMs who are looking for new ideas and who influence internal decision making. In other words, the supplier contacts in the OEM should also be truly cross-functional and should include product planning. The objective should be to develop a "research" relationship with the OEM as well as a sales relationship.

There is a large potential contribution that purchasing should make to a new product programme, not just in the area of new technology input from suppliers, but also in important programme decisions such as cost targeting, make-buy decisions and the contribution made by supplier parallel working in reducing time to market.

Make-buy is a particularly significant area. Many companies are getting rid of in-house manufacturing of parts of the product not considered "core business". High cost, inefficient manufacture is put out to suppliers that focus on a given technology, and that boast a sufficient base of expertise and volume because they supply several OEMs with the same product. Often their specialised approach enables them to beat the original OEM in-house manufactured cost with a fully absorbed selling price. This means more business for suppliers, but the planning and implementing of such actions requires delicate working between purchasing, product planning and the planning and personnel people from the affected production location. This is particularly so when the outsourcing involves a simultaneous change in the product. Hence major make-buy sourcing changes are often being built into new product programmes as a means of creating a better profitability base.

As with manufacturing engineering, the simple upstream involvement of purchasing is often a problem in itself. Most purchasing departments have their heaviest concentration in two areas; keeping costs down for purchased material and keeping supplies rolling to maintain production levels. Thus they have a main focus on current operations and budgets. Another heavy workload point occurs around the time of new product introductions where the burden of last minute corrective changes often falls heavily on purchasing and its suppliers. This creates a problem when product planners want to use purchasing resources for studies and decisions prior to, or early in, new product programmes. This is a case where budgetary constraints hinder the concept of "doing more early". Because of involvement in short term activities, there are many instances where purchasing lacks the resources to do anything early, and where the purchasing assumptions, good and bad, have to be made by product planners. It is necessary, therefore, that the early, cross-functional involvement of all departments in new product programmes is not just stated as a wish or objective but actually made possible in terms of budget, resources or whatever other means are necessary.

Other than long term, there have to be very close working relationships between purchasing and product planning departments. This has as much to do with running supplier relationships as with new programmes. In its negotiations with major suppliers, it is essential that purchasing should provide a vision of the future, beyond the short term component and material requirement schedules, so that the supplier can lay down or adapt the appropriate amount and type of capacity and make available new components and technology. Thus the combination of volume and product assumptions contained in the business plan and the details of product programmes must be used – but with caution – by purchasing in supplier negotiations. Caution is necessary because of the nature of supply contracts with volume guarantee clauses or the amortisation of development, capacity and tooling expenditure absorbed by the supplier and then included as a unit amount in the component price.

The illustration in Chapter Eight that connected the volume forecasting required to support a business plan with external planning dialogue between sales and its distributors, has an exact parallel in the need of suppliers for firm forward volume and other product-related information. In a multi-product company, much in the forward product plan will need to be communicated to suppliers at a time when it is still in a tentative or assumption state. In this regard, the heads of purchasing and product planning must have an excellent understanding of the risk levels inherent in any forward figures or product decisions provided to suppliers. They must carefully review the assumptions behind the information before using it for external commitment.

FINANCE

There are many different parts of the finance function that need to be involved with product programmes at all stages. Finance, like product planning, is a truly cross-functional department if only because of budgets and the fact that the operational success of all departments is ultimately measured in financial numbers. In some companies, finance alone is seen as having a official analytical capability with numbers. Of course, numbers are a main ingredient of any new product programme and its decisions.

There are, however, many situations in new product programmes where the two departments may not agree. The conflicts that arise come from their naturally opposing views: the one driven by the significance and validity of margins and returns; and the other more concerned with strategic issues, product and customer needs and the validity of the assumptions behind the numbers. However, there is still a very equal partnership aspect in the relationship between product planning and finance because of the need always to reach a good business solution. The following are the main areas of co-operation:

Programme Analysis

When product planning began, personal computers and spreadsheets did not exist and so they were very reliant on the finance department to do official analyses of product programmes. Nowadays this is less necessary because even a full business plan can be pre-formatted on a personal computer and alternative scenarios quickly calculated. Finance's involvement in new product programmes is not, therefore, just based on performing of analyses because product planning itself can undertake such tasks. Instead, finance should provide a financial view and contribution to the decision making surrounding the programmes.

Much has been said on product planning's involvement in evaluating potential new programmes in Chapter Three – the building blocks – and there the same conclusion is reached. Financial analysis and a strictly financial appraisal is only one of the necessary inputs to new product programme decision making. Financial views also tend to be driven by experience of historical numbers and are not over influenced by creative approaches suggesting that it will all be different this time. In new product creation, however, experience shows that only companies introducing new products with flair and imagination will lay the foundations for profitability and long term success.

Capital expenditure

The amount of capital available in future for new programmes, the exact amount estimated and agreed for each new programme and the timing-related release of funds all require constant dialogue and tuning. This dialogue starts in the business plan preparation phase and goes right through each new product programme, becoming particularly strong at each D decision point and at moments of capital commitment and release.

There is usually a separate approval and release cycle for capital expenditure that runs parallel to the programme decision process. Therefore, time has to be allowed for the necessary approval for funds, from shareholders, from parents, from corporate boards, or from the financial appropriations committee (often the same people as the PPC but operating with different constraints and objectives). The timing of capital release can lead to programme delays, so it requires careful attention. Particular difficulties crop up when advanced capital or tooling releases have to be made to support tight programme timing, even though the quality decision milestones appropriate to the release have not been passed. In the whole of this process, the product planners and financial controllers must negotiate because a combined effort can keep the programme on track. Separate ones will definitely not.

Budgets

Chapter Eight explains the relationships between the product cycle plan, the project plan and the annual start of the budget process.

There is very often a clash between what has previously been approved as a product or business plan element and the, often more strict, guidelines laid down for budgeting. It is impossible to avoid this totally because circumstances change from one year to the next and most European and North American companies are strongly driven by short term financial considerations. However, any forward planning activity becomes a nonsense if it constantly ignores or turns out to be at variance with the immediate short term needs. I have discussed this at length with financial colleagues and my conclusion is that at least the first two years of each round of a business plan should be evaluated financially with the same level of attention and discipline to the resource requirements as the budget itself. Thus, the first year of the plan is the draft budget for the following year. The second year plan is a firm link to less certain parts of the plan in year three and beyond. By doing this, a constant rolling check is kept on the financial resource needs of the forward plan and the actual financial capability of the company.

Budget conflicts over "do more early" approaches have also been mentioned where the product development expense hump at the programme start has to be compensated by expenditure reductions derived from efficiency improvements downstream. Particularly severe problems occur where several new programmes are initiated using the parallel working approach and the budget controllers cannot allow it. This emphasises that the implications of integrated new product development must first be thrashed out at board level. If not, then board strategy and objectives, however well intentioned and communicated, will not come to fruition because they clash with what the budget system allows or with what the company can afford.

Cost Targets

The process of setting cost targets has been discussed in Chapter Three and Chapter Nine. Cost estimating departments are often part of finance and in such cases a partnership exists in which product planning can provide many of the assumptions and product content for the costing while finance provides the estimating and co-ordinating expertise. Here also, official company assumptions about future exchange rates and cross rates and predictions of company, national and international inflation are made. The costing structure built into a company's information systems will also be a strong influencing factor on the type of cost information available for decision making. The use of activity-based costing systems is growing but still not sufficiently widespread. These systems allow the real costs of different parts of both the product and the manufacturing systems to be calculated. Activity-based costing is to functional costing and budgeting what matrix working is to over the wall functional product development. Many companies still rely on full cost accounting for products, which makes it difficult for their reporting systems to handle variable costs on their own, separate from amortisation and fixed costs – an essential starting point for design cost targeting for new products.

For product planning, the important thing is to be able to isolate those elements of the cost structure in each estimate – tooling, piece cost, capital, direct or indirect overhead – that invite actions and changes which can have a favourable effect on the cost outcome. The quality of the cost analyst input, especially from personnel experienced in design and manufacturing matters, is a major factor in arriving at good cost targets. This will also ensure good programme decisions and good trade-offs between competing requirements based on real, rather than artificial, cost structures.

Pricing

Many companies still place the ultimate responsibility for pricing with finance. This can be explained by a heavy emphasis on cost-plus and required margin pricing approaches. However, the real issues surrounding the positioning of a new product in the market are so complex and are so connected with non-financial issues such as strategy, product value, specification and competitive action, that pricing should be much more a marketing and product planning responsibility.

The concerns of companies with inadequate financial margins on products is understandable but the solution of continuous price increases, while it may work once or twice, will eventually drive customers away. Pricing and acceptable margins should be one of the outputs of the more efficient integrated new product development process that we are talking about. Hence responsibility for product pricing should be exercised initially by product planning for all new product programmes and should be handed over to marketing at a suitable point in the programme – before job one but after the cost targets, specification and option mix are decided. Sticking five per cent on prices, a common budget improvement technique, is no solution to a profitability problem. Equally wrong, is to calculate all prices from a margin on top of manufactured or variable cost, also a common practice. The finan-ce department is fully entitled to argue that margins on a given new product are inadequate and to expect corrective action, but their opinion on absolute price levels is bound to be biased, not to say uninformed.

The intelligent way to deal with the whole cost and price issue is in parallel. The positioning, the specification, and the top-down price value should be calculated at the same time as the bottom-up cost targeting. Thus part of the evaluation of the risk in a programme, carried out during the programme decision process by product planning, is the balance between the cost that can be achieved based on specification, design and process criteria and the price that must be achieved to make the necessary margins.

SERVICE AND PARTS

These are left until last because they come last in the product development value chain and are the people often left with the task of picking up the pieces to help the product survive in the marketplace. The last line of defence, as it were. They are not left till last because of importance.

This situation must change. As we strive more and more to make the product satisfy the customer, so the service and after-market aspects of that satisfaction are becoming more and more important. Service should not be seen as a last line of defence but as an integral part of the product character-istics and performance that in turn are part of the offer to the customer. The input from service and parts to product planning comes in four main areas.

Warranty costs

These are one of the principal single cost elements in the total product cost build-up and they can be targeted just like individual component costs. It is also the case that warranty or other service failures are a prime source of customer dissatisfaction. Much of the short term product change action accompanying new product launches occurs at the instigation of service to correct early life faults, lower warranty or increase serviceability. At this time, of course, remedial action is really too late.

During the start-up of a new programme warranty costs should be broken down and targeted along with the target for components and manufacturing cost. Expenditure on changes to improve warranty or serviceability can be justified as part of the initial programme concept and the service engineers should start work at this stage – just like their design colleagues. The time and effort versus expenditure curve is just as valid for warranty and service costs as it is for any other product aspect. Good decisions taken early are much cheaper than bad decisions corrected after production start. The differ-ence between service and design and process problems is that the time for correction is much longer because it takes time, after launch, for faults to feed back and for action to be taken. To correct these problems resources that should be working elsewhere are consumed and more damage is likely to be done to consumer confidence in the product. The warranty specialists must be brought in as early as possible in the product concept process and warranty history on existing products is a very important input to the product planner's specification planning and cost targetting process.

Serviceability

Serviceability may not impact directly on the customer but has a big influence on product faults' rapid rectification and on the efficiency of routine servicing and maintenance. Very often, service engineers get their first look at a new product when the first pre-production versions appear. This is far too late for any valid product layout or serviceability critique. Serviceability has to go hand in hand with the early input on warranty matters. By the same token, there must be trade-offs, visible and measurable, between product improvements, possibly at higher cost, and service cost or problem avoidance. There is no reason to consider service needs as different from any other customer input. For example, in a QFD exercise, service needs and costs must be included at the start.

Going further, there is no reason why serviceability standards based on experience should not be set in the same way as design, test and process standards. That is, provided they also stand up to the test of adding customer value to the product.

Reliability

Reliability is the ability of a product to perform in the specified manner, with the specified level of faults over the specified period, and in line with customer expectations. Reliability failures come both early in a product's life, when caused by incorrect processing of the agreed design: and later in the product's life, when caused by components that wear out too early. Thus a washing machine that works perfectly for five years and then fails totally could be said to be reliable if its price and image justified the expectation of that kind of life. A car that lasted twenty years but which required constant repairs to engine or electrics could be said to be durable – but not reliable. Hence our definition involves fitness for purpose.

Reliability is not always the concern of service but I equate the two in terms of new product programme input because warranty measurement is the first part of reliability and with increasing reliability in products and longer and longer warranty periods the two things are converging. Product planning cannot specify reliability targets for a new product without a major joint effort with service to evaluate current vehicle reliability and known causes of current reliability concerns. The achievement of reliability is a design, process engineering and supplier concern but the standard setting and deter-mining of the key issues should come from service and product planning.

Perkins Engines had a combined product planning and product reliability department in the 1970s. It was headed by a board member and was his per-sonal brainchild. There was a lot of logic in the approach. Product planning

set targets for products based on analysis of customer and market requirements and looking at the cross-company implications of what was needed to
achieve them. Product reliability set reliability targets for products based on
market and customer needs and worked cross-functionally to improve total
company performance in achieving the targets. Thus the activity of product
reliability planning is just like product planning. A large element of the
market input came from service: the field information and warranty tracking
was managed by product reliability.

The example simply emphasises the need for effective service and warranty
input to product programmes to ensure the improvement of product reliability.

Parts Planning

If service needs are left until last, spare parts requirements come even later.
The basic issues are the same: early input of requirements and the provision
of resources to meet them are desirable: the advantages or trade-offs to the
parts division must be clear. This can be more difficult than in the case of
service because traditionally, parts profit is not included in programme profitability analyses except by some rule-of-thumb profit or sales turnover of
parts per product sold. Nevertheless, there are costs involved in making provision for parts and accessories (both engineering and tooling costs) and
sometimes built-in penalties on the product itself, that must be justified.

The profit from parts and accessories is a very important element of operations for dealers and product manufacturers alike, and not just in the automotive industry, so it is essential to include provision for parts and accessories in a product programme. The input must also be made at the appropriate time and action taken before irrevocable commitment is made to
design layout or tooling.

In one example of late input, a car manufacturer once spent over £1 million
after the start of production, for tooling modifications to a car roof panel in
order to allow the correct fitment of a roof rack. Had the correct product decision been made much earlier, the design provision could have been made at
almost no cost.

Another problem area: often, the service condition of a part is not the
same as the production condition. Thus two releases have to be made, hopefully without extra engineering work. Examples include pistons, rings and
liners for diesel engines where several different versions, undersized or
oversized, have to be made available for repairing engines in service compared to the production standard. The availability of part body panels for
economical vehicle crash repairs is a similar example.

Name branding too is an issue; the high value and profitability of the after-market parts business has attracted many outside players who bring in so-called spurious parts. These may be made to the same general specification as the original equipment part but do not carry the product OEM's approval nor his warranty. Hopefully they don't carry his logo, either. Hence the parts division will want to brand everything on the product so that the repair station or the customer, in the case of DIY repair, will want to buy only a branded replacement part. Branding is in the first place a styling issue and so product planning are brought in to the discussion. It can also have a cost implication and, in the case of proprietory parts, a commercial policy aspect between OEM and supplier. Service parts profit and competition from spurious manufacturers can be defended with effective parts product planning within a new product programme.

Without a clear view of the profit effect of these issues, there is often a difference of opinion between parts and product planning as to what should be included. However, it is like all these other aspects of early input to new product programmes: the only time for effective input is early enough to make a change without incurring extra costs. While the product planner should be sufficiently on his toes to ask the right questions, the inputting departments should also be geared to the "do more early" theme.

CONCLUSIONS

The emphasis in this chapter has been on cross-functional relationships and cross-functional co-operation. Elsewhere in this volume, you may have concluded that product planning's characteristics make it a line function, or that in some ways it acts as a staff or advisory function, without a true line role. You may also have assumed that it is merely a part of the new move to cross-functional team working in cases where the product planners are included in the permanent staff of a programme team.

In fact, product planning fulfills each of those roles in different companies and organisations. Yet some special characteristics of effective product planning are particularly appropriate in the current climate of striving to be more efficient in new product development.

The assumption of staff or line role should not occupy much of our time in this context: product planning is a job that needs doing. This requires people who take decisions and risks and are responsible for performance. Thus it is a *doing* and not an *advisory* role. The major consideration should be the role of product planning in the major business processes of a company.

Throughout, I have emphasised the cross-functional nature of product planning, acting on behalf of the chief executive, co-ordinating inputs from other functions and making business decisions, managing a major part of the new product development process that itself is now recognised as necessarily cross-functional.

Programme management, the creation of teams and concurrent or simultaneous engineering are three other concepts widely discussed in almost all chapters. We must, finally, fit these elements into the product planning framework. Each helps to bring the new product development process to the more efficient performance level which we all seek. But none of them can achieve much without the presence of the building blocks of product planning to act as the drivers.

A badly conceived programme can be superbly implemented and fail. A simultaneous engineering team, starting without business and product planning preparation and input, must itself begin the product planning before it can start on the engineering. Multi-disciplinary teams have been adopted by many companies to achieve improvements in product creation – but with disappointing results because the product planning expertise required to drive the team working was absent. Successful teams should operate, in the first instance, as product planning teams.

The key point is that product planning has to be seen as an overall process, from the beginnings of the business plan to the point at which all the elements of a new product programme have been decided. Product planning also has to be seen as a professional area of competence populated with managers who operate throughout the entire product planning phase of business activity to ensure that each new product programme is well founded.

Chapter Three showed the total extent of this professional competence in its description of the building blocks of product planning. No definitive statement was made on how the blocks should be arranged organisationally, but they all need to be present somewhere. Chapter Four showed the potential for product planning activities and disciplines in a wide variety of industries and Chapter Five put the specific product planning activities into the wider context of a typical new product development process.

In Chapter Six a survey of the product creation organisations in companies and industries showed that the building blocks of product planning do indeed exist in many forms and permutations. Chapters Seven and Eight offered insights into programme management and business planning – two disciplines that have a strong inter-relationship and are often organised together with, or as part of, product planning.

Chapter Nine concentrated on the tools and techniques that make up the product planner's professional armoury. Chapter Ten showed several examples of product planning at work in industry, demonstrating that good product planning does produce more competitive, more profitable, more customer-oriented and more timely products. Lastly, in Chapter Eleven, I have outlined the kind of relationships needed between product planners and their counterparts in other functions, to ensure success in new product programmes.

Product planning, it remains to be said, is the driver of successful new product development, which in turn results in products that succeed in the market place.

Notes

1. Sir Terence Beckett, 'Design, Product Planning and Prosperity', paper delivered to the London Business School design management seminar, 1989.

INDEX